into the vortex

into the vortex

female voice and paradox in film

Britta Sjogren

University of Illinois Press
Urbana and Chicago

Library of Congress Cataloging-in-Publication Data
Sjogren, Britta, 1958–
Into the vortex : female voice and paradox in film /
Britta Sjogren.
   p.   cm.
Includes bibliographical references and index.
ISBN-13: 978-0-252-03028-4 (isbn 13 - cloth : alk. paper)
ISBN-10: 0-252-03028-1 (isbn 10 - cloth : alk. paper)
ISBN-13: 978-0-252-07267-3 (isbn 13 - paper : alk. paper)
ISBN-10: 0-252-07267-7 (isbn 10 - paper : alk. paper)
1. Women in motion pictures.
2. Voice in motion pictures.
3. Voice-overs. I. Title.
PN1995.9.W6S59   2006
791.43'6522—dc22   2005011374

for Sean

Neither I am me,

nor you are you,

nor you are me.

Also, I am me,

you are you

and you are me.

We have become one

in such a way,

That I am confused whether

I am you,

or you are me.

Rumi

contents

acknowledgments

The writing of this book would not have been possible without the influence and assistance of many, many people. Above all, I want to thank Janet Bergstrom, a truly inspiring scholar and incomparably generous mentor, for all that I learned from her challenging, brilliant intellect, her example of professional rigor, her flawless aesthetic sensibility, her encouragement and guidance, and the warmth and depth of her generosity and friendship. Her fingerprints are all over this book. Nick Browne, with his inimitable Socratic style and droll sense of humor, offered invaluable criticisms of the first draft of this manuscript that I very much appreciated. Teshome Gabriel and Frances Olsen, likewise, gave me sound advice at this beginning stage of writing. I am grateful for all that I learned from my exceptional friends and colleagues at UCLA: Alison McKee, Lynn Kirby, Nita Rollins, Vicky Callahan, Ayako Saito, Lynn Spigel, Jonathan Kuntz, and Rhona Berenstein. I owe Alison McKee, my dear, wonderfully sage friend, special thanks. Her exuberant and searing intellectual companionship is a perpetual gift, and her contribution to this book is profound in ways large and small. Without her support over the years, I doubt I would have mustered the confidence to write it.

The genesis of this project benefited from two years of study at the Paris Centre des Études de Cinéma et de la Critique. I sincerely thank the Department of Film,Television and Digital Media at UCLA for its generous support in awarding me the Charles Boyer fellowship and the United States Information Agency grant that made it possible for me to have this wonderful time of study in Paris. All my critical work has been inflected by the illuminating courses I had the privilege to take with Jacques Aumont, Raymond Bellour, Michel Chion, Agnes Minazzoli, Marie-Claire Ropars, and Charles Tesson. Marc Vernet, in particular, was exceptionally astute, kind, and generous in facilitating my work on voice during my time in Paris. My friends, James Schamus, Judith Shulevitz, Michele Zaccheo, and Jeffrey Ruoff were no less important in challenging me to their high level of thought and writing, and I thank them for their companionship at *Action Christine,* and insights into film. Kutlug Ataman, maverick thinker and fellow filmmaker, was like a brother to me during the years in which I was researching and writing this book: his lively wit and love of the absurd kept me from losing touch with reality while steeped in academic concerns.

The writing of the first draft of this book took place at the University of North Carolina at Chapel Hill, where I had my first teaching appointment in the Department of Communication Studies. I wish to express my appreciation to Bill Balthrop, in particular, for arranging for me to have a reduced course-load and research assistance to assist in the completion of the manuscript. My colleagues at UNC were all very generous with their help. Anna McCarthy, Vicky Johnson, Joanne Hershfield, and Hap Kindem especially were infinitely supportive during the long and sometimes painful period of writing, and I look to them as inspiring examples of scholarly achievement, and equally inspiring human beings. Erik Doxtader was utterly giving as a colleague and a friend, reading the manuscript in its rawest state, offering very helpful criticism, and suggesting texts for me to read that proved to be absolutely vital to the project, and I am very grateful for his help.

I wish to thank Dean Keith Morrison, Chair Steve Ujlaki, and all of my colleagues at San Francisco State University for their support of all my projects, and in particular for enabling me to take a leave of absence during which I significantly retooled the project and made it publishable. Many wonderful people (too many to list here) inside and outside of academia lent me assistance and/or cheered me on down the finish line, and their friendship has meant all the difference in bringing this project to fruition. In particular, I want express my appreciation to Judy Bloch, Susan Evans-Wickburg, Kathy Geritz, Steve Kovacs, Jennifer Hammett, Jenny Lau, Amie Williams, Miya Lippit, Ann Martin, Bill Nichols, and Bérénice Reynaud for their advice and moral support. It is hard to come up with words that seem remotely adequate to thank the peerless Akira Lippit for all he has done for me. He has championed the project, helped, and encouraged me in countless ways. The brilliance of his work, teaching, and personal grace is without equal: I count myself lucky to have had him as a colleague, and luckier still to have him as a friend.

Bertrand Augst's inspiring film courses at UC Berkeley, where I was an undergraduate, set me on a path that has become my life. His mode of teaching, so exuberant, so respectful of his students and so creative, is everything I wistfully aspire to. Likewise, the courses I took from Noël Burch forever altered and sharpened my understanding of cinema and its representations. I have the greatest admiration for his evolving and always iconoclastic relationship to film theory. His support of my writing and my films, so expansive and generous, has been a rare honor for me.

I want to express my appreciation to Joan Catapano for her guidance as editor and for selecting this book for publication. Thanks to all the other wonderful people at the University of Illinois Press, in particular, Angela L. Burton, who was so helpful to me throughout the production and editing process. One could not hope for a more accomplished, refined, and talented copyeditor than Julie Gay—I am extremely grateful for her dedicated work on behalf of the book.

My family has supported me both materially and emotionally through the various phases of writing this book. My heartfelt thanks to my mother, Christine Sjogren, my father, Per Sjogren, my sister, Lisa Naito, my brothers Rolf Sjogren, Lance Sjogren, and Chris Sjogren, for keeping me afloat in hard times, for all their encouragement, wisdom, and love.

My daughter, Asta, was three days old when I received word that this book was accepted for publication. Her birth brought me good luck in this and many other ways. The direct experience of the mysterious and ephemeral voice that connects child and mother helped me understand my subject better, and made this period of living and writing one of sheer joy. This book is the better for the influence of her sparkling presence.

Finally, one person has cared as much about this book as I have, (and maybe more so). My husband, Sean Uyehara, kept me from giving up during the arduous, lonely days of initial writing, gave me pep talks, talked over my ideas with indefatigable interest, came up with key sources to help bolster my arguments, gave me soup and chocolate, and still loved me at the end of what seemed like a long dark tunnel. His help on the revisions of this book has been crucial—I have relied utterly on the difference of his tenacious and incomparable mind, his editorial acumen, and the astonishing breadth and originality of his take on film theory. His voice-off is here alongside mine, on every page.

into the vortex

prologue:
voices, vortexes,
and dialectics

The propositions offered in this book arise from my love of classical cinema—in particular my fascination with those films that bear a female voice-off. Beyond these affinities, it has been my aim to question, refute, and rebut some strongly entrenched theoretical assumptions that have led many feminist (and other) critics to dismiss Hollywood films as invariably and monolithically "male-centered," as catering to a phallocentric gaze alone, as occluding the feminine, and as containing the woman, and her desire, within not only images that objectify her, but inside narrative structures that constrict and oppress her subjectivity and point of view. These texts need not be looked at so pessimistically. Feminine difference is a positive structuring force within these films—one sustained, rather than stifled, through the apperception of contradiction on the levels of consciousness, point of view, and discourse. Indeed, an orientation that presumes and insists that the woman cannot speak or be heard in the classical cinema may bar us from perceiving ways in which the feminine is represented, eventually suppressing what we seek to find.

Films from the 1940s possessing female voice-off offer a particularly generative vantage point from which to address these concerns and to rethink prevailing critical perspectives on the classical cinema. More than any other period in film history (aside from the 1970s feminist and other avant-garde movements), 1940s Hollywood *favored* this formal characteristic. Alongside the enthusiastic voice-off experiments of the film noir cycle proper, studios produced a veritable rash of films bearing female voice-off during the '40s—with a few examples trickling into the 1950s. These films cross genre lines, ranging from melodrama (*Letter from an Unknown Woman*), horror (*I Walked with a Zombie*), and noir (*Raw Deal*), to gothic (*Secret beyond the Door*) and combat films (*So Proudly We Hail*). Generally popular and classically styled films, they aimed to speak across class and gender, unlike "art" cinema movements, which address a narrower, more elite audience. Produced for general audiences, these 1940s films were tailored particularly to appeal to women. Their themes often directly addressed the home-front experience (*Since You Went Away*, *So Proudly We Hail*). Also, through more indirect representations of women facing difficult choices, separation from loved ones, and performing their "duty" under emotional strain (*Humoresque*, *All This and Heaven Too*), these films often made reference to the challenges newly independent women faced during wartime.

Though frequently directed by "authors" like Fritz Lang, Max Ophüls, and Joseph Mankiewicz, these films were produced under corporate, capitalist conditions and were thus quite clearly imbricated in the patriarchal system that engendered them. Moreover, most of the '40s films bearing this formal characteristic (and indeed all of the texts discussed in this book) were directed by men rather than women. Still, this book looks for feminine subjectivity within these films as a *positive structuring element*, a dynamic contradiction, rather than as a "subversive" thread woven in or "breaking out" of the text, somehow inserted there by a female filmmaker resisting patriarchy behind the scenes.

Films of the 1940s are of interest in this context precisely because they rise out of a period in which the relation of sound to image might be described as conventionally stable. Whereas in the late 1920s and the early 1930s, Hollywood cinema was still in a state of flux, "adjusting" to the discursive and formal possibilities and challenges ushered in by the introduction of sound, by the 1940s the industry had successfully negotiated this "transitional" phase.[1] Thus, this book takes an opposite tack from a feminist position that argues, "if we are to have any hope of finding a break in the hegemony of classical style (silent or sound), a time when a woman's voice could be her own, we must look closely at a limited period in American film history when the conventions of cinematic representation were for a time in crisis."[2] Indeed, one could say that in the 1940s, the cards were, in a sense, doubly stacked *against* the possibility for feminine subjectivity to be expressed through voice-off (or any other formal aural component). Not only do films from this period bear the political and discursive limitations imposed generally by a powerful representational monopoly (the studio system), but they are also representatives from an era in which sound's signifying "difference" had evolved from an awkward and often foregrounded formal "attachment" to a highly conventionalized, firmly integrated element of film form. Thus, the sheer unlikelihood that such films nonetheless offer a space for the feminine to be spoken motivated me, in part, to focus on them.

Representing the 1940s (or any era) as "stable," however, is inherently problematic—a generalization that is at odds with the larger spirit of this project. Representation proliferates: meaning is anything but static, despite the presence of stabilizing codes or conventions that may anchor its progress. At any point in history, contradictions—representational, discursive, ideological—exist in tension with a dominant order. On one hand, the choice of this era is decidedly pertinent for this project; on the other hand, one might choose another "era" (a subjective category in itself), a single year, or even a solitary film as an arena within which to study the process by which difference is sustained in film. This is not to say that historical context is irrelevant—any film or group of films potentially examined here would have been subject to the times and conditions in which they were produced. My project, however, is not "historical" in the sense that *only these films at this historical point* could give rise to the speculations that follow. Rather, these specific films provide an especially apt historical context within which to explore the theoretical issues at stake in this book. They also provide an arena within which to illustrate a method and model of analysis that expressly parts company with a strong feminist tradition that looks to "subversive" film genres, female authorship, formal ruptures, "progressive gaps," and periods of representational "crisis" in order to find the feminine. This project demonstrates the ways that such discordant elements may structure all films—the ways in which the feminine, too, may structure all films. Certainly, I see the role of sound, and particularly the female voice-off, as a marker of "difference," an undeniable asset that marks the creative flex of contradiction that runs through the group of films examined here. As Rick Altman has put it, "Cinema changes, and the action of sound is one of the prime reasons for that change."[3]

Still, to assert that historical context plays no role in the selection of these films for this study would be false. Despite their masculine "authorship," the films analyzed in this book all attempt to address a woman's subjective experience in some way, reflecting the industry's efforts to capitalize on the World War II home-front audience's new spending power. Targeted to this newly dominant, independent female market, these films articulate and respond to a socio-historical context within which the "voice" and the increased discursive visibility of women was a pressing issue. Not only are the narratives generally focused on female protagonists' negotiations of romantic, psychological, financial, or political problems, but the female voice-off strongly foregrounds the women characters' speech. There is no pressing need here to revisit the historical circumstances of wartime propaganda and capitalism's exploitation of women as consumers and second-class citizens. Others have strongly argued to these purposes, with depth and persuasive force.[4] Rather, this book looks at these films from another perspective, to consider the problem from the side of the female subject who speaks (and listens) from within patriarchy. In this regard, the appeal of these films to more contemporary audiences is striking, for, clearly, they were not addressed to the women and men who study them today. Yet, as the legacy of feminist film theory since the 1970s plainly illustrates, these films remain compelling sources of pleasure, antipathy, debate, and fascination. (One could even argue that these films are *more* pleasurable for us today than they were for their intended audiences, for although these were popular films, they were not all successful films: unlike *Rebecca* and *A Letter to Three Wives*, for example, both *Secret beyond the Door* and *Letter from an Unknown Woman* were financial train wrecks.[5] Whether all these films "spoke" to their contemporary audience is something difficult to affirm. It is clear, however, that these highly contradictory texts speak to *us*.)

Their cult-like status for many contemporary theorists was an important consideration in selecting these works. I wanted, on one hand, to propose my theses in regard to films that had been, so to speak, already run "through the mill" and about which, one might fear, there is "nothing more to be said," with the aim of opening up a fundamentally new way of looking at these canonical texts. Rather than searching out obscure films to render my arguments, I wanted to test them against texts that have, by virtue of their critical "popularity," proved to be of central importance to the field. On the other hand, I chose these films because of their strong affective pull. I had to question why and how I "loved" these films—whether my subjectivity was at stake or obliterated as I listened to the voices-off that leave such an indelible mark on the mind. Why did I feel that these voices manifested a powerful dissonance, something that I myself could exploit while making films?

The initial research for this volume coincided with the writing and directing of my first feature film, *Jo-Jo at the Gate of Lions,* and I was deeply absorbed with the tangible challenges facing any feminist filmmaker. Searching for ways to convey feminine subjectivity in film, for strategies to address other women, for a narratological means of displacing a "centered" objectifying point of view, I looked to these classical films as question marks, as sites of problems and possible solutions. My perspective on the issues raised in these pages is thus indelibly marked by the sense of urgency I have felt as a woman trying to "speak" through film. This book reflects, moreover, my longstanding effort to reconcile the infamous divide between theory and practice—a dialectic that has structured my own life as both scholar and filmmaker. As my theoretical interests have propelled my creative work in specific directions, so, too, has my creative work come to influence my perspective on theory. Making films has forced me to look for solutions to problems that theory suggests are nearly insoluble. A remarkable sense of freedom comes from such a dilemma: a certain naïveté allows one to take action *as if it were possible*. I must assume a woman can speak through film, and that feminine subjectivity can find expression within patriarchy: this stance encourages me to question theoretical truisms I find stifling. My own practical experiments with sound, voice-off, and narrative structure, then, bring me to many of the conclusions I offer in the pages to come. The time I have spent designing, editing, and mixing sound has also rendered me particularly sensitive to the possibilities of sound and voice, and has assisted me in appreciating the complexity of the sound tracks analyzed here. An intricate technology serves sound recording, editing, and re-recording, facilitated by the controlled use of microphones, digital audiotape (DAT), Nagra audio tape recorders, magnetic film, digital editing software, mix boards and the like. Through these tools, these apparatuses, sound is worked, directed, and manipulated; in fact, in a sense, sound is frequently more consciously crafted than the visual image. Where the image often contains many accidental and unforeseen elements that surface within the "real space" where the filming takes place (play of light, weather, etc., especially in on location shooting), the creation of a sound track is more often completely contrived—created artificially in an independent process and composed with elements that were not necessarily present during the filming.[6]

Sound thus emerges as a parallel process, powerfully structuring the meanings available to the spectator of a film. It is by way of stressing this "parallel" status of sound, moreover, that the term "voice-off" is used throughout this text, rather than the more traditional "voice-over." I prefer the term "off," in part, because it registers an independent space. Whereas "over" suggests a top "layer" or cloak of some kind, "off" connotes other-ness—a distinctness that moves alongside, "elsewhere." In this sense, "off" best evokes the tension of a dialectic to the image, a vital relationship to preserve in descriptions of the voice. Indeed, though the analyses here concentrate on the asynchronous use of the voice, the question of the synch voice is never far afield. I focus on films that stress this apparent separation because they amplify and render more obvious the degree to which all voice—all sound—could be said to be "off." All sounds, that is, are equally separate from the image track in that they are only "married" in the final instance, brought together in the composite film print: prior to this, they are separate elements which can be "placed" anywhere one wishes relative to the picture. In distinguishing "synch" from "non-synch" sounds as if they are in some ontological way quite opposite from one another, we may be forgetting the artifice of any connection they hold to the image. Synch, in this sense, is an arbitrary concept—for one "synchs up" "non-synch" sounds with as much diligence as "synch" sounds in film production practice. Thinking about synch as also "other" and "off" helps one keep in mind the multiple significations generated by any voice (or sound) during a film viewing.

In French, *voix off* stands in for any voice which registers as non-synch—whether a narrating voice that is never seen, a voice emanating from a character who stands just offscreen, or an interior monologue expressing the thoughts of a character visible to us. I find this idea useful in respond-ing to the taxonomies of voice that others have prepared before me. Both Mary Ann Doane and Kaja Silverman have taken great care to discriminate between different "kinds" of voice in cinema.[7] Doane's categories seem coined by way of preexisting tropes: (1) synch; (2) voice-off (where a character speaks from offscreen but is not seen); (3) interior monologue (where we see the character and hear his or her asynchronous voice); and (4) disembodied voice-over (no visible character or designated diegetic figure—usually found in documentary). Silverman takes these categories and remaps them expressly in terms of "embodiment": (1) synch sound (which she suggests binds the female film subject to the prison of the objectifying image); (2) the floating voice (one that at times emerges as detached, at others, attached to a specific female body in the film and thus enjoys a certain degree of subjectivity or resistance to classical cinema's normal vising in on the female body); and (3) the disembodied voice (a voice entirely without visual locus during the course of the film, which Silverman understands to be the most resistant to oppressive patriarchal psychology). The problem of the body that is broached in Doane's article becomes, within Silverman's account, the *ne plus ultra* of the voice—*the* critical focus of the problem. Hence, Silverman's schema unfolds as a complex grading of voice embodiments, from "disembodied voice-over" and "embodied voice-over" to (male) synch speech that is "coded" as relatively "exterior" to the diegesis and is thus more "disembodied" than certain (female) voice-overs. Within this demarcation (which Silverman spells out most clearly in her article, "DisEmbodying the Female Voice," but which she expands with great flourish in *The Acoustic Mirror*) an ideal (under a feminist optic) seems implicit in the "disembodied" voice, which, as she describes approvingly, is "freed from its claustral confinement within the female body."[8]

Although all these demarcations are extremely valuable contributions to the field of sound theory (and certainly of great interest), they are also somewhat misleading. The very stratification that these authors point out between "kinds" of voices or "degrees" of embodiment suggests a logic that sees each "class" of voice as bearing intrinsic properties which remain immutable from case to case, film to film, moment to moment. This is not to suggest that either Silverman or Doane uses these categories in reductive or rigid ways. Nor do I wish to throw out the baby with the bathwater: I will refer to these taxonomies at points in this book, as they are particularly useful in helping to "visualize" aspects of the voice's multiple spatiality in relation to imaged space. The very construction of a hierarchy, however—ultimately implicit in the mappings these theorists have made of the voice—invites us to forget the alterity that is always present, always structuring the asynchronous female voice in film. It is this otherness, again, that I am concerned to preserve and foreground throughout these pages: the residue of difference and plurality of which the voice speaks. A definition like "disembodied voice-over" subordinates supplemental meanings to a primary one (one of distance from the body), discouraging other possible simultaneous, contradictory meanings.

Separating off the voice into neat divisions may not only close down the play of the signifier: there is also a danger in overdissecting the mechanisms of meaning, inasmuch as we may forget that these categories are merely tools for understanding a larger system at work, a system that is, at the limit, abstract and unbounded. We may begin to believe in an empirical science of voice, or of art. This criticism extends not just to the kind of taxonomies of voice discussed above, but pertains to a whole tendency in much of film theory to isolate meaning. The fabulous and brilliant cognitive schemas proposed by Edward Branigan in *Narrative Comprehension and Film*, for example, run the risk of trapping the films he analyzes in a deterministic structure. That is, hierarchical models/deconstructions can ultimately come to "rule" the meaning of the film—confirming, in a sense, what we expect to find, rather than opening onto the unexpected or helping us to change the way we interpret a film. In critiquing such schemas, Gilles Deleuze and Félix Guattari have objected to linguists, such as Noam Chomsky, who carve from language *constants* or "a homogeneous or standard system . . . making possible a scientific study of *principles* . . . guaranteeing the constancy and homogeneity of the object under study."[9] They claim that these constants are in fact false and "superseded by variables of expression internal to enunciation itself."[10] These "variables of expression," they go on to say, "are then no longer separate from the variables of content with which they are in *perpetual interaction*."[11] In other words, in the designation of constants (such as "types of voices" operating in films), we risk losing sight of the process by which meaning is produced, the "perpetual interaction" of voice, narration, editing, the spectator, the image, and the excess that is always part of expression and communication. Without an analytic framework that allows for the unforeseen and for the contradictory exceptions enunciation produces, it is not, indeed, possible to account for *change*. Thus, to paraphrase Deleuze and Guattari in this regard, it is not that the categories Doane and Silverman offer are too abstract, "it is that [they are] *not abstract enough, [they] remain 'linear.'*"[12] Linearity, indeed, is a problematic model for the voice, as we shall see. It is in the spirit of change, then, that I embrace abstraction here through this term "voice-off." Like a talisman of difference, it stands in to remind of all that it simultaneously is and is not.

Abstract, amorphous, contradictory: the asynchronous female voice in these films constantly fluctuates from one "state" to another. These fluctuations themselves are my quarry—these traverses *between* the endpoints bounding them rather than the endpoints themselves. I propose, therefore, that it is perhaps pointless to try to pin down a voice as either "off" or "over" according to traditional definitions. It is the very mutability of the voice-off that characterizes it—the way it slips free of the image, glides in and out of its attachments to its apparent body, moving from (in Doane and Silverman's terms) voice-over to voice-off to embodied voice-over to badly synched sound and back again. Using the term "voice-off" allows one to follow these movements, unbiased by the assumption, for example, that the moment in which a voice seems "furthest" from a body correlates necessarily to a textual point of greater subjectivity. Indeed, a feminist project that looks for instances of truly "disembodied voice-over" in these films is something of a lost project from the get-go. Most Hollywood films from the '40s that do bear a female voice-off of any narrational weight, in fact, offer at best a "floating" voice, which at times speaks without visible corporeal support and at times is linked expressly to the female body. The only totally disembodied female "voice-over" from this period, according to Silverman, in fact, is that of Addie Ross in Mankiewicz's 1949 film *A Letter to Three Wives* (a contention open to debate, since we do briefly see Addie's fragmented body in the middle of the film). Given the categories she sets up, unfortunately, Silverman cannot find evidence of feminine subjectivity in these classical Hollywood films, for her definitions exclude the very possibility. In using the term "voice-off," then, I hope keep descriptions of this chameleon-like phenomenon from ossifying into predetermined strata, and to keep an open mind about the possibility for any voice—embodied or not—to speak of the feminine.

Like many feminist films that surfaced in the 1970s and 1980s (such as Laura Mulvey and Peter Wollen's *Riddles of the Sphinx*, Sally Potter's *The Gold Diggers,* the films of Yvonne Rainer, etc.), for which 1940s films provided a point of reference (if not inspiration), the films discussed in this book encourage spectatorial identification of a feminine order—an "address" to a female audience was implicit in their production.[13] The privileging of female voice-off, indeed, in these films seems an obvious textual strategy devised for achieving a certain aesthetic and/or psychological aim. That is, though different assumptions were of necessity made by the different writers, filmmakers, and producers who incorporated the female voice-off into their films, the primary significance of exploiting the female voice as a narrating presence in a film seems grounded in, it is tempting to say, a common assumption of the "essence" of this voice. The female voice seems to "speak" directly to women "from" a female subject. A female character vocalizes her thoughts or feelings to an audience of (assumed) women, and a "hailing" of the spectator is underscored in a way that rarely, if ever, sustains itself on the image track. It is problematic, of course, to suggest that any voice speaks "directly" in culture—ideology would seem to mediate what can be said. A voice represented as both speaking to and for women thus bears interesting social inflections within the wartime era. For instance, did films characterized by female voice-off in the early to mid-forties encourage a feminine consciousness or incite the discursive empowerment of women? Did films of the late forties bearing a female voice-off reflect the respective closing down of the same invitation? It is my view that the contradictions enounced in the discursive operations of these films may be seen as not only formative, but pervasive, in traversing the decade to speak of feminine subjectivity. That is, despite the Holly-wood/patriarchal "agenda" to rope women back into their pre-1940s role, the later films articulate strong ambivalences and conflicting discursive dynamics that remain a legacy of the ascension to speech promised by earlier experiences and prior representations. The female voice-off, in this respect, continues to speak of the female subject even as she is suppos-edly put to rest; moreover, much of the contradiction, we shall see, rests in the dialectic the voice offers to the *gaze*. As the work of Laura Mulvey has demonstrated, it is the (male) gaze above all that "seeks" to objectify and contain the woman.[14] Whereas many theorists seem to consider the gaze invulnerable to distraction, a monolith agency that always works to contain difference, I contend that the voice offers another perspective, a subject placement that allows for multiple subjectivities, rather than "centering" just One.

By taking up the female voice-off as the centerpiece of this manu-script, this book counters a number of essays and books dedicated to the soundtrack and the voice in film. While looking over these texts, all brilliantly written and groundbreaking in one way or another, I have been struck by a sense of progression between them, as well as by certain assumptions many of these texts share about the relationship of sound to image, about the subject's relationship to the apparatus, about point of view, and about narrative itself. It seems clear that the relative dearth of work done on sound by film theorists overall reflects a kind of "poor cousin" status for sound in general: most writers have dedicated the bulk of their work to the "primary" element of film, the image. Many of the authors who have dedicated considerable thought to the problem of sound and voice in film, moreover, seem to have come to a sort of con-sensus regarding the heterogeneity sound presents to image. Within this "camp" there is, as Edward Baron Turk has put it, a "critical bias towards the visual."[15] Either sound is understood as "just like" the image, though subservient to it in many ways (as in Christian Metz's writings), or sound is seen as posing a potentially radical difference (as in Doane's work, and Silverman's, in particular). This difference, however, is usually (if not always) viewed as constrained by being embedded within the image, "yoked" to a claustral body, or ensnared within narrative interiority. There is an underlying agreement, however, that sound in general and the voice-off in particular cannot "compete" with the image. For all these theorists, cinema is, indeed, primarily a *visual* art.

I have tried to critique this privileging of the visual over the acoustic register of cinema in a number of ways. In this endeavor, I am indebted to the pioneering work of a handful of critics and theorists whose writing on sound might be said to fall into a second "camp"—work which postulates sound's signification in cinema as at least bearing equal weight to the image, if not more. The importance of Rick Altman's book, *Sound Theory Sound Practice*, cannot be overemphasized as a vital perspective not only on the relationship of sound to image, but also on the heterogeneity, dimensionality, and materiality of sound itself. Altman's own writing and that of others (especially James Lastra and Amy Lawrence, in their own books) recall in important ways the legacy of "silent" cinema and the forms of sound and speech that predate and influence the development of sound's representation in the talkies.[16] Moreover, looking back to the origins of cinema, there is ample evidence that a "purely" visual filmic experience was never produced for, nor desired by, spectators. The representational history of film suggests that the alterity that sound presents to the image has always structured film texts, long before an optical recording was married to the celluloid strip. Beyond this, the fact that the sound demanded by early spectators distracted from the illusory pull of the image helps dislodge the commonsense thesis that sound is secondary since it merely helps to "add realism" to the image. Indeed, this "historical fallacy" about sound, which Altman has resoundingly refuted, is an important buttress to the observations offered in the pages to come.[17] My own critique of the primacy of the visible in film studies extends these debates into different ground. Altman, Lastra, and others have offered compelling scenarios of the ontology and perceptual status of sound and provocative histories of its unique representational development. This book is complementary to their work; its focus, however, is elsewhere, given my expressly feminist agenda. This book sees the primacy of the visible in film studies as more than an error. Rather, this "bias" leans, like an ace in a house of cards, on other "biases," assumptions about the nature of subjectivity and the threat of the body that naturalize and justify much of film theory's exclusion of the feminine from representability.

In these pages, I have attempted to situate some of the key issues in sound theory, paying particular attention to the feminist work that engages the terrain of female voice-off. The major debates need to be put into context if one hopes to move onto new ground. In addition to the problem of the relative perceptual and representational value to be placed on sound relative to the image, other questions that have surfaced in both feminist and sound theory remain vital: the "place" of the acoustic subject with regard to the voice; the spatial dimension and perspectival contribution of sound; the relation of voice to language, speech, and discourse; the problem of the body as material origin of vocality; and the textual and ideological implications of synchronization.

In much early film theory, one finds a predictable and, perhaps, understandable neglect of sound. For instance, Metz's influential study of the film subject, *The Imaginary Signifier*, still one of the most imaginative and compelling critiques of the psychoanalytic and ideological implications of the cinema written to date, offers little assistance in understanding the metaphysical relationship the film spectator may take up in relation to sound and/or voice. Metz undervalues the component of sound conspicuously in his famous dissection of the apparatus. Though the psychoanalytic writings of Jacques Lacan, upon which much of Metz' work relies, frequently point out critical differences between the scopic and invocatory drives, Metz invariably treats these as identical functions.[18] In another article, "Aural Objects," Metz explores the ramifications of sound more specifically; however, his conclusions betray an unwavering, underlying assumption that the image is always primary.[19]

This familiar bias toward the visual surfaces even in texts dedicated to sound and voice in cinema, most notably and surprisingly in Kaja Silverman's *The Acoustic Mirror*. Much of Silverman's work on spectatorial relations stresses the ways in which the (female) voice is pinned to the image, drawing it as ineluctably corporalized and ultimately doomed to signify as if it were specular. Though she does briefly entertain the idea that the spectator may relate differently to the voice-off than to the image, she discards this possibility before long, at least as far as the classical cinema is concerned, concluding that whatever potential exists in the voice-off to address or represent feminine subjectivity is squelched by the implacable textual grip of the male gaze. The interpretations Silverman brings to psy-choanalytic paradigms that specifically concern the voice (such as those written by Denis Vasse and Guy Rosolato), moreover, fail to address key concepts these authors offer that open the door onto other ways of look-ing at how the voice-off may inflect spectatorship. Among these, the meta-phor of the *traverse* of the voice, which both links the child to the mother (in the womb and after birth) and articulates their separation, has been a powerful figure for me in conceptualizing the spectator's relationship to the voice-off. Conversely, the term "acoustic mirror," coined by Rosolato and taken up by Silverman, has unfortunate limitations in describing the voice. This vision-based metaphor cannot adequately capture the most intriguing and provocative characteristics of the voice—its fluidity, its non-specularity, its heterogeneity.[20] Indeed, Rosolato's use of the phrase derives from his interest in the oscillating movement between subjectivi-ties, rather than an intention to cast the voice as a site of specular/imagi-nary identification. This *between* can be grasped as a psychological cur-rent, a "space" for a non-imaged body, a multiple or shared point of view, an active, dynamic discursive contradiction.

Given the bias toward the visual component of film and the phallocen-tric basis of much of Lacan's writing, the subject is invariably understood within most psychoanalytically informed literature as "male," "transcen-dent," "distant," "centered." Such a description obviously derives from the history of visual art, Jean-Louis Baudry's famous essay on the ideologi-cal effects of the cinematographic apparatus, Metz's compelling theses, and, finally, Mulvey's groundbreaking essay, "Visual Pleasure and Narra-tive Cinema." In this scenario, which presumes a transcendent distance to be synonymous with subjective power, an ideological premise can be observed which conflates subjectivity with a position "outside looking on"—a removed, yet central place of authoritative privilege. These val-ues clearly reflect a view of "masculine-coded" subjectivity, one based on the primacy of the phallus as a *visible* signifier, one that seems unlikely to account for an experience of feminine subjectivity, or for the effect or experience of the acoustic register of film. In looking to the voice-off as an arena relative to which feminine subjectivity may surface, then, I was not in the least disappointed to note that such subjectivity is often linked to positions of textual interiority, to poetry rather than logic, to vortexical narrative movement rather than linear progression. It is my position that, if we want to begin to conceptualize feminine subjectivity, the masculine model will not serve. Indeed, such a model hardly serves even the male spectator, the male subject. The male spectator's allegedly sadistic gaze has frequently been assumed to be unassailable, a powerful objectifying force. But if sound opens onto heterogeneity, and female voice-off operates to sustain difference (as demonstrated in the following pages), to express contradiction, to signify *between* male and female, then, I would argue, we also need to look more closely at the schemas that lock men, as well as women, to a depressing scenario that reduces desire to objectification. Feminists, as well as others looking to imagine subjectivity in a less pessimistic vein, need to interrogate this "masculine" model of subjectivity, and to question the valuation of a distanced specular transcendence as the only paradigm within which subject relations may be conceived.

Joan Copjec has argued, in fact, that this view of the Subject of film, and film theory's interpolation of Lacan, are not sufficiently psychoanalytic but rather are overly influenced by Michel Foucault's description of the panoptical gaze.[21] Her work has led to emerging theories sensitized to the order of the Real in Lacan's work, which in turn will doubtless unfold into less ossified models of subjectivity. The notion of consciousness as proposed by both Vasse and Rosolato relative to the voice provides just such a possible alternative paradigm. According to these theorists, the voice is both of the unconscious and the conscious, of the body and of the Other's body (anterior to the placing of a sexualized value on that body). The recognition of these differences "in" the voice, I argue, may remind of a state in which consciousness of self and Other does not imply dissolution for the subject. Such a voice may enable or incline the spectator to sustain difference, rather than to deny or punish (with a sadistic gaze) the images that accompany his or her sense of heterogeneity.

My approach, thus, in looking at the sound track and the voice-off of classical film, differs in important respects from those adopted by Metz, Silverman, and others who see the image as primary and the voice as, in a sense, its prisoner. This book disputes this basic assumption about the filmic experience and looks at the female voice-off as a strongly heterogeneous formal element that helps construct the film text along with the image. Neither image nor sound track, I argue, dominates in creating meaning, addressing the spectator, structuring narrative, evoking perspective, or producing discourse. This heterogeneity, sustained, works moreover in a paradoxical, dialectical sense: not by obliterating difference, but in accounting for the existence of contradiction. The dialectical potential of the female voice-off emerges less as a matter of degree of disembodiment effected "between" the voice and the body of the female, but rather more as the repercussion of the formal and textual relations the female voice-off structures progressively into the text, which contribute to the evocation of feminine subjectivity. The radical paradox evoked by these films lies not merely in the appendage of the female voice-off as a formal element per se, but in an intensification of a psychological heterogeneity implicit in the female voice-off through discursive strategies that open up the contradiction in its relation to the image. This book traces these textual structurations and seeks to elucidate the dynamic presence of sustained contradictions that shape the films.

Voice-off allows (narratologically) for the introduction of heterogeneous and seemingly incompatible perspectives or points of view in a film—perspectives that, moreover, do not necessarily cancel each other out in their contradictoriness. Thus, in an analysis of *Secret beyond the Door*, I attempt to demonstrate how the character Celia's narrating voice-off's perspective remains active even after it has seemingly "disappeared" into the voice-off "belonging" to her husband Mark, continuing to help structure our appreciation of point of view in this film as *shared* by them. Similarly, in *All about Eve*, point of view cannot be ascribed to any one of the voices-off in particular: our understanding of perspective arrives *between* them all. Indeed, it is not necessary for multiple voices-off to surface in a film in order to create the paradox that such simultaneous subjectivities suggest. In *Letter from an Unknown Woman*, for example, the strongly shared consciousness of the two protagonists, invoked by a sole female voice-off, allows for our recognition of such a "shared point of view." Such a perspective is echoed in the spectator's relationship to the text—he or she recognizes the voice as consciousness, as both "I" and "other," and thus sustains the paradox of difference in a positive sense. Further, I argue that for the spectator the voice-off acts as a kind of rhetorical "middle voice," neither active nor passive, but both at the same time.

The female voice-off tends to provide a plurality of points of view within a film text, influencing the textual form of a film in revealing ways. The narrative movement of the films discussed in this book proceeds by digression rather than the linear model of progression often cited as the model of the classical cinema. Far from seeing the delays, the flashbacks, the holding up of time, the privileging of space, the circularity and stasis of these texts as negative attributes that lock the female protagonist "inside" the narrative, I question the notion that "exteriority" to the text translates into a superior subjective placement for a character (or spectator, for that matter). Rather, these texts move in a vortexical fashion, with a verticality that flexes against the linear flow of standard narrative, the vertical vs. the linear posing, again, a fundamental contradiction. Thus it is my contention that certain indices of signification—linearity and time, rather than circularity and space—have been erroneously privileged as primary in the construction of narrative meaning. Stasis and repetition need not be seen as immobilizing, paralytic influences on female characters within these films; rather, their deviational and often dialectical effect may instead provide a vigorous contradiction to the lure of causal relations that inform forward narrational movement. In this sense, contradiction is formative, rather than hierarchized—both directions move simultaneously in a dynamic expression of difference.

While looking at the female voice-off, I have taken care to consider its function as voice, not wishing to reduce this phenomenon to the language it bears. However, the important discursive function of the speech borne by the voice, clearly, requires examination. For their part, many of these films seem to be "about" a struggle for mastery over discourse. The very emphasis on the voice "over" the body is pertinent in this respect. In a textual system that generally "pins" the female voice to the female body, their separation, in itself, may be regarded as a radical rupture to the norm, as Silverman has pointed out.[22] The female voice-off introduces a tension within the discursive practice of classical Hollywood cinema. This tension (which may be understood as a subtle undercutting of patriarchal discourse "about and for" women) is evident, for example, in the frequent "point-of-view wars" that characterize many of these films—for example, *Secret beyond the Door* and *All about Eve*. Many of these films also link female voice-off to the writing of letters, signaling an effort on the part of the protagonist to take discourse into her own hands.[23] The representation of feminine discourse in these films furthermore arrives in concert with a marked textual ambivalence toward the female character whose actions and voice-off have betrayed a will-to-power. Almost all the female characters bearing a voice-off are "punished" diegetically for the degree of subjectivity allowed them within the text. As others have shown before me, women appear to speak only to be elided (*Secret beyond the Door*) or silenced (as in *Rebecca,* where Joan Fontaine's character speaks less and less freely, or in *Kiss Me Deadly,* where the price of speech is death). Women in these films, it would seem, "learn," in the course of the narrative, to "hold their tongue" or suffer the consequences. As I will try to show in the coming pages, however, statements like these are often untenable generalizations. The heterogeneity characteristic of the female voice-off contributes critically to its discursive function in film. One voice can express contradictory discourses, embodying its own paradox.

These films, that is, may be said to countermand a view of discourse and ideology that understands patriarchal representation as hegemonic, as unassailable and homogeneous, always "containing" difference beneath a strongly worked coherence. Rather (as the writings of Michel Foucault suggest), discourse is constructed through its own contradiction—and this relation is a dynamic process of perpetual renaissance and proliferation of difference. Thus the speech borne by the female voice-off in *A Letter to Three Wives*, for example, enunciates both the patriarchal and the feminine simultaneously. Such films do not constitute sites of one "master" discourse (and certainly not one levied by the image alone) but reflect a dynamic relationship between conflicting desires, disparate discourses, different will-to-meanings. Moreover, the recognition of this contradictory discourse is rendered acute for the viewer in the case of these films produced in the 1940s, which specifically interpolate the "issues" women faced in society as their recent economic empowerment was being whisked away. The voice-off's address of the contemporary female spectator is implied, not only through the political and social tensions raised by the dialogue in the films, but in the subjective experience of contradiction the voice recreates and the representation of a consciousness of a paradoxical point of view. The specific contradiction of being female in patriarchy, thus, is *amplified* through the voice-off, in its evocation of a heterogeneous consciousness, of a self that is also other. This experience of sustained difference points to a feminine politic of sorts that exists in dynamic tension with patriarchy. These women's films speak, that is, of a plurality of voices—of the society within which they emerge, of the subjects they address and attempt to represent, and of their differences. The voice-off speech in these films exacerbates our awareness not only of the constructive force of difference between voice and image, but also leads us to recognize the plurality of subjects who speak, despite and through contradiction, in patriarchy.

Thus it is as *both* speech and voice that I will examine the female voice-off, tracing the movement of these *together* as they structure the narratives in question. Whereas, frequently, even in studies devoted to voice-off (or "over") more emphasis is placed on the content of the dialogue, on its overt signification and sense-making inflection relative to the image,[24] I will maintain a close vigil on the "other side" of the voice: its grain, its difference, its *non*-sense. Indeed, this is a tricky process, not easily achieved. For the voice is an elusive subject, and in trying to do justice to its ephemeral and contradictory qualities, I have been as concerned to avoid reducing it to a literary model of narration as I have been to paint it as more than a mere ornament that humbly serves to enhance the meaning dictated by the image. The voice-off works in many, often contrary, directions simultaneously: this is its provocative, intangible paradox.

Textual analyses of films seem increasingly infrequent in film theory. Specifically, much of the work that has been done on sound (excepting, notably, Amy Lawrence's) either tends to examine sound's role in general (if exacting) ontological and historical terms (Altman, Lastra, Levin) or, when couched in reference to film texts, offers only brief examples to illustrate larger principles at work (Silverman, Doane). Indeed, Altman himself has noted that, ". . . ontological claim[s] about the role of sound ha[ve] been allowed to take precedence over actual analysis of sound's functioning. . . . [I]t is essential that such speculation not be taken as a prescription, as a binding assumption about the way sound must work in all cases. . . . [We] must depend on historically grounded claims and *on close analyses of particular films* rather than on ontological speculations that presume to cover all possible practices."[25] I agree with Altman that close textual analysis is critical for an accurate representation of the experience of a film's sound. Film is a temporal medium, the affect and meaning of which cannot be determined by isolating a few key moments that "illustrate" the whole. Sound, moreover, is less easily reduced to "quotation," as the image frequently has been in the form of stills. Sound is perhaps more temporal than the image, unable to be indexed through a fragment, requiring us to listen to its traverse across and through the narrative. Sound, that is, has a specific contribution to our experience of film-viewing that merits the same patient articulation the image track has received in innumerable textual analyses produced by scholars since the 1970s. This method, certainly, best suited this book, given my desire to look at voice-off in its textual progression. The close readings elucidated the key issues to be considered here and moved this text in some unforeseen directions.

The vortexical nature of the narratives in question was one such discovery. This spiraling, internally directed progression that structures so many of the films I encountered while writing this book is a poetic form upon which I have modeled my own methodology. I am concerned, first, to simply elaborate this helixical movement—to articulate its spins, chutes, and curves, and render them poignant to the reader. I also wish to emphasize, through this attention, the formal beauty and poetic complexity of these structures. By demonstrating, through sustained description, how the internal spaces of these films offer deep evocations of character sub-jectivity, invite vertical signification as against linear, and allow for the rich dissonance of discursive contradiction, I hope to cast doubt on a strongly entrenched view in film studies that such narratives "obviously" work in one way—that is, to "fold" characters into "stasis," to "pin" their voices to the confines of an objectifying body, to trap them in "claustral spaces," "regressive positions," etc.[26] Beyond my readings of the films, I have adopted this circular structure as inspiration in elaborating my own larger argument. Though the chapters that follow have a linear arrange-ment, the issues raised within them inexorably relate back to one another, refracting and spiraling to remind of the fundamental connections between spectatorship, narrative, and discourse. Important, too, in response to authors who have previously tackled these questions, it seems vital to represent their ideas both as part of an evolving field of thought and as texts that must be read vertically themselves. That is, my own writing here embraces repetition, and circles "back" more than once to recon-sider ideas and issues in multiple contexts—as does, for example, Kaja Silverman's analyses of the voice's relationship to the body in film. I hope in this way not only to avoid reducing the complexity of her arguments to a single "refutable" point, but also to render homage to the intricacy of the issues at stake. The question of the body, like others that will be explored in these pages, cannot be "contained" in a discussion of psychoanalytic registers, but also pertains to textual structure. One needs a simultane-ous cognizance of both relations to appreciate how the voice-off works in order to begin to understand the multifaceted question that the body poses. In spiraling round some of the figures who have contributed most to laying the groundwork in studies of the voice, then, I mean to go deeper and deeper into the questions that have engaged them, and now engage me, each time they are reintroduced. I hope also to draw connections between ideas in multiple and even contradictory directions. My dialogue with these authors, indeed, is intended as a dialectic—my criticisms are offered in a spirit of creative contradiction. In this sense, too, I am con-cerned to take up a position that echoes what I have learned from these films: that as a subject, I may signify from a displaced position—a place of difference that does not obliterate its opposite and that does not privilege one centered meaning. The reflections I offer in this book are a contribu-tion to a larger structure than that embodied in chapters and pages. Each of us who writes, works—perforce—within a vortex of thought that powerfully conveys us in new directions. This book hopes to acknowledge, in its progression, the ideas that made its writing possible.

Many questions remain lively, still provocative challenges to puzzle out in time. For example, how directly can some of the ideas presented here "transpose" pertinently to films that do not bear a female voice-off? I would argue that films bearing male rather than female voice-off may also exacerbate the consciousness of sustained difference; however, the films discussed in these pages, I feel, most vigorously demonstrate this process. The strong attention to the sound track and the peculiar properties of the female voice-off conspire to create a heightened example of contradiction and paradox. For the purposes of clarity, then, I chose an arena of study that both pleased me aesthetically and supported most compellingly the propositions I aimed to explore. These particular films from the 1940s and the voice-off that distinguishes them were my route leading to the questions that concern this book—the possibility of representing feminine subjectivity in films made within patriarchy, the nature of spectatorial relations to the cinematic apparatus, the dynamic of sound and image, the ideological implications of contradiction, and others. I do not doubt for a moment, however, that other routes may lead to conclusions similar to those I have drawn here, and that other classical films, whether they bear female voice-off or not, allow the feminine to be expressed in sustained difference.

1

a metapsychology
of the voice-off

In this matter of the visible, everything is a trap. . . .
[C]ertain optics allow that which concerns vision to
escape. Such optics are within the grasp of the blind. . . .
They have eyes that they might not see.

    Jacques Lacan, "Of the Gaze as *Objet Petit a,*" *The Four
    Fundamental Concepts of Psycho-Analysis*

This phantom being of the voice is what is dying out,
it is that sonorous texture which disintegrates and disappears.
I never know the loved being's voice except when it is dead,
remembered, recalled inside my head, way past the ear;
a tenuous yet monumental voice, since it is one of those
objects which exist only once they have disappeared.

    Roland Barthes, "Fading," *A Lover's Discourse*

Footsteps and Rustling Leaves: The Gaze of Sound

Sound, and particularly female voice-off, renders acute a cinematic phenomenon of "blind images"—moments in which we are asked to lay down
the gaze, to "see" through our hearing, moments that are often identified
with a feminine subjectivity. Too strict a correlation has been placed,
in fact, within scenarios exploring the riddle of cinematic identification,
between "sight" and "the gaze." Jacques Lacan repeatedly distinguishes
between these two terms: he stresses that there is, rather, "a dialectic" of

the eye and the gaze.[1] In another fascinating description, he implies that the gaze is like an acoustic perception. Citing Jean-Paul Sartre's discussion of the gaze in *Being and Nothingness,* Lacan notes with approval that "far from speaking of this gaze as of something that concerns the organ of sight, [Sartre] refers to the *sound of rustling leaves,* suddenly heard while out hunting, to a *footstep* in a corridor."[2] Lacan goes on to remind that the gaze is not apprehended "in the function of the existence of others as looking at me . . . but in the subject sustaining himself in a function of desire."[3] The tendency to attribute desire to vision/the image in the cinema is understandable. Lacan's hint, however, that vision per se is not the primary issue (and that in fact, the gaze can be felt via sound) certainly opens up other ways of conceptualizing desire in the cinematic relation.

It is interesting to think, in this connection, of the numerous film scenarios that "castrate" a woman by blinding her, suggesting that the feminine can be seen but cannot see, not "externally," at any rate. This kind of (non) vision evokes Lacan's description of an "elision of the gaze" in the waking state, and his remark that the gaze does not only "look, it also *shows* (Lacan's emphasis)." This reverse side of the gaze is most evident in the experience of dreaming: " . . . our position in the dream is profoundly that of someone who *does not see.*"[4] The "blinding" need not be literal, as it is in Sirk's *Magnificent Obsession:* it may be figured as a peculiarly opaque vision, as when Lisa confesses, in *Letter from an Unknown Woman* (1948), "Somewhere out there were your eyes and I couldn't escape them," as the film offers us a glimpse of Stefan's face. Lisa, whose voice-off directs our attention to Stefan's visage, seems to "see" him differently than we do, since she cannot locate him visually in the theater. This image, in fact, may be her internal vision of him—her point of view of the man she cannot seize with her outward look, a point of view we access through her voice. Many films thus produce a sense that if the female voice-off sees the image we see, it is "internally." Such voices, as those in *Rebecca, Letter from an Unknown Woman,* and *Secret beyond the Door,* are often coded as a partaking in memory or imagination, "seeing" through an "internal (blind) vision," whereas the male voice-off more frequently comments in such a way as to suggest that it literally watches the image over the shoulder of the spectator. This kind of vision that cannot see, of images that cannot be seen, is moreover often overtly narrativized in films in which the female voice-off plays a vital structuring role for point of view. A central flashback spiral in *The Enchanted Cottage,* for example, suddenly introduces the shared voice-off of the characters Laura (Dorothy McGuire) and Oliver (Robert Young), who describe in rapturous tones their mutual metamorphosis from disfiguration to beauty since their wedding day. Their diegetic audience, a blind friend (Herbert Marshall), "knows" as we do as spectators that the characters are seeing each other "through" the filter of their love, and that this transformation is "not real." Yet, we see Laura and Oliver *as they see each other* in this sequence, bound to their perception. *The Enchanted Cottage,* moreover, represents this internal vision as both more subjective (linked to the bias of emotions that "color" what the characters see, and what we see) and more true (freed from the limitations of the visible, the images we share with these characters reveal the "deeper" spiritual perception they access through their love). It is also linked to (shared) voice-off and a point of view it inspires—shared between the two lovers *and* between them and Herbert Marshall's character, who is literally blind (and thus already knows what it is to "see" outside the limitations of the gaze). Thus, the female voice-off (here a shared voice-off) serves as a potential disruption to the specular female body. It connotes and is "used" to connote an intimacy, confusion of limits, and a loss of (objectifying) perspective, even as the image seeks to structure point of view, center and isolate the subject, and insist on the definite in sexual difference. Indeed, Lacan stresses the contrariness between the invocatory drive and the scopic drive: "Whereas *making oneself seen* is indicated by an arrow that really comes back towards the subject, *making oneself heard* goes towards the other."[5] The "difference" the voice poses to the body leads us, in fact, to a new theoretical model for film scholars and others to figure feminine difference in a positive sense and, more specifically, moves toward a fresh conception of a feminine subject as she may be represented in film or as she may be addressed by it.

The Phantom "Being" of the Voice

Efforts to describe a voice often betray a difficulty in naming the quality unique to it. Vague analogies and general adjectives seem to fall short of the peculiar tonality that is the essential interest of the voice—a voice said to be "metallic," "musical," "hoary," or "thin" still more or less eludes representation beyond a general sense of its tenor at a given moment. A single voice might bear, for instance, each of these attributes (especially if the speaker is practiced in modulating this instrument for dramatic effect) and yet still hold some distinguishing characteristic that allows for the recognition that this voice is "different" from all others. The voice is often

Oliver's scarred face

The lovers, seen outside the limits of the gaze

(*The Enchanted Cottage*)

thought to "belong" to someone, or more specifically, to some body, and, moreover, we tend to understand this proprietary relation as immutable. We think of the voice as being within the control of the speaker (except in those moments of physical or psychological fatigue when it betrays us). The voice also seems relatively immune to the physical toll that time takes on the body, remaining constant and recognizable, even when a person's face or figure may have drastically altered. This independence introduces a schism between the voice and the corpus it inhabits, countervailing the opposing representations that figure the voice as in some way attached or determined by the condition of the body. (In French, Roland Barthes notes, descriptions of the voice often bear a strong physiological connotation—it can be "toothy," "intestinal," etc. The "grain . . . is an erotic mixture of timbre and language . . . wherein we can hear . . . the articulation of the body . . . materiality . . . sensuality . . . the breath, the gutturals, the fleshiness of the lips . . .")[6] The voice speaks of "difference" thus in a double-edged sense: it speaks, on one hand, of the "difference" of this voice from other voices, inasmuch as it bears the mark of a particular body. It also speaks of the difference of the voice *from* the body itself—the voice bears witness to that which is unrepresentable about the body. It is "unrepresentable," first, in this sense: the voice resists efforts to image it. Like sound in general, the voice is usually described relative to the "characteristics" it bears—to adjectives, rather than to nouns, objects. Christian Metz has explained that the difficulty of "tracing" the source of a sound is linked to its pervasive ambiguity. Its mellifluous potentiality inspires us, he suggests, to specify or locate the object that produces sound, in order to understand "what" the sound is.[7] The sound itself, that is, defies nomination. The voice is unrepresentable also in the ambivalent relation of the voice to the corpus which "contains" it and yet contradicts it—the body's materiality controverted by the intangible, aphysical spatiality evoked by the voice. The uncanny way in which the voice suggests both a double for the body and a possible threat to its coherence (hence the desire to describe the voice, to imagine it as an object—visible and qualified—to deny its strangeness to a psyche that craves a certain mastery over the body and the world) may explain the Janus-like split in the history of its human representation.[8] On one hand, "the voice" is mythologized, romanticized in the mystic power of incantation, prayer, the ecstatic fusion with music in song. On the other hand, its ambiguity evokes terrors, the horrors of demonic possession, the lure of the Sirens, insanity, and death. The voice thus expresses the body and inhabits it: it is organic and foreign at once, a "characteristic" that also expresses a kind of subjectivity. It speaks not only *of* but *through* the body. The voice strikingly proposes a paradox, a contradiction in which heterogeneous signification dwells in dynamic, constructive expression. In its relation to speech, too, the voice is both "flesh" and "sense": in words we hear "a voice still mysterious, indefinite, on the slope of meaning."[9] The "oscillation," Guy Rosolato suggests, between these poles, "*between* body and language . . . is the vibration that gives the pleasure of *hearing*."[10] And where Rosolato compares this oscillation, at moments, to an acoustic mirror, it more properly is described in the less visual metaphors he adopts at other moments—such as the "between." "Between," this vibration is no ricochet but is rather a simultaneity in space of absolute difference. Thus, in the final instance, the voice and the body are not truly separable: instead, they form a paradoxical relation within which heterogeneity strongly signifies.

In its paradoxical effects, the voice can also be said to act as a "middle voice," such as Roland Barthes and Michel Foucault have described with regard to modern literature. Hayden White describes the middle voice as one in which "actions and their effects are conceived to be simultaneous; past and present are integrated rather than dirempted, and the subject and object of the action are in some way conflated."[11] Neither passive nor active, but *between*—the voice is both simultaneously. We will return later in this book to this notion of "middle voice": it is of interest both in its psychoanalytic implications (Freud linked the middle voice to a form of obsessional neurosis close to masochism he deemed "*without* an attitude of passivity"), and in its invocation of a specific consciousness of difference within/of the self.[12] The idea of paradox—which leads to the possibility of envisioning simultaneous (and multiple) subjectivities, of transcending "the problematic dichotomy of subject and object"—clears a path for understanding the voice as an index of difference: it is a difference, however, that eventually folds back onto itself in a constitutive way.[13] This difference is "recognized" as sameness, sustained as consciousness.

The symbolic heritage of Western representations of the female voice, indeed, amplifies the "difference" implicit in the voice. The legend of the Sirens who lure sailors to an ecstatic death epitomizes the power of the voice over that of the body. The myth of Echo and Narcissus similarly demonstrates the peril that the "unattached" female voice constitutes for the (male) subject, who, hearing it, is irrevocably lost to desire. Likewise, the female characters of opera possess voices that express the body and exceed it simultaneously, pointing to a desiring subject (one which inevitably undergoes severe treatment for the glorious threat her singing conjures). These female voices evoke the external (the voice as audible representation of desiring speech) *and* the internal (the voice as expressive of what eludes representation, feminine desire itself). Desire is both triggered by language, then, and heard *in* the female voice as such—voice produced by, yet never reducible to, the body. Desire and contradiction lead us to the Subject of cinema—the focus of this chapter. Where or what is the Subject in relation to the voice, and specifically in relation to the female voice-off? What is the nature of the link between the cinematic female voice-off and the "voice" per se, both metaphorically and psychoanalytically? What might be the effects of such subject positioning relative to the image that also "places" the viewer?

Remote Transcendence: The Myth of Distant Subjectivity

The female voice-off has often been described in film theory and criticism as a particular form of narrative overlay—as a purported authorial position granted to the female character. Writers such as Kaja Silverman, Mary Ann Doane, and Tania Modleski agree that the female voice-off preliminarily, at least, represents the female character's ability to speak, and to express her subjectivity. Thereafter (in classical cinema at least), these same writers point out that this gift is hauled back by "male-coded" narrative linchpins that work to suppress the feminine by defining the male at her expense. The female character bearing voice-off, that is, soon "loses" the subjectivity initially promised by her offscreen speaking; her figuration is re-rendered in the text as "object" or image. This movement of containment can come through, for example, the "loss" of the voice-off by a character who ceases to enjoy this speaking privilege, or the inscription of the female voice-off to the "recessive" regions of the diegesis. Whatever the mode of "containment," it is invariably viewed as evidence of the ineluctable overpowering of the female voice-off by a more powerful "off" voice, that of the dominating ideology of patriarchy. The female viewing subject, too, has been implicated in this containment of the diegetic female character. As we shall see, in the insistence on aligning subjectivity with vision, and centering vision to a masculine subject, the female spectator has been neatly tucked away, rendered "impossible." This "impossibility" derives from a misguided effort to figure the female spectator's "subjectivity" from within a set of assumptions that pertain more clearly to masculine subjectivity, assumptions that posit subjectivity as "bodiless," "imaginary/visual," and "distanced." These presuppositions derive in part from a bias that holds the image to be "primary" and sound "secondary." They also respond to a strongly entrenched analogy in film theory that aligns subject positioning with the transcendental "voyeur" encoded in Renaissance vanishing-point perspective, a spectator whose "pure gaze" dwells with pleasure specifically on the fetishized female form, from a distance.

The subject/spectator of film has persistently been cast in one of the following ways: "transcendent" (the universal/patriarchal subject implied by the metapsychological studies of Jean-Louis Baudry and Metz); "male" (the arbiter of the objectifying gaze first proposed by Laura Mulvey); or "male-coded" (the "transvesticized" or masquerading female initially constructed by Mulvey and later nuanced by writers like Teresa De Lauretis and Doane).[14] These scenarios have contributed crucial insights into the nature of the apparatus and of the viewer's contract. However, thus far, paradigms of spectatorship have invariably been figured as constituted through the cinematic *image,* through the subject's visual relationship to the imaginary signifier. The ideological lesson of Baudry's "eye-subject," constituted through a relationship to cinema's replication of a centering Renaissance perspective that constantly "lays out the space of an ideal vision . . . [and] assures the necessity of a *transcendence,*" stresses simultaneously that the illusory mastery of "reality" arrives specifically *through the gaze.*[15] Importantly, too, Baudry's "discovery" of the transcendental subject already dissociates spectatorship from the body and betrays an assumption that in spectatorship and subjectivity, the body must be left behind: " . . . the eye which moves is no longer fettered by a body, by the laws of matter and time . . . the world will be constituted not only by this eye but for it."[16] Baudry is critical, of course, of the "transcendence" he observes, as replicating and reinscribing an "ideological machine"—but his own ideological "limit" is evident in his implicit assertion (by default) of the visual axis as not only dominant over sound but occluding its very signification.[17] One may very well ask if, as Baudry asserts, "the ideological mechanism at work in the cinema [is] concentrated in the relationship between the camera and the subject," where does sound fit in?[18] Is it "less" ideological than the "camera"?[19] Does it "interfere" with the mirroring relationship that enables the subject to transcend the body? Can it be a "mirror" too, even if not a reproduction that traffics in images?

To Alan Williams, who transposes Baudry's arguments from the visual register to the auditory, the answer to this last question, at least, is a resounding yes.[20] Sounds, he reminds, are representations, reflecting ideological choices that serve to center a transcendental "hearing" subject. Williams's view of the ideological bias inherent in sound's representation is of great importance, for he strongly debunks the mythology that sound is merely "reproduced" in film, unaltered by the mediation of the apparatus.[21] Yet his article simply maps Baudry's scenario relative to image onto sound. Though his remarks on the explicit modulations and distortions of sound—and on the general Hollywood concealment of the signs of pro-

duction—are both valid and insightful, he disregards the crucial relationship of sound to image. This dialectic structures both the film and the
film viewer. The "centering" impulse of the gaze, in fact, is only with great
effort reconstituted as a centering of an acoustic subject. Where Baudry
is able to point to a long history of such "visual" centerings, the history
of acoustic arts is only beginning to be studied in this way.[22] Williams's
suggestion that sound's perspective reflects "one point of space," rather
than a spatial volume, works only if one considers each sound in isolation
rather than the mixed relation of multiple sounds, as is usual for a sound
track.[23] He suggests that microphones are "more like ears than they are
like rooms."[24] This may be somewhat true, though sound *is* affected by
the dimensions and textures of the room in which it is recorded, and it
necessarily takes on the acoustic quality of that space.[25] Though mikes
are held out from a point, they have pickup patterns that are diffuse and
varied, limited only in their directionality. (Some mikes, in fact, are omnidirectional, pulling in sound from a concentric volume.) Moreover, the
mike is not the only element that determines the perspective of sound
proper. Rerecording and mix technology allow perspective to be added
to sounds that are filtered through spaces and "rooms," usually to create
a stronger or richer sense of spatial volume. A sound recorded from "a
point" in one room thus bears a second spatial volume (or point). Indeed,
the use of multiple mikes is more than frequent both on the set and in the
mix room, where sounds miked at different times in different spaces are
combined to play back simultaneously.[26] Whether this spatial volume is
"real" or "represented" is, perhaps, not as important as how it differs from
the establishing of "one point in space" from which something is heard.
It is critical, that is, when thinking about the nature of the film auditor's
relationship to sound, to account for the degree to which sound recording
and mixing admit heterogeneity, evoke difference simultaneously, and offer
an alternate conception of "subjectivity" to the model of lines converging
to an "ideal" point, such as has been construed for the image.

The Many-Eared "Monster" Spectator

Thus the spectator who watches and listens to a sound film inhabits many
more than one "place." There is not one "angle" from which we hear—
rather, we effortlessly sustain a spatial volume, a complex web of contradictory sounds, some recorded "close up," some recorded for an effect of
"distance." As Rick Altman notes, "Just as cameras may have wide-angle

or telephoto lenses, changing the angle of image collection, . . . so microphones vary from omnidirectional to narrowly focused, thus changing
both the angle of sound collection and the apparent distance of the sound
source."[27] The difference for the spectator's relationship to the two elements of film leaps from between these lines—for the image track selects
one view seized by the camera for us to see, while many different angles
of sound are presented for us simultaneously.[28] The multiple spatial characteristics of sound, moreover—in sound's relationship to a spectator, a
recording instrument, narrative coherence, and the image—extend to each
sound in *itself,* as both Altman and James Lastra have pointed out.[29] Each
sound, that is, "includes multiple sounds, each with its particular fundamental and array of partials, each with its characteristic sound envelope,
each possessing its own rhythm within the sound event's overall temporal
range."[30] In addition, sounds depend on the acoustic chamber in which
they are heard: they change according to the place of the auditor who
hears them, becoming further multiple. That is, the "same" sound (Altman's example—a ball breaking a window) sounds *different* to the father
who hears it from the study than to the son playing outside in the yard.
Represented sounds (recorded sounds) exacerbate this inherent heterogeneity—given that the point of audition (the theater) differs markedly from
the space of the recording—it always sounds different than it did originally.
Indeed, people sitting in different parts of the movie theater will hear even
this "different" sound reverberate differently still. We are far, indeed, from
a cinema that plays to the illusory centering of a single subject. Rather,
sound constantly *divides* the attention of spectator/auditor, each sound a
complex of contradictions itself, signifying within a heterogeneous system
of sounds that offer contrasting, plural spatialities.

The *distance* so often proposed as primary to the spectator's psychoanalytic and ideological relationship to the film apparatus also comes into
question when one considers the specific characteristics of sound perception. As Metz's vastly influential insights into the workings of the "scopic
regime" of cinema have shown, the spectator enjoys a layer of "protective" absence between his body and the image, due in large measure to
the physical absence of the object seen, and the mechanisms of fetishism
and voyeurism that negotiate a position of transcendence for the troubled
Subject.[31] Metz has suggested that the auditory track works like an identical twin to the image, allowing for an auditory "voyeurism" that parallels
what the spectator experiences relative to the image.[32] Lacan, however,
suggests that the "desire to hear" (invocatory drive) differs crucially from

the "desire to look," proposing that there is "total distinction between the scopic register and the invocatory . . . field."[33] Guy Rosolato's findings confirm Lacan's: Rosolato stresses that "one could establish a system of opposition between the auditory and the visual."[34] Rosolato stresses that visual "interiority" does indeed differ markedly from its acoustic counterpart: the visual is always directed in an anterior sense, whereas sound allows for apperception of posterior space. In this sense, vision "keeps the index of spatial distance" oriented like a "continual confrontation opposite a staged scene."[35] A certain flatness seems to characterize vision, then, while sound constitutes "a spatialization of the outside in the inside."[36] The image that is "out there"—a distant and remote "staged scene"—is counterposed by sound that is both "out there" and "in here" simultaneously. The (meta)psychological experience of sound, then, amplifies the multiple spatiality, which, as we have seen, distinguishes it from the image. Moreover, this spatiality distinctly collapses distance and difference—even as it opposes (in Rosolato's words) the visual.

Where the seeing subject's "contact" with the object vised by the eye renders it (partially due to the mirror phase) "other" and "out there," sound confuses and links these poles, invoking not an oscillation but a continuum. This alignment of sound with the interior of the body (and specifically the cranium) explains, perhaps, the overwhelming tendency within cinema to represent "thought" and consciousness through voice-off. (*Female* voice-off, in particular, very commonly serves this representational function. Alongside the major examples explored in the chapters to come—*Letter from an Unknown Woman, Secret beyond the Door,* and *A Letter to Three Wives*—striking instances of voice-off as "thought-voice" can be found in *Raw Deal, Brief Encounter, Since You Went Away, No Man of Her Own,* and *I Walked with a Zombie.*) Sound seems, in fact, a closer cousin to the "senses of contact" than sight, as it penetrates the ear, activates the eardrum, inhabits the body. Moreover, whereas we can control what we see to some extent, sound is more insistently active, less easy to block out.[37] Metz notes that we only "need close [our] eyes to suppress [the film]," but surely this is untrue.[38] The sound track will continue to play to our ears, to be there, to amplify filmic space, drama, pleasure. Thus, sound is more invasive than the image—and also less distant. Sound must enter the body to be heard, but it also can enter without our permission, or without our "opening our ears" to hear. Sound's "object," too, is different from the object that is seen: it is more "active"—it emits vibrations. Whereas the image is seized (first by light and then by the eye, thus rendered, in a sense, passive or "objectified"), sound has, in a strange way, its own subjectivity. It "speaks" in two places simultaneously (or nearly so): at the source and in the ear. As a voice, it "speaks" doubly. The sound track of a film, then, seems, even in these very general and intuitive terms, to invite a "relation" with the subject very different from that triggered by the image. There are even "blind" spectators, apparently, who go to the movies for the sound track alone, spectators whose pleasure would be an intriguing arena for study. Rosolato notes, in fact, that hearing "is not a tributary of the light (one can hear in the dark) and it surmounts the obstacles of what is opaque to vision."[39] Thus, moments in which the voice or sound is accompanied by darkness (no image) should not be understood merely as signaling a frustration to sight—an absence of the visual signifier, the marking of a certain kind of phallic impotence—but also as a heightened moment of sound. Such moments represent an invocation of the specific apprehension of spatiality that hearing enables, and the breaking down of the visual threshold in order (in a sense) to perceive or represent *more, beyond, within.*

Sound's Absence: De-frauding the "Original"

The desiring Subject of sound should not be figured relative to visual scenarios inspired by the absent image. We need to consider the peculiar absence of sound in looking for alternate configurations of spectatorship. James Lastra's work on sound suggests, in fact, that it is always absent. Where Rick Altman, Tom Levin, and others suggest that an "original" sound exists that suffers some kind of "loss" or distortion through technological mediation, Lastra claims that there is no "pure" perception possible in any event, since *all* practices of audition are "socially constructed."[40] He claims, pointing to Altman's example of the sound of the shattering window (heard by father and son in different spaces differently), that by definition "there is no strictly definable 'original' event . . . each auditor gets a slightly different sense of the sound, depending on his or her location and the directedness of his or her hearing . . . [thus] . . . *every hearing is in some way absent. . . .*"[41] He continues: "The historical happening of the sound event, its spatio-temporal specificity, always appears to escape our apprehension. Whether we're in an auditorium, or listening to a relatively contextless, closely-miked recording, or to one which stresses the peculiarities of the room, the event, in its fullness, seems to escape. What is the 'real' of which these are the traces?"[42] Lastra's description is fascinating and extremely useful in moving this discussion forward to contemplate the specific psychoanalytic and ideologic positioning of a spectator/subject elicited by the female voice-off. Lastra's evocation here of the "absence" which distinguishes sound differs markedly from the kind of "absence" generally associated with the image. The "absence" Lastra observes seems not so much perceptual loss as perceptual contradiction. That is, in thinking of the image, we rarely doubt that what we see existed at one time, even if we appreciate that it is not really "there" now. With sound, as Lastra suggests, such a doubt always colors perception: there is no "real" "original" sound of which the recorded version is a shadow. Rather, all sounds are simultaneously "real" and "unreal," "there" and "not there," "like this" and "not like this." Thus, "'in the sound recording the original is still as present as it ever was, which is to say, just as absent."[43]

A paradoxical perception, then, is constitutive of hearing itself, both in our everyday relationship to sound as well as to the sounds we hear/do not hear in the cinema. This figuration of paradox, and of contradiction, implicit in Lastra's remarks, is central to my own analysis of the voice in cinema. It is my contention that the female voice-off makes these contradictions all the more pronounced, all the more acute for the spectator of film. Another dialectic that Lastra suggests structures sound representations should be mentioned here, a dangling caveat to his theory which has profound implications for the reading of film sound: recording technology can direct our attention in one of two directions with regard to a sound—to favor "intelligibility" or "fidelity." Dialogue recorded to maximize "intelligibility" strives, for example, to stress the comprehension of the words, where a "fidelity" recording might maximize the grain of the speaker's voice or the acoustics of the recording space. Thus, again, apart from perception proper, sound is "divided" into different sounds—in fact, we often "ignore certain aspects of the event because our hearing is directed towards certain ends" (usually understanding speech).[44] The way we listen thus affects what we hear. What we perceive is inflected by what we are listening for. The framework in which a sound is heard then, extends beyond physical—spatial and temporal—dimensions to include social, psychological, and, one might add, theoretical attitudes. As we turn from sound generally to more closely consider the specific contradictions that characterize the female voice-off in cinema (and the spectator's relationship to it), it is necessary to understand the "frame" that has surrounded this voice in film theory. Film theory has perceived the relationship between the voice-off and the spectator as fraught with a kind of danger, due to its potential contradictory signification—a danger which leads, ultimately, to voyeuristic/fetishistic positionings effected in concert with the image track. If one listens to this same voice "differently," however, another "frame" emerges from which to interpret the same phenomenon. One finds, in fact, that "what counts as a significant element (in what we hear) changes as we change our frame."[45]

Heterogeneity, the Voice, and the Body: "Risks" and Reverberations

The theoretical "myth" of the transcendent, distant spectator "centered" by the all-seeing/voyeuristic eye cannot account for the workings of sound in cinema. Sound does not "center," as it provides multiple spatialities simultaneously. Neither does it offer a position of "distant" protection from the (absent) signifier: rather, it places the viewer inside a continuum where the oppositions between object and subject, inside and outside, here and there coincide in vigorous simultaneity. Moreover, sound works in opposition to the image itself, in a radical heterogeneity that the voice-off renders acute for the spectator/subject. In *The Imaginary Signifier*, Metz broaches the ideological implications of such heterogeneity. Referring to "the anonymous 'speaker,'" he suggests that this voice-off, "beyond jurisdiction, represents the rampart of unbelief . . ."[46] He further indicates that the "distance it establishes between the action and ourselves comforts our feeling that we are not duped . . . [and thus offers the] 'alibi . . . [of a] naive distanciation.'"[47] As we have seen, the idea of "distance" when applied to sound has its problems. Crucially, though, Metz portrays the voice as working in the service of the image, even as it operates elsewhere ("beyond jurisdiction," behind "the rampart"). A gulf between the image and sound is drawn, but, significantly, not to open up the possibility of heterogeneity, but to close heterogeneity down. The distanciation the voice-off offers is "naïve," harmless, hardly worth mentioning except to dismiss as a ruse.[48]

Mary Ann Doane recognizes the heterogeneity of the voice-off as potentially much more disruptive. She observes that voice-over was a "late acquisition" after the introduction of sound to film, because of the spectator's desire for synch sound that coheres with image. Synch allows for a "unity" of the "fantasmatic body" reconstituted by the cinema and "confirm[s] the status of speech as an individual property right."[49] After a "'breaking in' period," she suggests, the spectator's insistence on lip-synch relaxed, allowing for more mobile and non-synch deployments of voice.[50] This "public demand" for synch supports Doane's suggestion that "[s]ound carries with it the potential risk of exposing the material heterogeneity of the medium," a risk that she stresses is "contained" by technicians who labor to "marry" sound to the image.[51] She contends that the voice-off is particularly "risky" in this regard, since it is "disembodied" from the synchronous signifier (what Silverman calls the "specific body") and that it is peculiar, "uncanny."[52] The voice-off, then, in her view, has no direct connection to the silent cinema; rather, it emerged as a new form of expression unique to the era of sound.

Charles M. Berg, however, suggests that the emergence of voice-off itself may possibly relate to its historical antecedents—the offscreen commentators and lecturers who spoke during silent films to "explain" their stories or speak "dialogue."[53] Although this tradition was fraught with annoyances (absurd juxtapositions of image with the "wrong" voice, clumsy attempts to emulate synch speech, sloppy elocution, etc.), it not only served the purpose of hiding the "disagreeable" sounds within the theater, but, along with music, made the otherwise (in Berg's terms) "flat," "lifeless," "colorless," purely silent film experience tolerable.[54] Thus at the dawn of cinema, the question of sound's heterogeneity is already at issue. Patrons demanded it—desired it—willing to abide some rift between sound and image rather than endure the stultification of "pure" image. But clearly, as Berg points out, the more "obvious" the gap between voice and image, the more the signifier's heterogeneity is underscored, to the point where absurdity can overwhelm the film's signification. The difference sound brings to image, then, seems more than surplus meaning—it is fundamental, able to construct or to destroy in its relation to the screen.[55]

The spectator's demand here, then, is somewhat paradoxical, insisting on having a heterogeneous signifier (the image is not enough by itself), and insisting that its heterogeneity adhere in a kind of union with the image. Sound, moreover, appears to provide much of the pleasure of film—early spectators found its absence grating, its presence soothing. Indeed, "the impression of movement in the early cinema appeared unnatural and freakish without some sort of acoustic correlate to the visual activity."[56] One cannot really attribute this pleasure to a surfeit of realism, since these "primitive" offscreen narrations and musical scores hardly contributed to ground the image in the real (indeed, they threatened at times to render it more unreal). It seems instead that it is the relationship of sound to image that brings pleasure, a dynamic that points to itself as heterogeneous.

Sound brings a spatial volume the image "lacks" while at the same time offering the perception of a "different reality"—a reality, as John Belton has put it, "one step removed from that of the images."[57] The "pleasures" of synch seem incidental in comparison, the use of asynchronous sound being very much "called for" throughout the "silent" era.

The spectator's awareness of this relationship of difference between image and sound, and of the "material heterogeneity" of the sound itself, is thus rendered acute through sound that constantly "threatens" to expose its own contradiction to the image. Yet Doane and others insist that this is a relatively idle threat, since classical cinema always works to buttonhole sound to image. However, Doane herself also frequently recalls sound's difference as though it were a ticking bomb. Though she sees sound as having its own ideological ax to grind (a discourse of knowing through emotion rather than intellection, buttressed through sound's "intangible" quality), she notes that the combination of sound and image "entails the possibility of exposing an ideological fissure—a fissure which points to the irreconcilability of two truths of bourgeois ideology."[58] Indeed, this fissure, in my view, can be said to structure all films. To approach this divide, to plumb its depths and scale its significance—how it relates to all the other "contradictions" that have surfaced already in looking at the "history" of the voice-off—it is necessary and instructive to look more deeply into the subtleties of Doane's arguments. For Doane's work is not important merely as one of the first to chart the metapsychological repercussions of sound and the voice for the spectator and within the narrative of film: her observations set out the terms of the major debates and her theses remain provocative and influential, offering numerous tangents ripe for exploration. Among these, the question of space—the visual and the non-visualizable—that she raises is particularly valuable. Space, I shall argue, constitutes a way to figure, relative to the voice-off, a place of subjectivity not contingent on the body and its visual restrictions.

In an early article dedicated to the voice in cinema, Doane repeats her view that sound "risks" exposing the heterogeneity of the cinematic signifier, but (significantly) she now shifts the emphasis and definition of sound/voice's ideological "message."[59] No longer does she associate the sound track (incarnated here as "voice") to knowing through feeling or emotion, but she suggests, rather, that its ideological burden resides in its relationship to the body. It is in voice-off's "detach[ment] [from a] . . . represented body [that] its potential work as a signifier is revealed."[60] Two issues seem raised by Doane's shift here. First, in separating out the voice from other auditory effects, she implicitly stresses that voice is a special problem in film sound, needing a more sustained analysis, specifically with regard to its particular relationship to the body and to its discursive power as a form of speech. That is, in important ways, voice is "different," even from the sound track itself. Second, she seems to cast the voice-off (and the voice proper) as having a discrete and possibly more intricate ideological function relative to the image than other sounds. This ideological complexity, in fact, relates directly to Doane's revised assumption that the "interior" spoken by the voice and voice-off in cinema speaks of the body rather than the emotions and feelings she mentions relative to sound proper. More material than other sounds, bearing the body that produces it, it is still acoustic, spatial—less material than the image. Her implied view of the voice here meshes closely with my own. Seen in this way, it threatens a heterogeneous contradiction to both the "image" and the "sound" tracks—it is somewhere in between, neither interior nor exterior, speaking from and of the body, rendering the corpus in space, as it floats alongside images to which it appears, at moments, to bind. In Doane's ideological arrangement, moreover, wherein discursive "types" of knowledge adhere to the two tracks, the voice again seems in a netherworld between—neither part of "the ideology of the visible," the real, the intellected that Doane attributes to the image track, nor entirely belonging to the ideology of "mystery" and immateriality presented by sound, which invokes knowledge through emotions, intuitions, and intangibility. The voice is both and neither simultaneously—an intangible evocation of an interior space, a cipher, a material effect of the body.[61]

In pointing to the body as the primary discursive and ideological "trouble" proposed by the voice, rather than to the sense-bearing power of speech, Doane moves the question of the voice's heterogeneity and difference into feminist ground. In post-1970s film theory, the question of the body necessarily introduces the problem of sexual difference. On one hand, the distinction Doane draws now between "embodiment" and "disembodiment" for the voice has important repercussions for the study of discursive movement and enunciation in films bearing voice-off. (I discuss these ramifications in depth in Chapter 3 of this book.) On the other hand, this demarcation raises some provocative new questions about subject relations to the apparatus. Here, we move past ontological debates about the relationship or hierarchy between the image and sound track to home in on a site where these two seem to "meet" and to signify their contradiction most strikingly and powerfully: the voice-off. Doane's point here is that the "meeting" between sound and image "in" the voice-off takes place expressly through the relationship drawn by the text between that voice and image-bodies seen or imagined relative to the diegesis. A second "meeting," however, is implied by Doane's terminology, which renders the voice and voice-off as though they achieve or reflect some degree of physicality, some incorporalization. This "meeting" occurs between the spectator's body and the "body" of the voice. The implications of such an encounter are radical, as we shall see.

Turning the Body into Space

In certain moments, Doane appears committed to understanding the "body" of the voice as synonymous with the visible diegetic signifier, stating that "the voice-off is always 'submitted to the destiny of the body,' because it *belongs* to a character who is confined to the space of the diegesis, if not to the visible space of the screen."[62] But, in other passages, Doane's writing seems to indicate that the body perceived in or through the voice by the spectator is not just the diegetic "anchor" provided or left in abeyance on screen, the image of the character who appears to speak or (in voice-off) to think aloud. She suggests, in one such remark, that in the "interior monologue," the voice "is the privileged mark of interiority, turning the body 'inside-out.'"[63] Thus the voice also functions in a fantasmatic sense, to suggest a body that cannot be seen, a body, in fact, that has been "emptied" into the voice, and turned, in a sense, *into space,* a space that is both interior and exterior—the "inside" no longer simply inside but also "out." Following this train of thought, we can look beyond the visible locus of the *character* to whom the voice is attributed in understanding how the body can "speak" through the voice. Indeed, the voice-off thus appears to create a space beyond the diegesis that confines the subject who "appears" to speak. (Vocabulary in describing this kind of "space" is tricky: it is beyond, but also behind, within, alongside, intersecting the diegetic space.) In fact, in a provocative digression from her main argument, Doane herself compares the relationship voice-off holds to image with the relationship voice-off holds to space, offering a hint as to what kind of "body" we might "hear" in the voice: "The voice-off deepens the diegesis, gives it an extent which exceeds that of the image, and thus supports the claim that there is a space in the fictional world which the camera does not register. In its own way, it *accounts for* lost space. The voice-off is a sound which is first and foremost in the service of the film's construction of space and only indirectly in the service of the image."[64] Although Doane means here to explicate how voice-off (which in her terminology refers to a potentially embodied "offscreen" voice rather than a disembodied voice-over) affects the construction of narrative space, a number of her statements open onto other possibilities. At every turn in this passage, Doane's vocabulary suggests that the voice-off introduces a non-visualizable construction of space, one that "exceeds" the diegetic space provided by the image and that in fact reconstitutes a "lost" dimension, space itself, heterogeneous to the image to which it offers a lively and constructing contradiction. At the very least, her final sentence makes clear that Doane sees the role of the voice in spectatorial relations as anything but "secondary"—it is, rather, responsible for the evocation of a fantasmatic dimension that "deepens" the diegesis, *but not in terms of the image.*

Thus, we find both a "body" and a "space" signified simultaneous to an image but not signified *by it.* The "body" of the voice-off, may, in fact, be understood as "belonging" more properly to the space than to an image that may retroactively come to "anchor" it, since it is coincident with the space and not with the image that is attached to it only through the logic of the diegesis. The voice-off speaks of a body in space, a body that is heard, not seen. Even if the diegetic anchor of a proffered body comes to "signify" its claim to that voice, the voice-off's "other" body constantly speaks alongside it, just as the space of the voice-off "exceeds" as well as "deepens" that of the diegetic image. One may argue that this logic works only when applied to what Doane calls "interior monologue," which turns the body inside out, funneling the body into space, bringing these two terms into a continuum, a congruence. But it is with regard to "voice-off" (a category which in Doane's view is much "nearer" to embodiment than "interior monologue") that she offers these provocative remarks about the space created through the voice. Indeed, these two textual placements of (in her taxonomy) "voice-off" and "voice-over" inhabit different spaces— one is "near" the image, just off screen; the other is "further away"—each troubling the image in its own way. Multiple spaces, multiple "bodies" inhabit the sound track as it interacts with the image. The dynamic here extends beyond a single contradiction or confluence between "image and sound," pointing to a plurality of spaces and bodies across the sound and image tracks.

The connection between the voice and space is psychologically deep. We know, for instance, that "space, for the child, is defined initially in terms of the audible, not the visible."[65] Rosolato notes that (as yet blind) babies recognize their mother's voice as soon as ten weeks after birth, where it takes five to six months for vision to become the "leading sense in delimiting the *exterior* of the object."[66] He stresses recognizing the importance "of early auditory and vocal introjections; for it is only in a later stage that the organization of visual space assures the perception of the object *as being exterior.*"[67] Though "difference" in the voice is recognized very early by the child, the separation of that difference from the self is only subsequently "perceived" in vision. The space of sound thus includes self and other as difference without the imposition of an "exterior," which the image seeks to elaborate.

In this light, Doane's reflections on space in relation to the voice-off provide a springboard to an alternative way of thinking about the problem that the body constitutes for feminist film studies. The fantasmatic body that exists as the space of the film rather than "in" the image speaks of difference that the spectator/subject may sustain, rather than seek to contain through objectification, fetishization, and other vision-based scenarios of spectatorship. In making this claim, in exploring the ramifications of this "other" body "in" the voice, my intent is precisely *not* to set up (against which Doane rightly warns) "a political erotics" that "overemphas[izes] . . . the isolated effectivity of a single signifying material—the voice—[and thus] risks a crude materialism wherein the physical properties of the medium have the inherent and final power of determining its reading."[68] Nor do I believe that the voice is "an isolated haven within patriarchy," a utopian signifier.[69] Film is a form of representation, and voice participates in its discursive operations. However, the voice (and particularly the voice-off) provokes a consciousness of heterogeneity and paradox that, rather than merely "opposing" the image, engages with it to construct contradiction. The "space of a body" inherent in the voice-off is not the body of "the other"—a female or male imaged body apprehended "out there." Rather, the body should in this case be grasped *as* space, *in* space—indeed, in multiple space(s). As space in sound, which we have seen registers as both "out there" and "in here" simultaneously, such space admits contradiction. A body as or in this space bears this same plurality—this evocation of a continuum, of a collapsed yet ceaselessly signifying opposition. Difference is not only negotiated thus by the spectator in perceiving how image and voice produce space between them within the diegesis—it is sustained as a peculiar experience of the other as the self, the body as interior and exterior simultaneously. This may sound like a phantasm, and indeed Rosolato constantly invokes the example of the hallucination to help illustrate "how much the voice . . . remains linked to a dynamic of the body and its *fantasmatic.*"[70] This fantasmatic body emerges through the voice and the space(s) it invokes. In turn, the (multiple) "spaces" of cinema structure the spectator's "place"—as precisely "in" difference itself.

Is the Subject Male?

The importance of a "body" *in space* for film theory lies in its relationship to that other "body" provided by the image. Neither supplants the other or dominates the signification either body may produce. We can no longer *understand the body purely in terms of the image.* The body, indeed, like all meaning in film, needs to be read between the image and the voice, alongside them, according to the spaces they construct, the subjectivities they sustain, the discourses they produce, *between them.* Doane has noted "it is precisely because the body has been a major site of oppression that perhaps it must be the site of the battle to be waged."[71] She stresses, however, that only to the degree that sound draws attention to its heterogeneity can it displace the body of the image—specifically through the disruption of imaginary cohesion through synch. Synch sound, throughout her article, represents patriarchal ideology come to roost in tying voice to image. Pointing to synchronization in itself as a (necessarily negative) proof of "embodiment" may lead us away from more desirable and productive possibilities, questions, and preoccupations. Understanding the coincidence of image and voice as synonymous with an objectified entrapment in a female body merely reconstitutes a logic in which "contact" with the image of the female precludes the representation of her subjectivity. Certainly, neither the voice nor the image "is" a body, female or otherwise. Rather, both represent and evoke the body differently: that is, the female voice-off foregrounds, exacerbates, intensifies, and poeticizes the heterogeneous signifier that voice constitutes relative to the image, but it may also bring the female body back into mind, as a place from which the woman speaks. This "place," (seemingly a kind of space, if the former conjectures lead us in the right direction), as everyone knows, is anything but "pure" subject, nothing like the masculine subject who serves as the model.[72] One cannot help wondering if we have been looking at the female subject all wrong—looking to conceive of her as if she could be seen, as if she were that image of a body, rather than a body in space, and, moreover, a (self)consciousness. The female spectator cannot "identify" with herself via a transvesticized "objectifying" male gaze that she puts on for the purpose of getting a little narrative action. At least she cannot know herself to be a subject in that image, though she can recognize an experience of her subjectivity: namely, objectification (for she knows herself to be an object in patriarchy). But in listening to the voice, perhaps, we can apprehend what the gaze cannot see but may hear—the space in which she experiences her subjectivity in difference.

Others have looked for a new way to cast the "problem" of the female body in film. Kaja Silverman's view that castration "belongs" more properly to the male subject than to the body of the female, for instance, redirects the objectifying gaze back onto its source, relocating the problem as the "male" rather than the "female," reversing the usual assignment of lack.[73] Her revision offers a springboard for feminists and others to begin rethinking assumptions that prevail in the field about the female body and the image that appears to bear that body in cinema, assumptions that construe the special "specularity" of the female as pure fetish, closing down the possibility for female subjectivity. Silverman's own efforts to elaborate the subjectivity of the female lead her in *The Acoustic Mirror* to propose a "phase" in which the daughter desires and identifies with the mother. This "negative Oedipal complex," she suggests, provides proof that the female subject can identify with femininity in a positive sense, rather than "through" the assumption of a male subjectivity that doubles back to objectify her.[74]

It should be noted, however, that Silverman's theorization of female subjectivity rests upon a visual model, as she slips from a discussion of the child's relationship to the voice onto an Oedipal scenario of symbolic castration. As Silverman notes, her "theoretical paradigm closes off the pre-Oedipal domain, both as an arena for resistance to the symbolic and as an erotic refuge."[75] In Silverman's view, then, a dividing line between the Oedipal and the pre-Oedipal (thanks to castration) exists, dictating that desire is possible only "from the shores" of the symbolic. She does note later, however, that an "oppositional desire" emerges in the retroactive friction of pre-Oedipal to Oedipal tableaux.[76] Where Silverman sees this pre-Oedipal "fantasy" as regressive, positing its interest as residing in the negativity it provides the Oedipalized female (a sort of positive lack), it can also be viewed as a component of the constructive contradictions with which the voice is charged. Thus, where Silverman sees "identity" firmly entrenched with the latter stage (albeit inflected by the former), it should be remembered that the unconscious knows no time—both "sides" of the divide effected by castration engage the subject constantly. Where in her view the visual demarcation of sexual difference determines the place of the subject, there is room to explore how other experiences of self and identity, such as may be invoked by and through the voice, may interact, reverse, or confound the limits set by the gaze. Thus, the pre-Oedipal—which we may preliminarily associate with the space of the voice and a consciousness of the self in difference—may be just as important a factor as the Oedipal in trying to understand the psychic relation of both the female and the male subject to the cinematic apparatus and its repre-sentations via both image and sound. Indeed, the voice's "role," inform-ing a different kind of subjectivity than what we associate with the gaze alone, seems still far from fully understood. Again, it seems, a dynamic is at issue—one fraught with paradox, a "dialectic" wherein synthesis main-tains difference.

The Feminine = the Body = the Image

Silverman acknowledges that "although on one level, [*The Acoustic Mir-ror*] is a study of the female voice in cinema, on another it is an investiga-tion of the verbal and auditory defenses by means of which Hollywood fortifies the male subject against his own losses."[77] Silverman despairs of "finding" feminine subjectivity within the classical cinema, which she sees as an implacable machine that chews up sexual difference and contains the female on every register of meaning. For this reason, she claims, she can only "approach woman as a symptom" when looking at classical cin-ema.[78] By her own admonition, neither does she expect to find the female subject represented as such anywhere in the classical cinema, nor does her approach reflect a conscious effort to even try to address whether such a subject may indeed surface in any way. Her stated goal—that is, to find ways in which the feminine is "contained" at every turn and in every register in the classical cinema—expressly declines to consider ways in which the feminine *speaks* despite processes of containment or alongside them. In Silverman's view, the woman (in the classical cinema) can never speak or see; she is but a "foil" for the male viewer, a "place" within the text where the male can project the recognition of his own "visual and verbal subordination to cinema's absent enunciator."[79] Further, "true" subjectivity, in *The Acoustic Mirror,* is always and only achieved via the "authoritative" exterior gaze. Since females have trouble assuming this gaze, and never do in the classical cinema (according to Silverman), the best subjectivity they can hope for, in her view, is a kind of "counterattack" wherein masculine subjectivity is displaced and frustrated via a radical separation of voice from body.

Moreover, when discussing Hollywood cinema, she seems to retrench the very problematic of castration that she seeks to disable theoretically—and projects negative values onto the registers inhabited by "femininity" in these texts. For example, while she reads Michel Chion's famously moody work on voice "symptomatically," she reiterates the negative connotation he places on the feminine relative to the masculine (with regard to the voice and the body) and transposes it wholesale in proving her point about classical cinema. That is, she essentially *agrees* with him that Hollywood films represent the female voice-off as invoking, unleashing, and representing a claustral site of non-meaning and immobilization, an "umbilical night."[80] She criticizes his alignment of the localization of the "source" of the voice (the moment of synchronization) as a kind of "striptease." However, she goes on to use his analysis as the foundation and support of her own postulation that the "embodiment" brought about by the "rule of synchronization" not only feminizes the voice but entirely disempowers it.[81] The critical moment in which the "speaking lips" are revealed by the camera, in both their views, betrays the voice's corporeal anchor, rendering the voice-off vulnerable and defusing it of its invisible authority. Interestingly, Chion's description of the striptease dwells more insistently on the latent power and the instability of the voice-off's relation to the body than does Silverman's, who later goes so far as to describe the woman's mouth in Hollywood cinema as the "organ hole," a "yawning chasm of corporeal interiority," which reveals only (discursive) "impotence."[82] Above all, Silverman limits the power of the voice by insisting that association with the body (or, as we shall see, anything connoting an "interior" space, like flashbacks) arrests and nullifies any subjective force.

Thus a marked bias *against* the "feminine" riddles Silverman's analysis of classical film and the voice, emerging most obviously in her complete rejection of the female body in film. Time and again, she points to the imaged body as a site of "claustral" containment, a "contaminating" influence, a constraining "limit"; moreover, the nature of this constraint relates to a condition of femininity expressed in the most pejorative terms. Though she considers that "the female voice has enormous conceptual and discursive range once it is freed from its claustral confinement within the female body," Silverman insists that the female voice in classical cinema never meets the level of "freedom" necessary for the expression of such mobility and is, rather, always subject to some tainting influence of the corpus.[83]

Synchronization (a worst-case scenario, to be sure) does not merely "yoke" the voice to a body, but, in Silverman's terms, always implies the imposition of a body that is, specifically, "feminine." The body can be nothing else in this system—always codified as the weighted signifier of lack.

In Silverman's view of the classical cinema, then, the image that provides the visible signifier of the body always represents a potential destabilization of male subjectivity and even of male sexuality. To give a male voice-off a body, for example, is (in Silverman's words) to "feminize it."[84] She postulates that "the voice-over is privileged to the degree that it *transcends the body*" and insists that "[m]odern male sexuality [is] defined less by the body than by the negation of the body."[85] Thus, in a logic that increasingly separates the body not only from male subjectivity but also from male sexuality, we are left with a representational system in which virtually every signifier outside the entirely disembodied male voice-off (which Silverman admits is "extremely rare" in classical narrative cinema) comes to represent the feminine, but not in any positive sense. In this peculiar isosceles mirror, the feminine = the body = the image. All these terms are, in a sense, "opposed" to the male, whose subjectivity they potentially threaten. Not only is the female defined entirely as image/body, but these terms also reflect back in kind: the image is feminine and a form of embodiment for the voice; the body represents the very condition of the female/image. Since all of these terms are seen as restrictive, precluding representation of subjectivity in themselves, there seems to be no way for the female to speak. Pushing Laura Mulvey's thesis in "Visual Pleasure and Narrative Cinema" beyond the pale, however, there no longer seems to be anywhere for the male subject to find "himself" in this cinema, either. If the image itself is feminizing relative to the voice, then "containment" of the feminine within the specular female body seems a tenuous effect/project at best. The cinema described here seems a scenario of crisis rather than one of pleasure, as Hollywood "erects male subjectivity over a fault line."[86] Pleasure, in these terms, entirely sadomasochistic, lies in disavowing not only the female body, but the image as well, which anchors the voice to screen space and renders even a male voice corrupted.

Embodiments, Feminization, and the Ruin of Subjectivity

But the levels of corruptions are (in this scenario) relative, hierarchized, with heavily feminized categories sinking to the polluted "inner folds" of the text. "Integrity" for a voice-off, in Silverman's schema, is defined in terms of its distance from the body (and the taint of the "feminine"/ image with which it is associated). She notes such disembodied integrity is "exclusively male" and suggests that more often voices-off suffer from some degree of "corporeal encroachment" or feminization.[87] However, as I shall discuss more fully in Chapter 3, she claims that Hollywood finds ways to mitigate against this onslaught of femininity, creating slides by which synchronous male voices nonetheless come to bear the privileges of the disembodied voice-over. Thus, she concludes, "At its most crudely dichotomous, Hollywood pits the disembodied male voice against the synchronized female voice."[88] These films are a site of struggle, then, where in her view "biology" would appear to be destiny.

The classical cinema she describes, a juggernaut, grinds up femininity, each film systematically operating to separate the disembodied male subject from the representation of his "mutilated" other. Classical cinema seems entirely programmatic—uniform, too—cut to order, to process difference the same way every time for the same results. One is struck not only by the gothic proportions of this ideological plot and its supposed efficacy and homogeneity, but by the idea, buried within Silverman's view of classical cinema, that it is really all "about" the feminine. Ironically, in a sense, the male subject is *nowhere* in this cinema—a bodiless, transcendent spectator whose pleasure it is to confront endlessly and on every level the spectre of a femininity he supposedly finds intolerable. Even the male characters—if one follows this logic to the end, where the image is always "feminizing"—might thus be imagined to constitute surrogate females rather than relays for male identification.[89] Indeed, synchronization itself infects every discourse with the weight of the body/female. If one looks at Silverman's writing from this perspective, her insistence on the perils of embodiment seems overwrought and forced, not to mention deterministic. For my part, I am no more inclined to assert that the classical cinema speaks only "of" the female body than I am to accept the dictum that it speaks only "to" a male transcendence. The classical cinema must be looked at less mechanistically, from less restrictive paradigms and less literal psychoanalytic logjams. Moreover, it is vital to begin with a logic open to rewiring concepts that have begun to fossilize the woman in the picture and render her an absurd category that both saturates all representation with threatening otherness and remains exiled "outside" or trapped "within" it. If we understand "identity," "subjectivity," and "address" as of and for the "male" and leave only "objectification" and entrapment in the "body" for the "female," we risk replicating and reifying constraint instead of breaking with it or questioning it.

We should therefore question Silverman's efforts to represent the psychoanalytic "practice" operated by the classical cinema as virtually concrete rather than metaphorical. Psychoanalysis, after all, is no more "reality" than is cinema.[90] Both are systems of representation that may help us to understand how we structure identity and sexual difference in our culture. In setting these two against each other tautologically, however, a certain amount of warp reflects back in ossifying ways. Constraining the representational edict of cinema to psychoanalytic scenarios alone verges on a distortion of the complexity of not only the differences between human psychic configuration and the spectator's "place" in the cinema, but within each of those systems as well. There is a level on which Silverman is primarily "psychoanalyzing" the cinema itself, rather than its spectator (à la Metz) or the film's characters (à la Doane—though she does venture into these arenas). But in her analysis, Silverman frequently skips from one psychoanalytic regime to another to find whatever works "best" to help prove her point. She "uses" a strict Lacanian/Freudian terminology to expose the neurosis of the classical cinema, then moves on to theorists with less "male-centered" views of identity and subjectivity (Julia Kristeva, Luce Irigaray) to discuss feminist film. There may be a logic in assigning the more "phallic"-based theories to mainstream "male-centered" cinema and more "feminist" psychoanalytical perspectives to more alternative, women-authored films. However, shifting theories in this way reveals a lack of consistency in method: as Silverman seems close to admitting at points, the psychoanalytic scenarios themselves are ideological constructions that determine which readings *can* be made of the films.

Where in Doane's system there is some room for beginning to figure the body differently (in terms of space, for example, rather than image) relative to the voice or voice-off, in Silverman's scenario the body is invariably equated with the image alone, and the voice is aligned with subjectivity only to the degree that it can escape all these negative entrapments. Embodiment of a male voice-off thus not only threatens what she calls its "integrity" but also implies an undermining of the codes of sexual difference that may be established in other ways by the image. To go along with her logic for a moment, however, it is still not clear *why* "feminization" of a male voice-off in this way must necessarily be read as a polluting, disempowering influence that closes down rather than opens up meaning. Surely there is something unusual and provocative, uncanny, in a "feminized" voice intersecting with a "masculine" image?[91] But Silverman's reading of classical cinema insists that anything feminized ruins subjectivity, which can only be male and bodiless. Her argument against the classical cinema thus rests on proving over and over that the "female" is always only a body, even when she seems represented as a voice. In Silverman's schema, then, the voice is always referred back to some visual signifier, reduced to it through a logic that understands the image as the ontological center of cinema, one which determines and rules its aural "accompaniment." She thus collapses the difference posed by the voice to the image, at least where classical cinema is concerned, asserting that its discursive power is disabled any time it comes into "contact" with the (feminizing) body.

The Voice-off in Hollywood: Patriarchy's Whisper

Silverman's unequivocal conviction that the female subject is "invaginated" by classical cinema, her vast array of guns that point at Hollywood and fire upon its oppression of the woman, unfortunately effect, on a theoretical level, a kind of "containment" of the female subject itself. Her insistence that the female voice-off in classical cinema has no chance against the systematic occlusion of feminine subjectivity mirrors a hermetic inexorability that she assumes governs every film produced in Hollywood. She is persuasive in pointing to ways in which both the image of the woman and her voice appear to be "[isolated] . . . from all productivity."[92] However, her argument strains when, suddenly, she is able to envision a release of the ideological/psychoanalytic burden of the apparatus when it comes to a discussion of more contemporary feminist films. The standards by which she judges these more alternative film texts, when set against many classical films, suggest that the classical cinema has gotten short shrift in her book. Many of the strategies she applauds in these feminist films—self-referentiality, the mobilization of a plurality of voices, exacerbation of a confused representation of sexual difference within both image and voice, underscoring of the reversibility between subjects, obsession with memory and unusual narrative structure, etc.—can be found (albeit, within usually less self-conscious implementations) in more traditional films. Indeed, one of the classical films she analyzes in depth in her book, *Peeping Tom,* is itself a good example of how unorthodox the representational systems of more "conventional" films often are.[93] Significantly, in a book dedicated to the female voice, she offers no sustained textual exploration of female voice-off from the classical period. She depends, rather, on the elaborate theoretical edifice she has constructed to keep the female subject "shut up" in the remote recesses of the classical texts, proving her points abstractly and punctuating them, so to speak, with an example here or there.

The isolation of moments within a text wherein the female voice is tied to a body, or her body held in a gaze, do not themselves suffice to support the claim that "she" is "isolated from all productivity," or fully "contained." A convincing proof that a process of containment works in this way really requires a much more thorough analysis of a text's movements over time, with great attention to the permutations undergone by the voice-off. Moreover, the implicit portrait Silverman presents of patriarchy here (via its representative vehicle, the classical cinema) comes across as monolithic, incontestable, absolutely homogeneous. If ideology, patriarchy, and subject relations are all so fully restrictive and efficient in closing off difference, it seems unlikely that women could speak or that films "outside" the Hollywood system (but still "inside" patriarchy) could signify differently in ways she suggests. Why is Hollywood alone susceptible to the vise-like grip of ideology, while feminists making films manage to wriggle through? Clearly, many feminist filmmakers have a strong critical awareness of the ideological implications of representation and struggle to open up space for the female subject in their films. But it does not go without saying that they are always successful, no matter how well-intentioned. Neither does it go without saying that Hollywood, albeit a capitalist, patriarchal industry, must always be unsuccessful (or rather "successful") at constraining the female, if that is its aim. In Silverman's approbation of the feminist cinema, the implied address is not a negligible factor in consideration: the films she discusses expressly look for ways to engage the female spectator. It seems important, then, to remember that Hollywood films were not solely addressed to a male spectator, and that certain of these films were hardly addressed to "him" at all. Within genres aimed at women, a privileged and emphatic address to a female audience is overtly underscored by the conspicuous presence of the female voice-off.

A grand and provocative loophole thus emerges in the theory that Silverman weaves in *The Acoustic Mirror,* implicit in her assurance that the voice-off works simultaneously in opposite directions (depending on the discursive context) to "objectify" or "free" the female subject. Unlike the visual signifier, on which much feminist theory has more or less given up, it would seem that some hope yet remains for the female voice-off, which, in the right hands, still has something to offer the female spectator (or filmmaker). The female voice-off, as implied in Silverman's writing, seems ostensibly "neutral," merely a tool which, within one woman-friendly system, poses contradictions and proposes differing subjectivity, but which, employed to contrasting purpose in the phallocentric order, works "just like the image" to contain difference.[94]

Thus, it seems as if the voice-off, in Silverman's view, is *enslaved* in the classical system, and *free* in alternative cinema. To what, however, is the voice first bound, and from what, then, unfettered? Although Silverman claims it is the body that keeps the female voice-off from expressing subjectivity, her argument more fundamentally presents the *image* as holding this constraining power. The problem of such enslavement thus emerges as ontological as well as ideological. Though Silverman works to represent this problem simply in terms of discursive operations, she is not entirely successful in defusing the strength of her initial argument that the female voice-off cannot "escape" the mirroring "encroachments" of the body/ image/feminine. All three of these (apparently negative) values collude to bring down the voice. The first half of Silverman's book strongly ties the psychoanalytic principle of lack to an ontology of the voice that represents it as inextricably embodied/imaged, even when non-synch. This ontology undermines the second half of the volume, where she claims the voice- off can indeed be "separated" from the body and the image of cinema, no longer "obliging woman . . . to assume a double burden of lack."[95]

The ontology she has constructed in this book should be reexamined. As we have seen, Silverman relies on a specularization of the voice to devise a psychoanalytic portrait of its classical Hollywood "spectator." She re-inscribes (for the voice) a constraint that is identical to the one Mulvey suggests the image operates on the female subject of this cinema. Redefining the voice in terms of the image misrepresents the specificity of its contribution to the cinematic experience. Collapsing the "body" into the image and understanding subjectivity purely in terms of separation from and rejection of both these terms is neither possible nor desirable. Disembodiment, within this scenario, becomes equated with relative sub- jectivity—both for the spectator and for characters bearing voices. Dis- embodiment of this order requires radical rejection of both real bodies and imaginary ones.

The ever-troublesome body, of course, pertains to both the male and the female (though the female body tends to be represented as the "problem" faced by both sexes). Silverman points at numerous strategies by which classical cinema disposes of this body—or, alternately, pins it to the voice, "yoking" it and "containing" the subject who speaks first *beyond* and then, dismally, from *within* the image. Indeed, examples of such anchorage leap to mind: it is the rule, rather than the exception, that the female voice-off in classical cinema is associated in some way with a represented body to which we assume it belongs. Interestingly, within the scenario Silverman constructs, the "nature" or specificity of the female voice-off is understood as the same, virtually, as the male voice-off—the difference between the two results primarily in the relative prevalence of male voices-off that bear authorial power and in the tendency to relate, or "anchor," the female voice-off to a woman's body in the text. The male voice-off is generally discussed with regard to its reign in the province of the conventional documentary, where, bodiless, it defines truth and epitomizes knowledge. Silverman claims that such voices are "exemplary" for male subjectivity, attesting to an achieved invisibility, omniscience and discursive power.[96] A search for an equivalent, "pure" female voice in classical Hollywood cinema, she suggests, is fruitless, and she dedicates the remainder of her text to discussion of feminist and avant-garde films that in her view move toward this ideal.[97] Throughout this early article and in *The Acoustic Mirror*, the stress is laid on *separating* the female voice from the body as a feminist strategy, and avoidance of synchronized sound that "entraps" the female subject and forces her to "emerge within a discourse contrary to her desires, and to submit . . . to a fixed identity."[98] The complete and utter disembodiment of the female voice-off is, in Silverman's view, the only way to challenge Hollywood, which sees the woman as *only that.*

Her argument and terms re-inscribe an identification between masculinity and subjectivity; that is, to achieve a subjective "position" relative to the text, a female voice-off must be as "disembodied" as the "disembodied voice-over" we associate with the male "Voice-of-God" prevalent in conservative documentary.[99] Understanding this kind of "disembodiment" for the female voice-off as synonymous with feminine subjectivity seems problematic, particularly as the subjectivity such male voice-overs suggest is that of the Father. By extension, it seems to imply that the female spectator/subject must emulate the male condition but from some undetermined "feminine" place relative to the image itself. Must female subjectivity also be defined in terms of the patriarchal ideal?

Though in the analyses that follow I look to the voice-off as a signifier that speaks of sustained difference from the image, my argument simultaneously reclaims the site of the body as something more than visual object. Indeed, I question the logic that leads Silverman to assert (as she does with regard to feminist films) that " . . . what is at stake in this disassociation of sound and image [is] the freeing-up of the female voice from its obsessive and indeed exclusive reference to the female body, a reference which turns woman—in representation and in fact—back upon herself, in a negative and finally self-consuming narcissism."[100] While "obsessive and exclusive" reference to the female body is indeed a serious problem for feminists to resolve in representing that body, her choice of words seems to exclude the possibility of representing women in visual terms that do not oppress and fragment them.[101] Moreover, along with an assumption that the voice-off can and should be "separated" as much as possible from the body in order to allow for a feminine discourse, her warnings against a "self-consuming narcissism" seem obliquely levied at the female spectator—in relation to textual processes she has already pointed out as tailored for stabilizing masculine identity.[102] One has the impression, from her article, that it is less a question of feminists needing to resist the "rule of synchronization" at issue here, but rather whether feminists making films must abandon the female body in order to speak. I do not pretend to be in a position to definitively answer this question. However, I would raise some others in counterpoint that may open up and clarify ways in which this dilemma intersects with the female voice-off. Can the voice really speak, as Silverman would have it, "outside" the body? To what extent can or does a female voice-off signify "differently" from the image of the female? Along the same lines, what degree of dissociation (voice from body) engenders such (if any) difference? Can Silverman's idea of a "pure" voice be observed or constructed? Finally, must feminists reject the possibility that the classical Hollywood films with female voice-off (many of which have cult status and seem to bring women pleasure) bear witness to a communication of feminine subjectivity or address a female subject in an observable way? I contend that a female subject is at stake—a female subject *with* a body. This subject, I submit, can be vised through the heterogeneous signification of the female voice-off and the identification with a space of consciousness that it engenders. In looking to describe this space—and its placement of the spectator relative to the difference of which the image, the body, and the female character of film all speak—let us turn to a classical Hollywood film that is legendary for its sustained and evocative deployment of female voice-off, *Letter from an Unknown Woman.*

Letter from an Unknown Woman

Kaja Silverman clearly recognizes that Ophüls's film merits attention in its possession of "one of the most extended voice-overs in classical cinema," yet she sums up the significance of this voice as more or less residing in the narrative relation it holds to Stefan's desire to hear. She contends, ". . .

Lisa speaks to a male auditor (Stephan [*sic*]) whose willingness to read her letter activates its discourse. In a sense what we *hear* is what he *overhears;* her voice is his mental construction. (In the same way, what we see is what he imagines, as the final montage flash-back makes clear.) Lisa's narration is obedient to Stephan's [*sic*] desires, to his ear."[103] Whether Lisa's voice depends on Stefan's "willingness to read her letter" seems debatable—the letter and the voice are linked to Lisa's production of discourse and her power to fascinate Stefan (as evidenced by the trance that brings him to lose track of time, a trance that proves fatal). Describing Lisa's voice as a "mental construction," too, is problematic. From one perspective, this analogy serves well. As with many female voices-off that "inhabit" a foreign body, as Lisa's voice inhabits Stefan's expressive face when he reads her letter, it holds an implicit connotation of vicarious hallucination, or an imaginary excess. However, Silverman insists on an equivalence between Lisa's "voice" and her "narration"—as well as on the "obedience" of these two to Stefan's desires. But the voice cannot be simply identified with or held indissociable from the language it bears. Nor is it self-evident, in this case, that the voice appeals to and obeys the same "desires" as speech. In fact, if Lisa's narration is to be understood as being in the service of Stefan's desire, what is one to make of the power her speaking holds over him? He does not leave, as he intends at the beginning of the film, and though we know he is reading the letter, we experience the letter, as he does, as a voice—a voice that holds him in sway. Thus, I would question the statement that "we hear what he overhears."[104]

Lisa's voice triggers a fascination that we share with Stefan—he is more obedient to the voice than it is to him. It interrupts "his" narrative, just barely begun and associated with the exterior social world within which this "internal" hiatus into reverie and nostalgia provides a radical break. We do imagine that Stefan hears the voice in his mind, and he is in his room—a space we come to associate with Lisa's desire, not his. In fact, he seems unable to resist the voice or to distance himself from it as it resurrects his past in its own terms, ones unknown to him. Moreover, the flashbacks at the end of the film (where Stefan looks back to imagine what he never "saw") function in a manner quite different from the voice-off that forces itself on his consciousness. The images interrupt, again, the "external" male narrative that has picked up its original thread. They echo, visually, the lost time that makes up the bulk of the film, the time conjured up by Lisa's voice, the "internal" narrative of the film. Yet they also may be understood as Stefan's interpretation or resolving of the loss

"Stefan's" narrative interrupted by the letter . . .

. . . and by his (lost) memory of Lisa

(*Letter from an Unknown Woman*)

that Lisa's voice has brought up and his effort (and the classical text's) to symbolize and close off what her voice "opens."

"Stefan's narrative," as I refer to it here, opens the film proper as we are introduced to him and to the possibility of his death, as well as to the transgressive attitude that brings his "word" into question.[105] He is singled out as the protagonist of interest in an explicitly "exterior" setting to which he returns once the lure of the letter has run its course. "Lisa's narrative," the story "behind" or "within" this first story of a man and his destiny, begins with the letter and her voice and is linked to the internal space of the house and to an interior journey of the imagination; her voice liter-ally *accompanies* the unpredictably wayward consciousness of the mind she hopes to reach, for whom she often "translates" the past into her own terms, helping him (and the spectator) to "read" the images her voice trig-gers. Demarcating these two narratives, the "external" and the "internal," I should note, is a way of describing a peculiar narrative movement, not an assertion of two distinctly gendered perspectives to the film. But it is important to remember that even on this overt level there is an effort to "represent" a woman's enunciatory position, and even if this position is stereotypical in its association to the "interior" of the text, it suggests that this narrative presents itself as in some way "shared"—relayed between the two principle agents.

This "shared" point of view has repercussions for a psychoanalytic read-ing of the female voice-off in this film. It also discourages a premature con-clusion that the sound of Lisa's voice translates as a mere aural reverse-shot of her image that Stefan "also" imagines (even if we choose to accept that Stefan ultimately controls its signification, a position with notable fis-sures). Differences can be located, moreover, between her voice and her image for the spectator, for Stefan, and in the way the two characters relate to desire—differences glossed over, for example, in Stephen Heath's "psy-choanalytic" reading of this film. Heath insists on the image (of the woman) as the privileged signifier troubling a male gaze that orders the text: "At the centre of *Letter from [an Unknown Woman]* is the full image, sexuality as look, the *looked for image* . . . the perfection of the flawless—*whole*—body . . . of the female *as beauty* . . . the desired and untouchable image, an endless *vision*. . . . [At the Opera] Stefan turns in his seat trying to seek out Lisa's face, the face of the woman who now—as always—is gone . . . with Lisa commenting in her voice-over letter-narration that 'somewhere out there were your eyes and I knew I couldn't escape them.' . . . [A]nd so it goes on, the entire film a problem of seeing and knowing, of the image glimpsed and lost and remembered—as of *the* woman, the mother . . . the goddess."[106] Given the unusual emphasis that the film places on the voice-off, it is extremely curious that Heath describes the problem of the film as wholly one of "seeing and knowing" without ever considering, beyond the brief mention here, how the voice fits in to this theory. His point, that the gaze and the image are privileged in the film-work, and that the problem is one of "'seeing' *for the spectator*" seems based on an assumption that the voice-off is insignificant or merely literal (an unaccountable assumption for a writer as sensitive to the aesthetic and ideological permutations of framing and montage as Heath is.)[107] It would seem that sound makes no difference—or that the difference it represents for the image is either too weak or too disturbing to be articulated. Fundamentally, Heath's elision of Lisa's voice as such drives home the point he wishes to make about the image—it also perpetuates a logic that looks to the ordering of a male-coded gaze as the basis for all meaning in film. It overlooks levels of signification that may allow for a less rigid conception of spectatorial pleasure than one locked to the mechanisms of voyeurism and fetishism. It participates in the ideology of the visible (and the patriarchal) it purports to critique.

Lisa vs. Stefan: Who Sees, Who Speaks?

A passionate debate has emerged over the years about *Letter from an Unknown Woman,* wherein critics and theorists invariably come down "on the side of" Lisa/femininity or Stefan/patriarchy as the site of subjective structuration for the film. Significantly, most discussions of this film dwell on the immaculate and elaborate camera work that characterizes this Ophüls text and on the complicated flourishes of the temporality engendered by its flashback structure; very few address the equally prominent formal feature of female voice-off. Theorists who do mention the problem of voice in this film still tend either to reduce the voice-off to the words it pronounces (forgetting that while voice may bear speech/narration, its own ontology as a complex sound phenomenon should also be acknowledged) or look to ways in which the voice-off is "folded in" to the image, and thus rendered, supposedly, powerless. Gaylyn Studlar, in an article dedicated to masochistic performance and female subjectivity, merely notes that "Lisa's voice-over and her letter guide the narrative to [the] end . . ." without delving into the performative aspects of the voice per se or of the seductive or leading activity of the voice which "guides."[108] Her article, instead, centers on narrative action and causality in order to display Lisa's "masochistic aesthetic."[109] Lucy Fischer suggests Lisa's voice "is subsumed by . . . [mediation through] male consciousness; she is 'read' by him."[110] Her essay conflates the voice with the text of the letter she has written, overlooking its potential signification as sound. Tania

Modleski, in an otherwise compelling article, strangely stresses not Lisa's access to voice-off but her *silence,* barely referring to the voice-off except to posit it as a cathartic medium through which Stefan's "hysteria" may be cured.[111]

Those critics who are expressly interested in the potential "difference" in the female voice-off of this film see its power as severely constrained. Silverman claims that the film "situates the female voice at the interior of the narrative by contextualizing it within a written rather than a performance text."[112] Because a letter launches the voice-off, she argues, no subjectivity can be attributed to it, and it is, further, "enclosed" in Stefan's consciousness. Silverman's insistence on denying any subjectivity to Lisa's voice-off and her alignment of that voice with the "interior" recesses of the text as well as with the image (it is "embodied") seem implacable. Its status as a voice is at every turn, in her view, compromised by the dominating image track. Interestingly, however, whereas Silverman claims that a letter is not a "performative" text, Linda S. Kaufmann's work on epistles by women describes such writing as "revolution"—specifically in amorous letter writing by women to men whose indifference or abandonment has triggered this passionate, transgressive act. The furious letter writing of that "other" voice-off in *All This And Heaven, Too*—that of the repressed and ultimately murdered wife—richly illustrates Kaufmann's point.[113] In another text that strongly stresses the duality of sound and image in the Ophüls film, Susan White notes that Lisa's desire for Stefan may be triggered by his embodiment of the phallic Mother through his production of an "aural bath" of music that captivates her transgressive imagination. White also stresses that Lisa "resists" visibility throughout the film in important ways ("masquerading" as feminine to attract the gaze, even while trying to "deflect" it in order to assume a subject position).[114] White is more interested, actually, in the role of music on the sound track than in the voice-off, though she claims that Lisa "*narrates*" Brand, in an active, creative sense.[115] White, moreover, strongly argues that contradiction permeates the film, which sets up "the male-female, image-music, subject-object oppositions that produce both love and violence in the tale," though she insists these oppositions are "undermin[ed] . . . even as they are produced."[116]

The notion that contradiction structures this text is central to my own view of *Letter.* In this respect, I find Edward Branigan's complex dissection of the narrative workings of this film provocative, even as I disagree with some of his conclusions. Branigan frequently refers to the voice-off in *Letter* as "words" that accompany the images, or alternately as Lisa's "narration," and he ultimately claims that Lisa's subjectivity is sorely compromised by a "hidden and powerful masculine discourse" levied via the objectifying image that precludes her ability to sustain a visual point of view.[117] Branigan's analysis depends primarily on a discussion of point-of-view structures as they are presented by the image track of the film, notably in the famous "stair shot" in which Lisa's vantage of Stefan's late-night philandering is reprised "without her there to see" on the fated evening she herself becomes the object of his attentions. Branigan describes this scene as "excluding" Lisa, in the first instance because she has an illicit view that separates her from her object and in the second because she is "no longer [there to] be a witness because she has become Stefan's object."[118] But Branigan's clinching argument "against" Lisa comes though a meticulous tracing of a retroactive point-of-view shot—a "reverse shot" given prematurely in an early scene when Stefan plays the piano as Lisa swings in a reverie outside—a low angle close-up of his hands. This shot indeed seems retroactively elicited in a scene toward the end when, in medium close-up, Lisa dreamily watches Stefan's hands on the keyboard as she kneels next to him at the piano. This "*delayed* or suspended POV structure" as Branigan puts it, defines her as "absent" in the later scene, "for now she exists only in *his* memory; her POV remains fragmented."[119] That Stefan's memory itself exists *grace à* the spiral reverie brought on by the instigating movement of Lisa's voice-off is something Branigan never addresses adequately in his essay.

As indicated earlier, I am skeptical about a project that represents female subjectivity though the same visual constructions (in this case a "non-fragmented" point-of-view shot) that have traditionally been ascribed to masculine subjectivity. Indeed, it seems far from incontrovertible that a "delayed" point of view can only be understood as one that elides Lisa here—for Branigan (surprisingly) appears to understand the temporal structure of this film in a strictly linear sense. The film itself, however, ceaselessly buckles against linear temporality (a characteristic of films bearing female voice-off, as we shall see). *As a voice-off,* Lisa is very "close" to this displaced reverse shot at the beginning of the film—having "introduced us" to the scene moments before and being Lisa's aural corollary to the sound of Stefan's piano.

Moreover, as Branigan notes, within this early scene, marked dissolves blur the spaces Lisa and Stefan inhabit, enabling a traverse of sound from one space to another (just as dissolves mark the traverse of the voice-off in every movement from Stefan's room to Lisa's flashback memories elsewhere in the film.) Whereas Susan White sees the flashbacks as "separating" (Lisa and Stefan), the use of dissolves (the conventional effect of which is to link overlapping spaces) would seem rather to connect them.[120] The repetition of the dissolves, in conjunction with the music and the voice, go a long way toward suggesting the simultaneous experience of two spaces at once—a simultaneity that the later scene renders acute with Lisa's happy awareness of being there, where she once was only in imagination, "under Stefan's hands."

Indeed, Lisa's voice-off has a marked capacity to traverse time, to force connections (for Stefan, for the viewer) across the film to evoke a consciousness of her "place." (The repetition of certain phrases over key scenes reiterates the mobility of the voice-off, its "hovering" spatiality, its strange verticality across the narrative's trajectory through represented time.)[121] If the low-angle shot is to be thought of as Lisa's point of view, however, it is not so much delayed, as *anticipated* by the young girl daydreaming as she listens to the lyrical prelude he plays. Looked at this way—as an imagined premonition of what she will see when she has attained her place of desire and made her fantasy come true—her subjective powers seem mythic, aligned not with a non-place but with authorship.[122] Moreover, despite Branigan's argument that "what is deferred and finally denied in *Letter from an Unknown Woman* is a position for its heroine, Lisa," he admits that to understand the film's complexity we must "search for opposing, masculine discourses *interwoven* with feminine discourses."[123] Thus his own reluctant project, to "prove" that Lisa is nowhere in this film, is subtly undermined, as he acknowledges that contradictory subjectivities coexist here. Indeed, I agree that heterogeneity is at stake in this film, and that "the splitting into many voices is the voice."[124] Where Branigan means to remind of (among others) the author's "voice," I am concerned to retrieve the phenomenon of the voice per se (and female voice-off especially) from this literary analogy, to examine the ways in which it appeals to the spectator, along with the image, to create a meaning *between.*

Consciousness and Sustaining Difference

In looking for a psychoanalytic model that can account for this notion of "between" as well as one that explores the possibility of contradictory and simultaneous subjectivities (something the voice-off brings into relief in a classical film text), I have found the work of Denis Vasse and Guy Roso-

Lisa's place of desire, anticipated . . .

. . . and realized

(*Letter from an Unknown Woman*)

lato compelling. Lacanians both, their perspective seems nonetheless to resist, to a degree, an automatic privileging of the phallus as *the* signifier of value, a privileging that also may on a symbolic level presuppose a higher psychoanalytic and social value placed on the visible over the heard.[125] Their writings on the voice open up provocative repercussions for film studies and offer a refreshing rethinking of the seemingly inevitable conflation of "difference" with "sexual difference."

Vasse's explication of the voice as a signifier of difference, and his notation of the various symbolic representations offered of it, underlie, in a fundamental way, Michel Chion's efforts to metapsychologize the voice in cinema.[126] Chion links the female voice-off to the Mother and to loss, noting the many cases in which the female voice-off leads a character to death ("sa perte"), calling like a Siren that compels the transgression of a limit that leads to the eradication of the subject.[127] In pointing out this tendency within cinema to "use" the female voice to represent such oblivion, he offers no theory as to how this voice-off may function relative to the spectator. Nor does he explain the relation between this "use" of the female voice-off and others to which it has been put in cinema. To move toward this end, I want to offer my own examination of both Vasse's work and that of Guy Rosolato.[128] The notion, explored by both Vasse and Rosolato, of the voice as related to the Mother and to a "transgressive" union anterior to the Symbolic is of central concern. My interest in this pre-Oedipal domain is heightened by the concept of consciousness that Vasse elaborates in his discussions of voice. In thinking about subjectivity in consciousness and space rather than in terms of a gazing position relative to an image, I hope to outline a general "psychoanalytic profile" of the voice that "speaks" of a difference sustained. Bearing in mind my limitations (I am not a psychoanalyst, and I look at much of this theory metaphorically), I offer here a "portrait" of subjectivity experienced relative to the voice and female voice-off, before relating it back to *Letter from an Unknown Woman*.

Mary Ann Doane's admonition that "[s]ound carries with it the potential risk of exposing the material heterogeneity of the medium" should be recalled here, as well as her view that the asynchronous voice is particularly "risky" in this regard, since it is "disembodied" from the synchronous signifier (Silverman's "specific body").[129] This risky "otherness," she contends, makes the voice peculiar, "uncanny." Her remarks coincide suggestively with Vasse's work on the voice. He points to a split inherent in the voice—the voice is not the same as the words it conveys and yet cannot be distinguished easily from them. The voice, as it was before language, simply can no longer be heard—yet it is always there, "in" the words, in the "grain," in, as Rosolato puts it, the "flesh" of the voice.[130] The voice, then, is a site of potential loss, like the image: it signifies the illusion of its own plenitude, recalls an "empty" state that is its "pure" condition, a condition outside of the Symbolic. This "voice beyond sense" is a correlative to the gaze.[131] As Vasse puts it, the voice (like the phallus, the "rien," the gaze) evokes "the pure and impossible materiality of the thing (*la chose*)."[132] He explains that "the voice inscribes itself in the umbilical rupture . . . [making of birth] . . . the first separation and the first reunion. . . . Heard, [the voice] re-establishes the relation of difference that founds the unconscious *and* speech. . . ."[133] He continues: "The umbilical is closure (*clôture*). The voice subvert[s] the closure . . . *traverses* it, without breaking it.[134] [The voice] transforms the silent body into a sonorous space [that receives sound] and lets the speech of the other *resonate* . . . in a suspension of all *reason*. . . . The voice is neither in the order of representation (knowledge/*savoir*) nor in the order of presence to the self (place/*lieu*). It is not conceivable except as the passage (*franchissement*) that *founds the limit it traverses*. . . . It manifests presence, outside place, in the concept that is representation of presence. Outside of the concept of which the voice is the mechanism, there is neither presence nor knowledge. *The voice is the originary between (entre-deux) of knowledge and place*."[135] A traverse, a passage, the *between,* the voice eludes the refractive ricochet that drives opposition and objectification in the subject/object relation.

The voice, then, belongs simultaneously to the mother and to the child in the womb: it opens and closes the difference between them after birth. The voice always carries the suggestion of non-differentiation within it and simultaneously articulates the very loss of the fetus's union with the mother, in the cry of birth. Like the umbilical cord, it connects subject to subject even as it separates them. Fundamental to Vasse's description is this notion of a limit that is both articulated and traversed by the voice: the voice is both of the conscious and the unconscious, of the body and of the Other's body (that is as yet only "understood" in terms of the voice, i.e., not a body as we inevitably "imagine" it, male or female). Voice, moreover, "transforms the body into a sonorous space." Here, Vasse's description opens onto Doane's intimation of a body in space discussed earlier. The voice is the "traverse" itself that marks these differences and allows for symbolic difference while at the same time uniting them, identifying them. It pronounces the "in-between"-ness that makes for the subject's speaking and triggers desire.

The interest of these speculations regarding the voice relative to cinema seems to me not only to lie in the apparent intensity that can be inferred of the "invocatory" drive. Vasse's theory also bears implications for the voice-off as symbolic of difference in a way that may "trouble" or destabilize the structuration of sexual difference effected by the image of the classical text. That is, if voice "replaces" the umbilical in this way and signifies for the child the articulation of separation and reunion with the mother, his description of this experience expressly enounces the child's difference from her in terms of consciousness rather than "identity." (I am taking the liberty of summing up Lacan's mirror phase as involving this new sense of the self, wherein the small human first comes to appreciate her or his place in the Symbolic.)

Vasse and Rosolato both suggest that the Father's voice also immediately comes into play as the third term and functions not as the voice of desire, as does the Mother's, but as the voice of interdiction. One might question, in fact, whether it is the "voice" of the Father that functions in this way or what the voice *represents:* language and the sense of the voice's modulation. Doane, concerned to avoid an essentialist equating of the voice with female subjectivity, points out that the voice cannot be separated in a symbolic system from the "politics" that underwrite it. She warns that an "erotics" of the voice may simply lead to the articulation of another "form of 'otherness,'" yet indicates that the "place" of the voice is a crucial feminist investigation.[136] Her point, that the voice must be considered within the politics of the representation within which it is deployed, is well taken. My interest in signaling the heterogeneity of the female voice-off is not to suggest that it reflects an essential female subjectivity but to indicate how the "feminine" is retroactively placed onto the voice as a psychical distancing itself. In this way, however, the "feminine" may be more than the "otherness" Doane speaks of, or, at the least, may speak through it. In any event, any notion of feminine subjectivity in a culture that defines the feminine as unrepresentable might inevitably be figured as indirect, a translation brought into terms that the culture can access and symbolize. The female voice-off in classical films may often provide an example of such rendering; however, the "voice" in the female voice-off is often the best translation we have of what we cannot imagine—a voice in its "pure materiality," as Vasse calls it.[137]

Inasmuch as the voice speaks of the traverse of a limit that is not as yet based on the symbolics of the visible, and if it is *"the originary 'between' of knowledge and place"* (*savoir et lieu*) (my emphasis on "between"), or the unconscious and consciousness, it may be construed as evocative of difference that is not "sexually" or gender determined. (That is, difference here is not attached to an appreciation of the physical characteristics that distinguish humans.) Rather, this seems to be a peculiarly mutable

difference, one that allows for the simultaneous consciousness of self
and other in a way that does not yet imply dissolution for the Subject.
Such "consciousness," for the infant, clearly differs from the notion of
"consciousness" we attribute to a socialized individual whose separation
from the Mother has already been (un)successful. For the child, then, the
voice would not only be perceived on a conscious level (*savoir*) as that
of the Mother, but also unconsciously as his or her own voice, the body
a place (*lieu*) where the voice resonates, "speaks."[138] Not only may the
"memory" of the mother's voice within the womb inflect the impact that
the voice holds on the child's psychical development, but this early consciousness of difference may not be traumatic in the same way that the
mirror phase in some sense may be seen to be. The difference the voice
traverses ought not to be described as an "oscillation" or as an "acoustic mirror" as it often is, but as the "in-between" that Vasse describes.
Difference, in this sense, allows the subject to "be" heterogeneous "as"
a voice.

Voice and (Non)Vision

What I earlier called the "fascination" of the female voice-off may be linked
to this heterogeneity implicit in the voice itself and "opposed" to the
"male-centered" image text of classical cinema. As we have seen, the
spectator's relation to sound differs in (at least) one radical respect from
that which he or she holds to the image: the spectator cannot "close the
eyes" to block out sound. The importance of the permeability of the spectator's psyche relative to sound lies partly in the notion of "blindness"
that accompanies it, as discussed earlier: what cannot be shut out also
cannot be seen. In a symbolic system where vision is a privileged sense
and synonymous with a kind of control, the "blindness" of the hearing
Subject suggests a relaxing of the limits that "center" the seeing Subject.
But another question surfaces here: can the Subject "hear" sexual difference in the voice as he or she sees it in the image? That most people
seem capable of distinguishing between a man's voice and a woman's
voice without seeing the person speaking seems to indicate that sexual
difference nonetheless "inhabits" the voice as well as the body. But the
sexual specificity attributed to the voice arrives with the cognizance of
sexual difference—the androgynous connotations placed on women with
deep voices and men with high voices seems to corroborate that such
identification is a retroactive placement on which the psyche insists,

particularly inasmuch as it also allows for a visual symbolization of the voice as "part" of the body.[139]

The voice-off in cinema, as we have seen, is often "placed" in this way, more or less anchored to a body, especially if it is "feminine." Indeed, given the mechanisms that suggest that the gaze is male and that the text works to resolve the "problem" that the female body signifies, it hardly seems surprising that the female voice, too, is "pinned" to a specific signifier of difference, i.e., (as Silverman points out) to a specific female body. However, the problem is not this simple. For one thing, in Hollywood films, particularly of this period, the female voice-off is generally coded as more of a "voice" (or an object-voice) than the male's, a richer signifier of this pre-Symbolic dimension, whereas male voices-off seem more transparent, coded as "language," speech. One obvious sign of this distinction lies in the more poetic, less "sense-bearing" use of language prevalent in female voice-off, compared to the caustic, take-no-prisoners relationship to speech that usually characterizes male voice-off. (One need only compare the lyrical language of the female voice-off that introduces *Rebecca* to the dry verbal style of the male voice-off in *Detour*.) Many female voices-off, also, are expressly musical, both in their interwoven relationship to the score and in their carefully modulated, expressive tonality, as opposed to male voices-off, which tend to be matte, dry, ironic—the "grain" receding into the words uttered. These emphases are due to "maximizing" technical preferences (fidelity vs. intelligibility) in both recording and re-recording. The melodious quality of female voice-off moves it away from speech— puts it on the side of the "unrepresentable": Guy Rosolato claims that a strong link associates music and the "Voice" as such.[140] (Indeed, as Edward Baron Turk has suggested, there are even "cinematic environment[s] . . . that [privilege] maternal incantation over male logocentrism.")[141]

Thus, even if the female voice-off is often "constructed" with respect to the female body, it is also powerfully wrested from it. Female voice-off signifies in its own terms as a voice, as, in some respect, bodiless, reminiscent of that "originary" difference that is traversed. One may very well object in this case that the male voice-off operates in the same way, speaks of the same traverse. And, to a degree, this is indisputable. However, aside from the fact that the voice heard from within the womb is that of a "feminine" register (a register, of course, placed on it later) there is also the symbolic dimension that the feminine seems to take on relative to a state that cannot be imaged. Thus the alliance of the feminine to offscreen space may well be privileged in some sense. The female voice-off not only sees what we cannot—the "blind image," the "off" screen dimension—but it is aligned with that which is not seen (that which cannot be seen) and the space(s) from which the non-visualizable emanates: the space "outside," "beyond" the visible frame, the space of imagination, and the space of radical interiority.

Subjectivity in Difference

A return to *Letter from an Unknown Woman* assists in clarifying these abstract thoughts about the female voice-off. In what way, for example, does the voice of Lisa communicate to the spectator as such, as "off" and as female? The first time we hear it, the image has made the transition from exterior to interior space: Stefan is privileged as the focal character as we watch him take the letter from the hall into the sanctum that his room later represents in relation to Lisa's desire. The camera movement expressively traces out this further movement toward increasingly interior space. Suddenly, the musical theme that will be associated with Lisa's voice in this space begins, underscoring the melodic quality her narration will hold. A few other discrete sounds reach the ear—the sound of the water in Stefan's basin as he washes his face, the ticking clock. Just as Lisa's voice breaks in there is a hush, an anticipatory hum of muted strings and silence. This overture to the "appearance" of her voice and the quietness out of which it rises heightens the impression of its strangeness to the space it comes to inhabit.[142] The grain of her voice is resonant and amplified for an effect of intimacy—rendered in "close-up." Most important, we do not at this point know who is speaking—Lisa's voice is unknown and anonymous, just as the title prepares us to find her. Magnified, lyrical, and invisible, her voice comes out of nowhere to speak the letter to Stefan. The quality of her voice here is at least as remarkable as the words. The words clearly are significant, with their melodramatic confessional message—yet, so is the emphasis on Fontaine's celebrated voice, with its hushed mellifluousness.[143] Stefan, indeed, can be said to be "listening" to both. He "listens" to what is written; we understand this as spectators to be his imagining of the source of the words, as his phantasm (and in this respect it is not incidental, in terms of the retroactive symbolization of the voice, that the voice he imagines is feminine) and also, simultaneously, as her voice-off speaking directly to him. Thus it is both his voice and her voice: it is a voice that replicates very clearly Vasse's description of the "traverse" that bridges the conscious and the unconscious, knowledge and place. Stefan does not speak: he receives the voice, desires it, and in this sense "speaks" with it as it "inhabits" his image. The voice of Stefan's interior monologue then, is Lisa's, and "feminine." More precisely, perhaps, the letter triggers what could be called an "interior bi-logue" between Stefan and Lisa, where her voice permeates, fascinates, and is heard "in" the words he reads. The female voice-off here connotes hallucination, the dissolution of limits, the presence of absence, but, most important, a "shared," heterogeneous consciousness (in the sense of these terms that I indicate above), one that the spectator may also assume.

Lisa's voice suggests images to Stefan, describing "the scenes from our youth" that were shared without his knowledge. It lures him further and further into the imagination, into memories he loses in having now to imagine them, memories that by the end of the film eclipse the reality of the life he has led "outside" them. Her voice leads him in a transition from what I will call "the first level" of Lisa's narrative (in Stefan's room) to the second, "shared" imaginary level (the "external" images of Lisa's life that are also read as "internal," part of memory or imagination). Lisa says, "I believe everyone has two birthdays—the day of his physical birth and the beginning of his conscious life," and her voice changes as the image dissolves to the unloading of the moving van and the revelation of Lisa as the camera pans right. As a result of this transition into the second level, her voice must compete with sounds in the image and with the image itself, saying, "I wondered about our neighbor who owned such beautiful things." She raises her voice to be heard above the din, and the voice thus bridges the two imaginary spaces—still "in Stefan's room," speaking to him, she is also "in the story," "the past," seeing the images she conjures up and hearing the clatter and commotion that threaten to drown her out.[144] Thus, though still directed at him, the recipient of her confession of love, the voice as such is not foregrounded as in the former scene, where her voice seems to so fully inhabit the image and his thoughts. The grain is less resonant, flatter, and the narrative function of the words thus seems stressed over the imaginary relation that the voice articulates. This is a more "ordinary" voice, less saturated with connotations of enigma, music, and loss that characterized it in the previous scene.

This "ordinary," narrativizing voice-off continues and perpetuates the digression that the more "intimate" voice-off began in interrupting "Stefan's" narrative. In short, it propels the narrative "forward," but in the interior direction with which this voice is by now associated. The narrative progresses inward to the "place" that the voice is imagined to come from—the "past" Stefan must come to "see" and "recognize" a past invoked by the voice that cannot be shaken once he's seen/heard it. The "internal" narrative that the incantatory sound of Lisa's voice triggers, in this light, thus acts as a vertical movement such as Maya Deren describes in relation to her own films, though it is also circular, vortexical.[145] Within the flashback structure, the voice arrives to remind of the "other" narrative (Stefan's vigil with the letter and the duel that is its consequence) that is held up, waiting for this long associative spiral to return, recoil, allow the release of the first.

The returns to Stefan's room emphasize, on one hand, the emotional effect that this evolving consciousness of loss wreaks on him. On the other hand, they insist on the contradictory stasis that crucially links the internal narrative propelled by Lisa's voice and the external narrative that the letter interrupts. The word "stasis" here is by no means meant to imply that the internal spiral movement is a dead zone, a "claustral" site wherein the feminine is imprisoned.[146] Rather, it is an opposite drive to forward linear narrative movement. The bulk of the film, in this sense, is one long hesitation, where the spectator "waits" for the first narrative to return and the film centered on the "male" subject to proceed, just as Stefan "waits," despite himself, for his seconds. The flashbacks within flashbacks to Stefan's room underscore the stasis of the "present" of the narrative tense that allows the vertical signification of the "past" to continue its unfolding motion.

Tania Modleski figures the film's resolution as a *containment* of Lisa's difference as follows: " . . . just as Freud said that the hysteric is a visual type of person whose cure consists in making a 'picture' vanish 'like a ghost that has been laid to rest, . . . getting rid of it by turning it into words,' so too is Stefan cured when after reading Lisa's letter, he looks back at her image behind the glass door, and looks back again to find that the picture has vanished. The ghost of femininity—that spectre that haunts cinema—has been laid to rest."[147] Whether Stefan can be described as a "visual type of person" seems debatable, given that he is a musician and that he listens, as we do, in rapt attention to the voice-off. His vision, in fact, seems poor: he misrecognizes women, confuses one with the other. One should also question whether the "spectre" of Lisa's femininity must be understood as relating only to her image. Modleski sees Lisa's disappearance as equivalent to containment, and I dispute this conclusion. The "ghost" shots that reappear at the end of the film suggest that Stefan sees her rise up before him in an "internal" kind of vision, emphasizing that he cannot see her in the "external vision" that has always kept him from recognizing her. When he "looks back to look" with the intentionality of the male gaze, he sees nothing. Lisa's "spectre" may then be said at this point also to relate to her voice, inasmuch as it is as voice in which she has been conjured up in Stefan's mind—rendered in an imaginary space he cannot otherwise access.

Moreover, one might well question Modleski's subsequent assertion that a film like *Letter from an Unknown Woman* appeals to men and male critics because it " . . . provide[s] them with a vicarious, hysterical, experience of femininity which can be more definitively laid to rest for having been 'worked through.'"[148] Possibly, in such a film, male pleasure may to a degree coincide with female pleasure in the relation that the voice-off evokes, a pleasure that may override, or at least alleviate, the allegedly sadistic designs of the male gaze. One way of understanding this is to observe the degree to which male and female desire are identified within the text itself—how pleasure and desire are represented as both heterogeneous *and the same*. In this respect, the linking that the letter and the voice-off represents between Lisa and Stefan also proves instructive in considering the spectator's own relation to the film.

The letter and the voice, both bearing Lisa's longing to exist in Stefan's mind, are two relays in a kind of translation that the film offers of feminine desire. The letter, a form of discourse that in many "women's" (and other) films symbolizes the difficulty for the woman to pronounce her desire directly, also is symbolic of a secret communication, a private declaration that nonetheless demands a response, forces something on the recipient—if only the momentary sharing of the sentiment in the mental reconstruction of what is written there. In *Letter from an Unknown Woman,* the letter comes literally from a radical "beyond": written by a dead woman, it challenges Stefan with an absolute love he can only reciprocate in death, or madness. But the letter also belongs to the "external" narrative that is Stefan's domain. "Taken up" from within this exteriority by the voice, it becomes Lisa's narrative that then forays into the Viennese society that in many ways thwarts her love for Stefan. The two "spaces" of the letter, linked in this way, represent the traverse of the voice, the bridging of consciousness and the unconscious, knowledge and place, and allows, ultimately, for their confusion in a way that the text leaves unresolved. Near the close of the film, Lisa's voice-off tells us, over an image of her son's deathbed which pans to frame her own torso bending over the letter, "Now I'm alone—my head throbs and my temples are burning. If this reaches you, believe this—that I love you now as I have always loved you." This shot is likely that which Silverman signals as "anchoring" the female body to the voice-off, thus constraining its potential subversion of the image. The effect of this shot is, to the contrary, to radically *disrupt* the segregation of imaginary levels that heretofore governs the structure of the film.

As we have seen, "Stefan's" narrative begins the story, then "Lisa's" narrative breaks in with its internal flashback spirals. These spirals resurface into the stasis that interrupts Stefan's narrative, her voice holding his story back to force Stefan's recognition of their mutual loss.[149] Thus, in the shot where Lisa writes (described above), these two narratives now seem simultaneously to "speak." It is the only space represented in the film, other than Stefan's room, in which the voice-off and the letter meet up. Yet it cannot strictly be understood as part of the "internal narrative" that the letter in Stefan's room initiates, since the writing of the letter "precedes" the movement into the past for Stefan *in* the "external" space from which the letter arrives. Nor can it be considered proper to the "external" space of Stefan's narrative, as it is Lisa's letter as voice which signifies its own writing in the "internal" narrative linked to her figure. Lisa's voice here seems equally the voice as Stefan imagines it in reading *and* that of her writing, imagining him reading. The letter, here, replicates the con-

Lisa writes, imagining Stefan reading, imagining her writing.

(*Letter from an Unknown Woman*)

tinuum of the voice, with sender and receiver taking up both positions with respect to it simultaneously, in the imagination. Like an "acoustic-verbal hallucination," this is a moment that "present[s] . . . the ambiguity of a confrontation between the 'I speak' and the 'I hear.'"[150] A lover's discourse, it "goes towards the other."[151] Barthes writes movingly of the solitude of the lover's discourse and how this solitude, "driven . . . into exile," becomes the site of affirmation. His description is singularly apt for the "lovers" in *Letter,* embodying both the terrible burden of solitude and the solace attained through a discursive gesture affirming it. Indeed, "[the love letter is] purely *expressive.*"[152] In Lisa's writing the love letter (as she does here, in her letter, in her voice, in the very film), she "engage[s] with the other [in] a *relation,* not a correspondence: the relation brings together two images."[153] Two "images," two subjectivites articulated in the traverse of the voice, sustained in the difference in the writing/reading/speaking/hearing of the letter.

The Middle Voice

This intersection of the letter and the female voice-off, the sense in which the letter is literature and the voice is a kind of writing, and the way in which both represent a passage of limits and the establishment of a relation within difference returns us to a concept introduced briefly at the opening of this chapter—the "middle voice." A grammatical and literary voice, the middle voice articulates clearly the strong coexistence of "contradictory" subjectivities. Indeed, it leads, at the limit, to a kind of redefinition of subjectivity itself, for it opens onto possible ways of describing subjectivity within what we "normally" think of as "the place of the object," by demonstrating agency within both the space of "interiority" and the "passive" voice.[154] The Greeks, according to Hayden White, used the middle voice to "designate the subject's 'interiority' to a variety of actions . . . especially [those] informed by a heightened moral consciousness." The "subjectivity" articulated by this voice comes in part through this kind of consciousness "and the force of involvement" it implies for the subject.[155] As opposed to an expressly passive/active split, where "either the subject or the object remains outside the action," in the middle voice "the distinction between subject and object is obliterated."[156] Thus, a subject need not, as in the "voyeur" model of spectatorship, be "exterior" to the object or "distanced" (nor indeed, is the "exterior" narrative region thus privileged as the arena of agency), for a model of subjectivity does exist in which "interiority" connotes a special heterogeneous agency in which "subject and object . . . are in some way conflated."[157] Martin Jay notes, moreover, that the middle voice, "if spoken aloud . . . would sound more like a hallucination than a communicative speech act."[158] His description seems peculiarly apt to the ambiguous "origins," multiple subjectivities, interior bi-logues, and the blurring of consciousnesses often represented by the female voice-off.

The "middle voice," a peculiar mode of address which I am claiming the female voice-off frequently expresses, seems to refute the easy alliance of the "outer regions of the text" with subjective privilege and authorship per se. It also suggests that the so-called "inner folds" of the film may offer a place to begin looking for subjective agency. Moreover, the middle voice relates crucially to the longstanding opposition of active/passive modes, in which passivity is always on the side of objectification, impotence, non-(self)expressivity. Freud's discussion of the drives of love and hate is brought up by Hayden White in this respect, specifically in regard to the "defenses of 'reversal of an instinct into its opposite' and 'turning round upon the subject's own self.'"[159] Freud sees sadism/masochism and the turning of the subject into the object as manifestations of these two defenses. Where usually these processes are linked to simple subject-object/active-passive reversal, White claims that Freud "posit[s] a third position in this process . . . [in which] 'the desire to torture has turned into self-torture and self-punishment, not into masochism. The active voice is changed, not into the passive, but into the *reflexive, middle voice.*'"[160] White goes on to note that this view of the middle voice relates to "obsessional neurosis . . . characterized by a 'turning round upon the subject's self' but '*without* an attitude of passivity' (the subject's attitude remains *active*)."[161]

It is not my desire, in bringing up this psychopathology, to present it as a "role model" for feminine subjectivity, such as is represented in *Letter from an Unknown Woman.* Though this may be a promising area of inquiry, and certainly as viable an allegory for feminine spectatorship as masochism, "aesthetic" or otherwise, my aim in bringing these ideas forward is simpler.[162] I merely wish to establish the existence of a psychological model in which passivity does not translate simplistically into objectification and non-agency, and moreover to stress the heterogeneous constitution of subjectivity as pronounced by the middle voice, in which both subject and object signify in all their apparent contradiction, *simultaneously.* White stresses that "actions and effects [in the middle voice] . . . are conceived to be simultaneous," as opposed to the usual "separation between the time of the inauguration of the action and the time of its completion."[163] In this I see a strong explication of the prevalence in films bearing female voice-off to adopt a spiral flashback structure, in which past and present are often collapsed and rendered indistinguishable. The structures of *Letter from an Unknown Woman, Secret beyond the Door, Brief Encounter, No Man of Her Own, So Proudly We Hail, A Letter to Three Wives, The Locket,* and others all bear this marked preference for temporal "simultaneity" over "separation."

Finally, the issue of consciousness raised by White with regard to the middle voice seems particularly relevant to the voice *en soi,* in the way Vasse has described it, and to the female voice-off of cinema, which represents this "pure" voice, this voice "beyond sense," most closely in film. The simultaneous evocation of difference expressed by this voice has to do not only with the "force of involvement" that renders subjectivity through an attitude of consciousness, as it pronounces its linking of the conscious to the unconscious, but relates also to the phenomenological problem of dialectical relations in general. For, as I am sure it is clear by now, the paradoxical dynamic of the dialectic is of crucial importance in understanding the work of the voice. Such a dialectic is implicit not only in Vasse's theory (of the voice's traversing of difference to engage the subject in space and consciousness rather than "identifying" (him) "as" a locus of sexual differentiation), but also in the theorizations mentioned here relative to the middle voice. Not only does the middle voice suggest an experience "with more than one subject inhabiting the same space," but it also fuses subject and object, a primary trait of phenomenological definitions of "self-consciousness."[164] In self-consciousness, "the conscious subject makes itself into its own object, or conversely, a particular type of object in the world grasps itself subjectively. Secondarily . . . self-consciousness makes possible a fusion of mental entities which would be judged merely contradictory by the standards of ordinary logic."[165] This "fusion of mental entities" is created not only between characters in films (for example Lisa and Stefan as they blur consciousnesses through the voice-off) but also between the voice-off and the spectator. Indeed, it is a question of "multiple subjectivities"—the "many voices" Branigan describes.[166] And in this dialectical self-consciousness, the problem of "synthesis," the transcendence of the impossible coexistence of contradictory subjectivities, should not be misunderstood as an obliteration of difference. Such synthesis does "not do away with oppositions through compromise but preserve[s] and transcend[s] them . . . often in explicitly paradoxical form."[167] Yet the opposites come together "in such a way that they are no longer opposite in their former and *univocal* sense."[168]

There may be something unlikely or even sacrilegious in bringing together such disparate notions of consciousness as those invoked by Freud, Vasse, Benjamin, and Hegel; yet all these writers point to a way of figuring subjectivity that slips out from the subject-object paradigm, a paradigm within which the "feminine" has been incessantly locked to a passive, receptive position that precludes agency. Moreover, the masculine has also received a raw deal, if agency and sadistic objectifying are always to be conflated with the male "exterior" position. In bringing these various and provocative figurations of another model of subjectivity together, my aim is to activate a criticism of the kind of "subject" that has become a monolithic presence in film theory—one without a body, all-seeing, strictly "male," holding itself at a distance to maintain control over its "other." The Subject, if one reads Lacan, is never as well-constructed as it seems to be in film theory—the Subject, in fact, *is not.* Lacan's invocations of "the subject" are famously indirect, oblique, paradoxical. Conceived in a "split," predicated on a "gap," "brought into the light of day . . . to clos[e] up, . . . vanish," the subject is "at home . . . in the field of the dream."[169] The middle voice embraces the contradictions on which the Subject is founded, reactivates them, and allows for the perception of paradox. What was radical, according to Martin Jay, about Flaubert's *Madame Bovary,* written *style indirect libre,* (often compared to the middle voice) was not the matter-of-fact discussion of adultery but the inability of the critics "to attribute with certainty the shocking sentiments . . . to either the character or the author."[170] The reading Subject, then, perceives the contradiction expressed in the middle voice as the concurrent activation of two (or more) "subjectivities" in sustained, contradictory signification. As a type of "middle voice," the female voice-off similarly evokes textual heterogeneity and subjectivity-in-difference, as *Letter from an Unknown Woman* beautifully illustrates.

In expressing the dichotomies of active/passive, interior/exterior, masculine/feminine simultaneously, then, the entire film folds back onto itself, but not to close itself off. Rather, the bridging of imaginary levels as Lisa writes the voice and Stefan reads the voice reaffirms the notion of a heterogeneous consciousness in the voice, one in which desire in difference can be sustained without trauma, without the necessity of deferral, mastery, and containment. Read in this way, the film is atemporal in its temporal movement, a spanning of the voice, as represented by the female voice-off, across stasis that opens up a vertical depth of signification. The meaning of the film, really, is determined by the nature of the voice, its utterance and its reception bridging a narrative that represents in many ways its poetic form. The problem of the image, for this film then, should be viewed from a perspective that considers this evocation of a "shared" desire, an intimate consciousness of difference that may explain not only the symbolics of the story but also the quality of the spectator's relationship to the film.

A famous moment in this film has been singled out by many critics—understandably so, since it pits the voice and the image directly against one another. Over a close-up of Stefan at the opera, Lisa says, "Somewhere out there were your eyes and I knew I couldn't escape them." This moment need not be seen, as Modleski has described it, as a "hysterical moment" in the text for the male spectator to endure and ultimately repress—"the passive, eroticised male . . . briefly glimpsed while being explicitly denied at the verbal level."[171] Nor should it be reduced to a moment that figures Lisa as pure Other, the female image as Object, as Stephen Heath has suggested.[172] Rather, as Lisa's voice speaks over the image of Stefan here, she expresses what is valid for both of them at that particular moment—the voice represents her, disembodied, "looking" at his body as she speaks of his "eyes . . . out there" trained on her. There seems no reason to place perspective in the figure of one or the other: both "see," both "are seen." In the voice, Lisa "inhabits" Stefan's body as she does at the beginning of the film, speaking his and her own desire simultaneously, as it were.[173] For, as demonstrated above, there is more than one body in the voice—difference "there" is also reunion, as this film suggests.

Thus, the ending of the film may be viewed as something other than the ruthless boot-heel of patriarchy grinding the spectre of feminine subjectivity into invisibility and giving the feminized male a swift kick. Instead, Stefan's fate may also be seen as his answer to the voice, his response to the letter. Our sense that there is something sweet in his tragic end does not seem inspired by the desire to see Stefan punished, in the name of the Law, by Lisa's über-patriarch husband (who is anything but sympathetic at this point in the film's narrative). Rather, the fatal resolution responds to the wish to see him share in Lisa's suffering and loss, to recognize her by mirroring her self-sacrifice and thus to acknowledge her as his lost love. His death results, in short, from having heard her, finally, and from having stepped out of the external narrative associated with his gaze to "share . . . in what was never lost." His deflection is provoked by a voice

"Somewhere out there were your eyes . . .

. . . and I knew I couldn't escape them."

(*Letter from an Unknown Woman*)

he neither flees nor resists, a voice he might very well be said to desire. His response to Lisa can be taken, too, as an analogy for the "dissolution" proposed above relative to the cinematic subject whose sensitivity to the voice should not be forgotten. For if Stefan's "love" for Lisa is inspired by the intimacy represented in her voice in reaching him from the beyond, it is also a love that agrees that "suffering . . . grants access to the joy of being recognized."[174] As he "recognizes" her, the spectator "recognizes" him. Such a relation may well bear relevance for the spectator of this film (and others bearing female voice-off) and suggests another way of figuring pleasure in pain than the model of sadomasochism suggested by theories of spectatorship centered on the cinematic image alone. It also hints that in the effort to describe feminine subjectivity, we need to start looking for a register of value that, while not denouncing or rejecting the body, may question further the valuation of the visible relative to other regimes of signification. The notion of a "heterogeneous consciousness" that the female voice-off in film evokes (and on which women's films in particular may capitalize) offers a way of figuring the feminine in terms that do not reflect the flip side of the masculine, nor a biological essence, but a means of communicating or of relating through difference, sustained.

2

point of view and
paradox

Say I am you.

    Rumi (Sufi poet)

The Disappearing Voice: Tracing a Silenced Point of View

In the cinema, the woman screams. This moment, full of terror, unseeing
and unseen horrors, is reserved for a female voice, a voice that seems to
have reached some sort of apogee. The scream reaches us, usually, from
offscreen space, as a manifestation of female voice-off. It is difficult, in fact,
to remember any film in which a man screams. A certain form of crisis
indeed seems "best" expressed or represented by the female voice raised
in an inarticulate cry, a sound that Kaja Silverman claims the Hollywood
film is "at the greatest pains to extract."[1] The female cry/scream represents,
frequently, a body's (impending) mutilation, and, subsequently, the female
character's subjective disappearance from the film text. This association
(terror/disappearance) takes varied manifestations—and it often links
characters as it powerfully halts the narrative to highlight the reverberation, tone, and affect of the scream. In *Cat People,* for example, the character of Alice becomes trapped in a dark swimming pool, "surrounded" by
ominous growls of some supernatural killer "panther." Dog-paddling fran-
tically in the center of the pool, her figure dwarfed within the wide-angle
framing, Alice screams—but her screams do not belong to her.

Wrested from synch by the reverberations of the aquatic space, the

In the cinema, the woman screams.

(*Cat People*)

surreal feline shrieks link her voice to the voice of the "cat" that similarly distorts and echoes—and by extension to the character of Irina, whom we suspect to be the "real" monster. We (barely) see Alice in the water, but it is Irina's "disappearance" from view that is underscored as the narrative pauses to dwell on the terrible voice that ricochets through the dark. A moment of terror for Alice, it is also a moment of power for Irina—stressed by her location in offscreen space, allowing us to imagine that she has transformed from a tentative, neurotic young wife into a jealous, violent beast capable of destroying its rival. This scream is shared by the two women; it is uncertain who emits the sound, or whether the scream is a response or demand. It is unclear whether the scream expresses Alice, recognizing her peril, Irina, triumphant in her malevolence, or indeed, the "cat," about to strike (or stricken itself): all of these possibilities resonate in this drawn-out, bloodcurdling, sonic representation. The scream fore-grounds the female voice as a site of crisis, and the narrative is held up while we are held captive to sound. The scream moves vertically against the linear flow—arresting time and expanding it—focusing our attention on a battle between subjectivities, ultimately implying their convergence, their simultaneous expression. Of course, the narrative of *Cat People* over-all is obsessed with the paradox of "being" two entities at once—osten-sibly both a cat and a woman. The beauty of this film, its subtlety, lies in its refusal to separate Irina into two halves—or to let us "see" that she really "is" a cat. Rather she embodies heterogeneity—the desire and the power of the *between*.

The scream marks a moment of heterogeneous subjectivity, a moment that the text dwells upon with eruptive insistence. The scream traverses between subjects—allowing a "disappearing" subject to speak despite apparent elision from the text. In a famous sequence from *M,* a series of shots represent the little girl Elsie's murder. The sound of her mother's cry, "Elsie!" over "empty" images (images significantly represented as such, to a great degree by their contraposed silence) finally fades away over an image of Elsie's ball rolling out of the bushes, and the little girl's tethered, torn balloon. Christian Metz has pointed out a simultaneous metaphorical and metonymic signification of Elsie's body in the use of the ball and balloon, and Thierry Kuntzel has noted how the "presence of [the mother's] voice . . . lets . . . another person's absence [Elsie's] be read."[2] What Kuntzel leaves unarticulated in his discussion of the final frame of the sequence, in dwelling on the simultaneous designation of Elsie's body and the murderer's desire, is how silence, in "replacing" and articulating the mother's voice, also represents Elsie's unheard scream. For it is partly the silence that makes the balloon appear, like Elsie, so "pathetic" (as Metz so eloquently notes) as it too is mutilated noiselessly. Thus, like the mother's voice-off, Elsie's repressed voice/cry is strangely echoed in the silence here: metaphorically (the voice that is stilled), metonymically (silent as her objects—an object, now, like them), and psychically (if the cry is the child's first expression of life, the umbilical connection to the mother, silence represents the death drive, a "silencing of the drives" themselves, as Michel Poizat puts it. Poizat cites Lacan to clarify: " . . . the cry is first of all not a call, but it makes silence emerge [*surgir*]. It is not that the cry is supported by a silence which is its base, but the opposite").[3] The silence in this scene is "supported" by a cry inaudible but present. This scene from *M* articulates a triangular connection between the scream/cry, offscreen space (linked to voice-off), and silence. Silence, that is, is never "nothing" (film recordists understand this better than anyone—silence must be created, laid down). Silence has a presence, and should not always be associated to "the void," especially when it is marked as filling in for a sound we imagine (a much more terrible cry, in Elsie's case, than any recorded sound could ever be). As Poizat's remarks imply, the voice and silence are engaged in a dynamic dialectic: in silence, paradoxically, we can "sense" the voice rather than hear it. Thus Elsie's voice, her subjectivity, does not go *unheard* in this scene; rather, it is perceived powerfully as silence—a silence into which both her and the mother's voice "disappear" and through which both "speak."

The peculiar shared subjectivity implicit in the scream is something we shall return to later in this chapter with respect to a critical transition point in *Secret beyond the Door*—a moment that articulates and highlights a shift of possession of voice-off privilege from the main female character (Celia) to the main male protagonist (Mark). This moment constitutes, among other things, an apparently brutal suppression of Celia's point of view, which "disappears" along with her voice-off. Where many critics see this supplacement as a repression of the female protagonist's subjectivity in favor of the male protagonist,[4] such transfers in voice-off, in elaborating a shift in perspective, do not necessarily elide an originary perspective. As *M* illustrates, a character who has disappeared, who is "silent," may yet be heard. It is not enough to point out that a character has lost her audible voice-off to conclude that she also been deprived of her power to transmute her point of view. We cannot simply assume that point of view "belongs" with or to the character who is speaking, at the cost and suppression of the subjectivity expressed by a character who has ceased to speak.

Yet, undeniably, possession of voice-off in cinema does imbue the character speaking with a privileged point of view. It not only suggests that this character has a perspective to which the spectator is privy, but it offers the protagonist a pronounced "subjectivity" within the narrative. When one character dominates in possessing sole access to voice-off within the film, such as is the case in *Letter from an Unknown Woman,* her or his point of view is thus underscored, made emphatic and of central interest. But what of films in which more than one voice-off compete for the privileged "place" of subjectivity? In these films, the possession of voice-off emerges as unreliable, marking point of view as potentially contradictory, polyvalent, in conflict. Moreover, when plural voices-off surface in the course of a film, the shift seems to take place at the expense of the female protagonist. The female is granted voice-off only to lose it halfway through the film, her voice-off is "buried" deep within the web of the narrative, or her voice-off is replaced by the voice-off of a male character.

The majority of 1940s films bearing female voice-off, in fact, are characterized by such "shifts," by multiple voices-off, or a female voice-off that "disappears." *All about Eve, The Enchanted Cottage, The Locket* (male and female), *Rebecca, I Walked with a Zombie, So Proudly We Hail* (disappearing female), *A Letter to Three Wives,* (multiple female), *No Man of Her*

Own, and *The Two Mrs. Carrolls* (sporadic female) all share this incon-
sistent voice-off, giving rise, as we shall see, to an understanding of perspective that may include the perspective of another—a heterogeneous
point of view.[5] In exploring this alternate reading, the expressive uses to
which the female voice-off is put relative to male voice-off are crucial. As
mentioned earlier, a certain "kind" of language typically (in classical Hollywood cinema) distinguishes female from male voice-off—"poetic" vs. a
more "transparent prose". (One should not misunderstand such tendencies as demonstrating that certain types of voice are essentially "male" or
"female"—the emotional, poetic thought-voices of the anonymous male
soldiers in Terrence Malick's *Thin Red Line,* for example, break with such
conventions.) The context within which these voices-off are often set,
narratively and formally, as well as the rhetorical values ("irony" vs. "sincerity," for example) which underpin them are also key considerations in
linking character voice-off, a representation of consciousness and point
of view. Point of view as suggested by possession (or "dispossession") of
voice-off also necessarily involves the question of sexual difference and
the representation of gendered subjectivity and power relations within
such texts, leading to a number of questions. Can point of view be simply
asserted as adhering to the sex of the character bearing voice-off? Is it
possible to conceive of, for instance, a male voice-off that is "coded" as
feminine? Are there deadlock point of view wars waging in these films? Can
a suppressed voice still "speak"? Finally, what conclusions can be drawn
about the description of perspective implied by the image relative to the
point of view suggested by the voice-off? Does the image always prevail
over sound, as so many theorists have suggested, especially in pinning
down or containing the female character within her status as looked-at/
objectified image?

   The textual relations between the protagonists within a rhetoric of sound
to image must be carefully considered in interpreting the representation
of perspective in a film. This rhetoric might also be described as a complex narrating process, wherein sound and image, and representations of
"listening," "speaking," "being seen," and "seeing" interplay to produce a
recognition of point of view that enables the spectator to negotiate difference (rather than to repress it). Seen thus, point of view emerges as a
complex construct brought together through the cognitive processing of
narrative schema by the spectator as he or she thinks through the text.[6]
Certainly, moreover, the formal specificity of voice-off offers a range of
expressive relations between voice and image in a film, a varying alliance

to the visible and to the imaginary that evolves along the temporal span of the film. A film that employs (in Doane's terms) a "voice-over" may be said to exploit the perspectival ambiguities of a voice emanating from off screen space in a particularly charged fashion. The symbolic presence of offscreen space, in such a case (even the seemingly "ordinary" sounds attributed to it) is overdetermined, reflecting a representational logic that the "voice-over" inaugurates and constructs throughout the film text. This "logic," a consistency to the manner in which the text relates offscreen space, symbolically, to visible space, is played out not only on the level of "voice-over" but also when that same voice (or other voices in the film) arrive from diegetic offscreen (Doane's "voice-off"). When, for example, one "voice-over" gives way mid-film to another, offscreen space and the orienting perspective have already been aligned with the first voice. This originary point of view inflects our reading of the voice-off and perspective that come to "replace" it. The female voice-off is strikingly unstable, in fact, constantly mutating, shifting, slipping, and transgressing both "bodily" and textual boundaries. The logic that associates an originary radically asynchronous voice to other voices into which it transmogrifies enhances the spectator's sensitivity to fluctuations between voice and body, on-screen and offscreen sound, and multiple points of view. The perspective inaugurated, ultimately, is one of fluidity and multiplicity rather than a single vantage point or "point of audition."[7] The heterogeneity of such a perspective is aggravated by the apperception of a consciousness through voice-off, a recognition that elaborates point of view as a kind of "middle voice." That is, the convergence of more than one voice-off and the representation of more than one consciousness lead not only to a multiplicity of perspectives, but these points of view exist in a paradoxical relation that allows for such difference to be expressed actively throughout the text.

Although sound and voice are often considered significant elements that affect our reading of a narrative and the expression of character point of view therein, they are more frequently viewed as cosmetic appendixes to the more primary constructing power of image and diegesis. But the contribution of voice and sound to the articulation of point of view "of" a text or character, in fact, is anything but secondary. To the degree that sound emphasizes offscreen space (both the diegetic imaginary space we imagine conjoins the image track and the nonvisual register of space that sound evokes), its constructive contribution seems amplified. Noël Burch has demonstrated how, in offscreen space, a dialectic of difference is continually present to the image, a difference rendered acute through formal emphasis on asynchronous sound.[8] This persistent alterity relates importantly to our apprehension of perspective throughout the film. Underscored by the pronounced "difference" of voice-off within the text, point of view, to a significant degree, is "determined" on the level of the sound track through its often radical disruption of what the image relays. Voice-off leads the spectator to recognize character consciousness as at odds with the image, to "see" beyond or through the visual register of the film, to perceive a point of view that is constructed " . . . on *the difference between* the opaqueness of visual appearances and the report of the depth of feeling of the interior world."[9] That is, in many ways and in many films—among these, *Secret beyond the Door*—hearing "trumps" seeing. It is not that the image track ceases to signify, leaving the voice-off alone to evoke point of view. Rather, voice-off participates in the structuration of point of view, establishing a strongly present perceptual framework at the onset of the film and evolving during the course of the narrative into a powerful representation of a "middle voice" between characters.

The dynamic view taken here of the transformative operations of the voice-off is sparked by the logic that underlies Edward Branigan's understanding of narration itself as, " . . . not just a structure but as a process . . . where[in] two narrations cease to be perceived as simply a mixture of separate features but instead become a blend with entirely new properties able to generate entirely new effects."[10] Where Branigan is concerned with how (and how many) different "levels of narration" interact to produce meaning, my analysis in this chapter maps the principle behind his analysis onto one of these specific levels—point of view—with an eye to uncovering its processes. It is in some respects difficult to elaborate character point of view as such, abstracting its "role" in the play of a text from the other levels. I aim, while concentrating my discussion on point of view, to respect the complexity from which it emerges, tracing a nonvisible structuring signification—a voice-off—as it signifies apart from (or, more accurately, *alongside*) the visible image—its frame, angle of view, mise-en-scène, lighting, etc. Point of view, in this sense, emerges *between* the voice-off and the image: it relates crucially to the spectator's apprehension of characters as consciousnesses and the degree to which they express, represent, and elicit recognition of perception and subjectivity. This "between-ness," indeed, comes out strongly in films bearing female voice-off. The female voice-off signals the heterogeneity of point of view, rendering it audible. Films that explore the repercussions of such a voice, moreover, represent such heterogeneity as a sustained, rather than foreclosed, difference.

The "Chattering Wife": The "Place" of Voice

Eric Smoodin suggests that the "voice-over . . . narrator is not the 'author,' [but] seems nonetheless to be the organizing force behind [the film's selection and ordering of images]," adding that "the equation of image to narrator's speech has become so conventionalized . . . that even after the spoken narration has vanished from the sound-track, the spectator still *feels* the narrator's presence and *senses* the narrator's control over the story."[11] Smoodin's evocation of the spectator's visceral apperception of the lingering presence (a physical manifestation?) of an absent yet structuring point of view resonates with a revelatory contradiction. On one hand, his description implies that the voice (and the words it pronounces) is conflated with the image, rendered doubly invisible, so to speak, in that we see "through it," perceiving the visual register as the primary signifier of point of view. On the other hand, the image has become a ruse, a mirage. It is "controlled" by what is absent, inscribed in a perspective that is sensed (intuitively) rather than seen. Voice-over works as a structuring absence, masquerading as transparency.[12] Or, perhaps more precisely, it offers a structuring contradiction, a meaning lent by paradox.

In layman's terms, Smoodin's point is obvious: the spectator takes what has come before into account as he or she follows the film's narrative. One's perception of point of view is constructed *in time,* through a process that, in Smoodin's description, seems progressive, complicating. Moving from the implications his statement holds for the spectator to how it may bear on the workings of the text, however, another important consideration arises. Smoodin's statement suggests that image does not necessarily dominate sound, even when that sound is not present "on" screen. Smoodin's description implicitly inverts the dictum that image comes "first" and sound "after," along with the ideological primacy accorded to the visual register that implicitly guides much of the work done in film studies. Metz's infamous adage that sound is like a "chattering wife," stems from what Sarah Kozloff has described as a kind of theoretical and critical "revolt" staged by many major film theorists, against what she calls "iconophobia."[13] This critique of sound stems from a political and aesthetic interest in dislodging the centering logos of the word. In a searing analogy, Kozloff alludes to the bizarre underpinnings of this "faith in the image" as fittingly dominant over sound: "... the image is cast as the husband/father and the sound track as the wife/mother. The proper power relationship is made abundantly clear."[14] Strikingly counterintuitive (for, generally, in film theory, the feminine is invariably associated to the image, where, it is suggested, she can never speak, but only signify her difference), Kozloff's description fascinates me by pinpointing a subliminally "feminine" affect to sound in general (one we might assume that comes across even more glaringly in a voice that is expressly coded as female).[15] This affect might also account for early theorists' phobic rejection of sound's contagion of the image, its rendering impure the (Apollonian, masculine) visual signification.[16] (The female voice-off, in this light, represents a highly "contagious" sound indeed.) Kaja Silverman, perhaps seeing such contagion as a weapon, has posited female voice-off as a feminist interventionist tool for destabilizing the male-centered image (in films made by women). I would carry the idea further: the alterity of sound is a perpetual and illuminating "trouble" for the stability of the subject's gaze, even in films constructed without the bent of a feminist author's intentions. There is something misleading, however, in the vocabulary used here for illustrative purposes—in suggesting that the image's meaning is "there," uninflected, prior to being "troubled" by sound. Rather, in their dialectic, their difference produces the meaning. To sum up: sound and image work off each other—neither, in a sense, can escape the signifying effect the other brings, once they are connected as a relation.

A tired adage warns that voice-over narration is a redundant "literary device" and/or a lazy last-ditch solution to make a badly constructed screenplay comprehensible in the final mix. This cliché is belied not only by the intricacy such voices often lend narrative structure but by the perspectival subtlety they promote. Kozloff has persuasively illustrated the complexity of voice-over narration, mapping out the different configurations the voice-over can assume relative to the diegesis. Throughout her book *Invisible Storytellers,* moreover, she points to two expressive tendencies "attached" to the use of voice-over. The first is an ironic distanciation, as in voice-overs that slyly pull the rug out from the image or undercut narrative events in some way. (Voice-overs can also make the viewer conscious of the unreliability of voice-over itself.) The second lies in its frequent invitation to identify with the character with whom it is associated, and "the voice's power to create a feeling of connection and intimacy."[17] Kozloff sees voice-over films as "hybrids,"[18] where these two seemingly contradictory modes of expression—distanciation and identification—coexist peacefully. Kozloff herself does not expand on the nature of such "hybridity" to explain, for example, to what degree these qualities co-exist within single films, to what degree they are properties of narratological strategies, or to what degree they are properties of voice-off per se. The path she leaves untraveled presents an important conceptual direction for this book. This chapter traces the implications of "hybrid" texts wherein the deployment of voice-off allows for the simultaneous articulation of heterogeneous, seemingly incompatible perspectives within the film text. With an agenda to topple the usual hierarchy imposed in film studies, where image figures an originary perspective and sound merely inflects or recontextualizes what visual information decrees for character and point of view, let us turn to *Secret beyond the Door.*

Levels of Narration: Multiplicity and Voice

An uneasy example of *film noir, Secret beyond the Door* does, nonetheless, bear what Christine Gledhill calls a "typical plot" of this genre—"a struggle between different voices for control over the telling of the story,"[19] or, as J. P. Telotte puts it, "a fight for the right to speak."[20] As discussed earlier, many films made during the '40s bear witness to the political and discursive struggles between men and women during this era.[21] But the notion of a discursive "fight" can also be taken quite literally in certain films, in which more than one character vies for the powerful position of offscreen narrator—the governing consciousness through which the viewer identifies a point of view. In *Secret beyond the Door,* an abrupt and disorienting shift in voice-off occurs midway through the film: the main female character's (Celia's) narration gives way to her husband Mark's spoken thoughts. To what degree does this shift alter the spectator's understanding of point of view? If the voice-over always " . . . testifies to a subjectivity at work, an 'I,'"[22] what happens when more than one subjectivity surfaces during the course of the film? Does one character's point of view simply cede way for that which comes to replace it? Or must the spectator, faced with a number of subjective viewpoints, "abandon all notion of an objective vantage or . . . possibility of ever synthesizing [the] multiple perspectives," as Telotte warns?[23]

Multiple points of view need not predispose the narrative to a kind of narratological chaos. The spectator always negotiates complexity as he or she engages with a film. The discernment of character point of view directly relates to our reading of narrative, our alignment with discourse, and our (and the film's) imbrication in and resistance to ideology. Understanding how character point of view is constructed, then, in a dynamic sense—as one level of a textual process—is fundamental if we are eventually to grasp the complex intersections of character/text, author, spectator, and culture. Branigan, for example, has separated out eight "levels" of narration in his study of narrative film: what I refer to here as "character point of view," would, under his taxonomy, be associable to the lower half of his pyramid, the levels of "focalization" attached in some way to characters' experience and consciousness. Branigan's dismantling of narrative levels is brilliant and extremely helpful in many ways, but it is also dizzying in its compartmentalization and exuberant dissection of terms, to the point of often occluding what he wishes to render clear. Branigan's view of focalization, however—particularly as it detaches character point of view from literal camera emplacement—allows for a reading of a character and its perspective from a more synthetic approach. His schema opens onto the possibility for structuration of meaning across a dynamic of representational cues, across contradictions and associations that progressively invite new interpretations of where or how to read point of view.

Multiple voices-off represent a fascinating cross-section of the kinds of structural intersections Branigan notes at work in film narrative. Separating off the workings of character point of view in this chapter, however, is not a strategy to imply that other narrative levels (the "narrator"/extra-character-linked levels, in Branigan's schema) do not contribute to the spectator's reading of the film. Though female voice-off can represent and offer to the spectator a feminine point of view, other readings of these films are possible, and other narrative levels may work similarly or at cross-purposes to the effects described here. This "cross-purpose" friction, however, cuts both ways: Branigan's demarcations of narrative levels and the absolute hierarchization he sets into place between them are unnecessarily rigid. There is no reason to ascribe greater weight or thrust of meaning to the "higher" levels ("extra-diegetic," "objective," etc.) than to the "lower" ones that may actually at moments confound, contradict, or destabilize the suturing of meaning. The idea of "gaps" and "excesses" in a text, and their revelation of something that the dominant ideology cannot contain, surely is not new. Branigan's model fails to come to terms with this idea, however, except by default. Though he defines the hierarchy in terms of "the number of assumptions that must be made [which] narrow the range of knowledge available to the spectator,"[24] this notion of "knowledge" slips onto a larger assumption about "objectivity" and "truth" that leads to a dominant reading of the text. Branigan's implicit assertion that the patriarchal "objective" narrational level supersedes other readings of a film (such as comes forth in his examination of *Letter from an Unknown Woman*) makes it clear that this hierarchy is anything but a mere theoretical convenience, free of ideological implications itself, in its valuation of "objectivity" over the "subjective."

If, for example, the point of view of a character represents the discursive problem of the text, might not the level of point of view expand to "bracket" the level to which it is, in Branigan's schema, "subordinate"? Branigan's model, meant to provide a means of elaborating how meaning is processed, opening up various strata that interact, paradoxically visualizes meaning in a funnel-like shape that maintains certain levels as superseding and dominating others. Thus the level of "thought" (in my view, connected to point of view and to spectatorship) at the "bottom" of Branigan's paradigm is always "subordinate" to the level of the "text" (connected to extra-fictional constructs and ideology) at the top. As these levels seem so different as to defy strict hierarchization between them, the construction of an absolute relation seems unwarranted. (It would not be hard, for example, given a different interpretation of "knowledge" such as is implicit in psychoanalysis, to turn Branigan's pyramid upside down.) With a slightly more free-flowing approach, however, the powerful implications of his model unfold. Surely, if the classical Hollywood cinematic text is the "chameleon" he describes elsewhere, it allows for the various levels to be exercised in multiple directions for multiple meanings.[25] Must the more "detached" voice of an implied author or "nondiegetic narrator" necessarily "count" more for a viewer processing the film? Is it not possible that viewers may latch on to the meanings that attract them most deeply or which reflect the subjective contradictions of their own lives—even as they discern and process the other, more "objective" narrative levels? Indeed, despite the limiting of meaning that some of his specific analyses represent, Branigan's work overall supports the possibility of plural address.

Part of the purpose of this work, then, is to show how the "level" of character point of view itself can simultaneously work on different narrational strata to affect our more "objective" reading of the larger film narrative. As a site of discussion, films with multiple voices-off bring the particular problem of character point of view into relief, as it were: they accentuate the idea of shifting point of view or conflicts in point of view amongst characters. Multiple voices-off also underscore the importance of examining character subjectivity relative to a dynamic reading of voice-off, the images it inhabits, and the progressive working of narrative movement. That is, point of view does not "belong" with or to the character who is speaking, at the cost and suppression of the subjectivity expressed by a character whose voice-off has stopped speaking. This is too rigid a notion of subjectivity (locked to speech), of narrative (locked to an idea of the present), and of space (locked to a privileging of presence). Rather, point of view emerges "between" the image and the voice, belonging to neither, but marked and generated by both. In such films, this "between-ness" is doubly represented—part of the signifying process (in which the difference evoked between the image and the voice constructs a point of view dependent on both) and part of the narrative (in which the different "subjectivities" of multiple characters allow a heterogeneous point of view to emerge). The point of view that emerges from such plurality is not ultimately, as Telotte has suggested, a "single," "limited" perspective.[26] The voice-off exceeds limitation. The voice, as we have seen, always admits something of the Other (the image, the absent, the offscreen, the Mother). Films with multiple voices-off represent more than battlegrounds for dominance of meaning or "point of view wars" waged by competitive subjectivities. Rather, they crystallize a view of paradox: in them we may observe difference sustain itself. Point of view in these films emerges "between" the characters, traversing boundaries, opening onto heterogeneity in a positive sense. The multiple voice-off renders the consciousness of the characters as a kind of "middle" point of view—not attributable to one or the other alone, but to both, together and in contradistinction.

The term "consciousness," used loosely above, is loaded with rich and often contradictory meanings attributed to it from a long history of philosophical, Marxist, psychoanalytic, and even linguistic explanations. For the present discussion, its very vagueness, its vernacular use, denoting an awareness of a point of view, or a subjectivity, is of central interest. In this sense, one that probably finds its roots in the cogito (and the pre-Lacanian/Freudian subject), consciousness could be described as an idea, a representation (that could be figured linguistically, politically, or discursively) of the mind's eye, rather than a state of being (or impossibility of being) per se. This is how a spectator could perceive consciousness as a place, a position, a point of view. Consciousness, moreover, can be seen as a process, one that reflects the dialectical dynamic of the middle voice, or of a paradoxical relation, recognized, apprehended. A split is embodied in consciousness, as is a transcending of that split—between voice and image, between voices-off, between the spectator's hearing and seeing. This dialectic, the paradoxical movement by which, on the various levels, "opposites . . . [are brought together] . . . in such a way that they are no longer opposite in their former and univocal sense," also situates the subject's experience as a kind of "self-consciousness"—a state of synthesis.[27] This "self-consciousness," which allows for the recognition, rather than the foreclosing, of difference, which frequently finds paradoxical representation, has discursive implications that I will address in Chapter 3. Thus, films interpolate the viewer's consciousness, and they also *represent* consciousness per se, illustrating and evoking the "field of the mind's eye" that Kawin describes.[28] The prevalence, in fact, with which the word "consciousness" surfaces in studies of voice, is notable. It speaks to the effort, within many different theoretical approaches, to account for a psychological connection between the voice and thought (as demonstrated in Chapter 1), and the difference between the mind's eye and vision. As a character expresses the workings of the inner mind through voice-off, these connections flex powerfully to link consciousness to point of view—a point of view that "cannot be seen" in the image.

Inner Vision: Seeing through Blindness

Secret beyond the Door opens with Celia's voice-off accompanying a sequence of abstract images all connected through a stylized dolly move— drops in a pool of dark water create languorous, ringed ripples, a floating paper boat drifts offscreen as drowned daffodils rise to the surface, their roots exposed in ominous shadows. If we imagine for a moment that the film is silent, and that Celia's voice does not reach us to color this abstract sequence with the imprint of her subjectivity, we can know nothing yet of the story or of how to interpret these mysterious images.[29] Without the sound of her voice, and the meaning of the words she speaks, these images as such "belong" to no one, neither to us nor to a character. No visual logic links them: they are remarkably opaque and resistant, almost defying signification beyond a primitive recognition of the referent. But Celia's voice-off, which accompanies these images, in fact, underscores that they are not meaningless at all: rather, they represent a component of a highly subjective and textually privileged point of view. Her voice-off helps us to "see" what these images relay to our eyes—the internal landscape of a character's dream. Celia tells of "remembering long ago . . . reading a book that told the meaning of dreams," and then lists a num-

Celia's vortexical vision

(*Secret beyond the Door*)

ber of "Freudian" symbols that map onto the image suggestively, ". . . if a girl dreams of a boat or a ship, she will reach a safe harbor. But if she dreams of daffodils, she is in great danger. But this is no time to think of danger—this is my wedding day."

At the very outset of this film, then, image and voice-off conspire to signify what could be termed an impossible view: the visual and auditory articulation of Celia's internal experience, the images and sounds of her mind, a blurring of unconscious and conscious representations. The voice-off, in its relation to "inner vision," calls upon memory, inspiring the spectator's empathetic understanding of the images seen as nonvisual—not apprehended by the gaze, at any rate. These are curiously blind images, images that cannot be seen except through the highly subjective, "deeper" vision of the mind. Sharing them with this mysterious character, we participate in a point of view that as yet defies the limitations of the visible.

Which signifier—the dream "image" or the dream "voice" (here representing her internal thoughts, to which we are privy)—initiates the journey that takes us inside this unusual point of view would be hard to pin down. Where do we place Celia? Is she offscreen somewhere, recalling the book that triggers these images for us? Does she inhabit the screen, like a ghost inhabits a house—there, but not there, recalling the images the book once triggered, her remembered visions obscuring the representation of the "real"? Or is Celia alongside us, "watching" these images that provoke her memory of the book? Certainly, we have inadequate information at this point to determine what part these images and sounds play in the diegesis. But we can at least say that the voice-off here directs, in a fundamental way, the viewer's perception of what he or she is "seeing": the secret images of a "girl's" dream, images that appear from an indeterminate, ambiguous space, providing the impossible look "inside" the narrator's head, to her conscious (and unconscious) thoughts.

The voice-off here, however, insists on more than the meaning of what we see, as it launches a narrative movement (implicitly promised in both the voice and the camera's traveling motion) that will take this "girl" from safety to danger. The voice-off, that is, expressly inaugurates a point of view, an "I," where Celia's voice and Celia's internal vision both merge and split into what could be described as a "mind's eye."[30] This "I" should be vised as the emissary of the middle voice, in this context, an ambiguous, dialectically driven subject. This "I/eye" emerges *between* voice and image, conceived in their radical heterogeneity, so to speak. What makes this initial sequence so fascinating is how completely offscreen space dwells in the image and how this evocation of what is not and cannot be "there" urges us to recognize a kind of mental awareness. The dream images have no meaning in themselves, needing the interpretive work of the voice-off to designate them, to place them. But the voice-off, here, can only explain these images as absent signifiers of a point of view so denuded of character, of context, of presence, as to be entirely abstract, figural. Celia's voice emerges from an indefinite space, addresses no one specific, but, reaching us via the images of a resurrected dream, initiates the viewer's apperception of her as consciousness. Not yet a character (we have not "met" her, except via the signifiers of her internality [her voice/her "vision"]), Celia, for the moment, *is* this point of view, this organizing mind—and so, via her voice-off, is the spectator. Her words, set out against a complete lack of ambient sound, wield an effect Amy Lawrence has described as "[denying] the particularity of the voice in space, allowing it to fill the theater, becoming something inside the hearer rather than 'out there.'"[31]

The voice-off that inaugurates this film, coincidentally, sets out the primary symbolic axes that will structure the film as a whole: the linking of love and marriage (for a woman) to death and danger; the "key" of Freudianism for opening onto the latent and manifest symbolic work of the film; and the evocation of narrative as an "internal" journey into the recesses of the brain.[32] It would not be realistic to undertake an extended textual analysis of each these trajectories here, but they all factor significantly in tracing point of view in relation to the voice-off, and hence will surface in tangential ways throughout this chapter. This opening sequence, more abstractly, represents a textual "navel," such as Freud has described exists in the dream. The narrative emerges in some originary way from this prologue, but these images also remain "outside" the diegesis, never really assimilated into the space of the film. This sequence in the film, a "tangle," remote, inaccessible, is "a spot where it reaches down into the unknown."[33] Connected powerfully to the voice—like the voice itself—this opening is umbilical.

From Consciousness to Character: Point of View as Textual Evolution

Secret beyond the Door's narrative structure refracts endlessly, like the mise-en-abîme of two mirrors. A dissolve links the opening abstract images to the interior space of a church—wedding/funeral bells toll as a shadowy wedding ceremony begins. The anonymous voice-off finally is attached to the image of Celia as she prepares to walk the aisle/plank. But this "attachment" of voice to body is loose, unconfirmed as yet, as we still hardly perceive her features and have not yet heard her "real" voice confirm itself as belonging to this particular woman's image. No synch sounds soften the juxtaposition of voice to image: their originary disunion is stressed. This is again, like a "silent film" sequence, set up against the sound that has equal weight. The over-determined "dreaminess" of the image suggests we are still in Celia's dreams, still seeing images internal to her brain. But a sudden shift in the expressive tonality of the voice-off brings us into the diegesis with dramatic emphasis, suggesting that this dream may have suddenly turned out to be the story. As Celia steps out of the shadows, she suddenly whispers (and her whisper brings the music and the tolling bells to a stop), "My heart is pounding so—the sound of it drowns out everything." Significantly, we do not hear the sound of Celia's heart; we hear only her voice and the silence from which it abuptly emerges. This silence is what "drowns out" everything and simultaneously "brings out" the voice. The silence underscores, on one hand, what she is saying (she is afraid/excited). It also represents a filter, one that mimics her state of mind. Like Celia, we only hear one thing: what is in her head, and in ours—her voice. That we hear her whisper, instead of a pounding heart, brings us to the crux of what is at stake for this character, for the film, for the spectator. We are not "one" with Celia, in the sense that we share her body (her heart is not our heart, that is). Rather, we are near her, so near that her whispered voice effortlessly reaches and reverberates in our ear. We are "with" her. Since we know, moreover, that she is not "really" whispering (we see her lips are not moving)—we understand that this whisper represents her thinking mind.

Moreover, a mutation has already occurred in conveying her point of view as "thoughts." Where earlier she is "represented" entirely by the voice—"she," as a voice emerging from the space of a dream that may only be the imaginings of the words in a book, is pure point of view, an impossible subjectivity, so to speak—here she assumes visible form and begins to represent the point of view of her character, a point of view that seems more "objective" inasmuch as it gives us a "place" from which to view the story.[34] There is a sense here of an evolving point of view, one that is in both instances linked to Celia's interiority (emerging from "inside her head") but which opens up from a hallucinatory space to one of narrative functionality. We advance in our understanding of "point of view" in this film via a progressive representability of Celia's voice as point of view, moving from abstraction to increasing referential specificity and yet saturated with the very fluidity of its signification. The voice now chimes poetically "with" the bells, underscoring our sense that we are no longer "in" the dream but "seeing" it. We begin to suspect that the dreamer is awake but perceiving her world, her situation, as dream-like. Her point of view, now, implies a distortion, a "veil," a curious awareness of being in the story *and* outside it. The wedding may well be "happening" in the diegesis; the spectator, however, cannot tell, as he or she shares Celia's point of view, a point of view that is anything but stable at this point. Celia, in fact, recognizes, as she returns to a normal speaking voice, moving out of the hyper-subjective connotation of the whisper and putting on a new hat, that of "narrator," that her subjectivity is in crisis. She muses, "It's said, that when you drown, your whole life passes before you like a fast movie." The implication of the words, that she is a drowning woman about to "see" her whole life flash before her as she prepares to meet her death in marriage, eases the way for a structural conceit—a flashback (of her "life"). Simultaneously, she recasts this dream scene as part of her story, the moment when the narrative of her life simultaneously stopped *and* replayed itself so we/she could see as she drowns. In watching what follows, we again gain access to what is "inside her head," what projects in her consciousness "like a fast movie."

Spirals, Vortexes, and Vertical Temporality: Radical Inwardness

Indeed the next scene, highly expositional, does give us a quick sketch of Celia's life history. "Holding out" for someone as "good" as her brother, she has a history of broken engagements. Celia acts like the stereotype of the commitment-phobic man, refusing to "tie herself down." Moreover, for a moment we consider that perhaps we have not flashed *back* at all but, rather, *forward,* for the previous "dream" scene could easily be interpreted (at this point, anyway) as Celia standing up her most recent fiancé at the altar. This intriguingly inspecific narrative time, and the ease with which it conveys forward and backward movement simultaneously, pervades this film on many levels. The narrative overall is composed of several spiral movements that turn in on each other. Much like in *Letter from an Unknown Woman, All about Eve, A Letter to Three Wives,* etc., the voice-off in this film propels a narrative movement in an internal, vertical, "vortexical" direction. *Secret beyond the Door,* however, could be said to have an even more radically spiral construction than does *Letter from an Unknown Woman,* the in- and out-points of the flashback slipping back and forth, rendering a temporal topography of a structure composed of crisscrosses, slidings, gaps, and excesses. Yet, if the web of scenes is brushed away for a moment for us to get a look at what begins and what ends the story, it seems, in a sense, that very little "time" elapses over all—that this is the story of Celia's thoughts as she *walks down the aisle,* her "fast movie" about the life to come (and the life which must end, as she "drowns," her identity dissolving into Mark's). The tale of a "marriage" that separates the opening wedding scene from the "return" to the honeymoon site functions like a ready-made fantasy that works out Celia's ambivalence, allowing the story of the couple to "resume" in its wake. In a sense, then, the narrative plays out the female character's desire like a troubled fantasy. It circles in on itself: the horizontal/ temporal motion of the narrative stands still, while the fantasy drives down with spiraling vertical deviations that respond, here, to the crisis engendered by the character's desire to both desire *and* to be. Freud tells us that the fantasy, in a sense, has already been written and can be "edited" wholesale into the dream, allowing for what we might in a movie describe as a long vertical narrative digression, like the one here.[35] This diversion of narrative energy in a perpendicular direction should not be confused with paralysis, or with suppression. As in *Letter from an Unknown Woman,* the point of view associated with the female voice-off, the point of view that prevails here to subject temporality to space, strives, in prevailing, to sustain the difference posed by the Other.

Much of contemporary narrative theory is predicated on a linear, horizontal model that privileges the "forward" motion of cause and effect, a model which seems singularly irrelevant to a narrative that "moves" in a vertical or spiraling fashion, a narrative that folds in on itself, rather than unfolding. The prioritization of the linear progression of narrative over a spatial, vertical digression from causality often leads theorists, also, to use metaphors of containment and suppression when describing such structures. Moments of "stasis" or circularity, and the characters associated with them, are represented as "trapped" or stuck within the dominating, sense-bearing advance of narrative movement. Mary Ann Doane, for example, describes the repetitive, cyclical structures of films like *Letter from an Unknown Woman, Humoresque,* and *The Letter* as " . . . (transforming") repetition from a tool of cognition into an instrument of pure affect," one that is played out textually as "waiting" by a "woman who *has the time.*"[36] She continues: "A feminine relation to time . . . is . . . defined in terms—repetition, waiting, duration—which resist any notion of progression." Films bearing this kind of time, she notes elsewhere, "immobilize."[37] Raymond Bellour and others have many times pointed out, however, that cinematic narration *depends upon* repetition (and difference) to progress at all.[38] Undue pessimism has frequently been attached to the repetitiveness in "women's" films, in understanding the repetition that characterizes them as, for example, solely "about" inertia. One would be hard pressed, indeed, to distinguish an "active" repetition from a "passive" one: such definitions seem tautological, biased by predisposed assumptions about films of this kind. There is no reason why the complex relations of time and space in film (or narrative per se) should be predicated on a model where time determines meaning (any more than the image should be read "alone" in a film bearing sound) in suggesting point of view. What of space, for example, which seems particularly invoked by the "vortexical" temporal movement described above? The maze-like quality of many of these films render them "rhizomatic"—"burrows" of multiplicity that "deterritorialize" film form.[39] As for the "diversionary" structures of these films (where flashbacks distract us endlessly from the story's "track"), it may be worth repeating that both Roland Barthes and Stephen Heath suggest that the very pleasure of narrative, in fact, lies in a principle of digression, of diversion.[40] Moreover, Barthes stresses, this digressiveness is "<u>paradoxical:</u> [the text] must set up *delays* (obstacles, stoppages, deviations) in the flow of the discourse; its structure is essentially reactive, since it opposes the ineluctable advance of language with an organized set of stoppages."[41]

Bearing this dialectical movement of the text in mind, Noël Burch and Jorge Dana's view of the narrative structure of *Secret beyond the Door* proves somewhat misleading. Burch and Dana, in outlining the economy of signification of the classical Hollywood cinema at large, with its overdeter- mination and obviousness of codes, notes this film as one of camouflaged linearity, wherein noticeable departures "from the norm . . . [are] only pass- ing stylisations."[42] They suggest that "from the very first shot, the whole film is organized to facilitate . . . [the] flattening [of] every signifier under the tyrannical weight of the signified. This economy of expressiveness, in which everything is determined by a single-purpose articulation, clearly defines one of the basic ingredients of linearity, the mechanistic relation- ship of cause and effect."[43] Although their observations of the predilection toward linearity as an effect of narrative in Hollywood cinema cannot be denied, it also merits some rethinking. Their analysis of linearity in this film does not account for the simultaneous and considerable pull of verti- cal movement. Moreover, far from being "determined by a single-purpose articulation," *Secret beyond the Door*'s narrative structure is excessively complex, and its "causality" is in many respects oblique. It may be help- ful to provide a quick overview.

In short, the structure is composed of a series of spirals and inversions that empty out at an ambiguous "time" at the narrative's conclusion, a nar- rative time one could read as very closely following the opening scene of the film. Moreover, these spirals ultimately insist on the spatial over the temporal. I map the structure as follows:

1. Prologue: Celia's remembered dream (a possible flashback, flash- forward, or extradiegetic scene).
2. Wedding A: Celia realizes she's marrying a stranger (possibly a flashback [from extradiegetic space of voice-off], simultaneous to prologue or following prologue *or* still entirely extradiegetic [dream]).
3. Flashback A: Celia remembers Rick/meeting Mark (possibly a flash- back within flashback [from wedding] or flashforward [Wedding A could be a remembered wedding of an earlier jilted suitor]).
4. Flashforward A—Wedding B: Celia returns to church (possibly a flashforward from Flashback A *or* another flashback [principle of deferred crosscutting] *or* simultaneous [principle of deferred alter-

nation]—i.e., both the wedding and the flashbacks all are "happening" in Celia's mind).
5. Hacienda A—Honeymoon #1: possibly *flashforward* (from wed-
ding/Flashback A) or flashback—Celia's voice-off "looking back"
("I should have listened to the dark voice in my head").
6. Levender Falls—The Honeymoon's Over, Part 1: possible continuation of Honeymoon #1 *or* flashback or flashforward (same principles as above).
7. Mark's voice-off confession—The Honeymoon's Over, Part 2: same
as above—Mark imagining/looking *back* (on having murdered her)/
looking *forward* (to his trial).
8. Hacienda B—Honeymoon #2: flashforward (imagined "happy ending") or flashback (imagined relived Honeymoon—maybe the story
was Celia's nightmare?) Other permutations are possible.

It should be clear from this sketch of the plot that the structure here is
anything but "linear." The movement rather *spirals*—spirals in a number
of directions simultaneously, both temporally and spatially. Moreover, it is
far from clear "which direction" we are to read these spirals as going: the
causality of narrative logic is anything but obvious. The helixes architect-
ing the film make our reading of the diegesis complicated (this is a story
of a woman who meets a man who tries to kill her—it is also much more
twisted than that). For the helixes are not only in the service of the story,
its temporality and narrative space, but they are also in the service of the
point of view. As these spirals move into the past, into the future, and into
imagined space, they create a crosshatched narrative movement. They
map out levels of knowledge (restrained by temporal order), imagination
(conducted by the associative paths of dream and memory expressly
evoked here), and space (linearity bracketed by verticality).

With regard to this last category, clarity is crucial. The most linear part
of this film (the events at Levender Falls) is deeply embedded "inside"
the scenes that are most unstable, spatially and temporally. The spectator accesses the post-Honeymoon crises via a progressive unsettling of
temporal cues. The linearity of this "inner" part of the narrative itself,
then, is brought into question, since its context is ambiguous at best. In
particular, two sets of scenes—the two hacienda scenes and the two
weddings—echo each other and retain an unstable place in the "linear
plot." The scene sets present an unbalanced reciprocity (the two weddings
"folding" in and refracting an uneasy construction of time/space toward

the first third of the film, the two hacienda scenes refracting "across" the second two-thirds), and contributes to the sense that this narrative's movement works along strongly spatial lines—relations between scenes and other signifiers being detached from a pure cause-effect chain linkage, one that linear temporality and coherence underscores.[44] Rather, the scenes connect vertically, poetically, and the narrative movement unfolds inward. The idea that such an "inward" motion, as well as an insistence on space, necessarily renders the narrative "static" or paralytic, seems a socially-inspired reflection on the "stigma" attached to the coincidence of the spatial and the female in cinema—connoting confinement, claustrophobia, madness, death. Temporal ambiguity and spatial complexity, as suggested to a large degree by the voice-off, here render this narrative dynamic and elaborate an articulation of point of view that moves past literal "alignment" with a specific visual field into a deeper affiliation with a process that sustains and recognizes both the lateral temporal progress and the vertical spatial movement of the narrative.

Identity-in-Difference: Vocal Fusion

After the death of her brother, Celia, on the brink of a safe engagement to reliable (but boring) Bob, takes a "last fling" in Mexico. In a central city square, she is transfixed by the spectacle of two savage "Latin" men fighting "with bare knives" over a sultry gypsy. Her voice-off tells us she was "strangely held," both by the idea of violence attached to love and by the recognition of the "pride" she imagines the gypsy woman feels (having inspired murderous desire). One of the men's knives sails through the air, hitting shockingly close to Celia's hand. But she does not flinch, nor does she comment on her near brush with death. Instead, we cut to her in close up as her voice-off describes her sense that she's being watched: a "cold" feeling of "eyes touching [her] like fingers." The reverse shot of her questioning gaze into offscreen space reveals Mark, staring at her. This shot-reverse-shot inscribes a reciprocity to their desiring gaze, much like the famous scene at the opera in *Letter from an Unknown Woman* in which Lisa senses Stefan's gaze upon her. In both scenes, the woman's voice-off speaks of being "watched," and the reverse-shot that comes to confirm the male gaze explicitly marks the male character as desirable himself. Both Mark and Stefan, in these scenes, appear out of context, a pure refracting look that exists only to mirror the woman's consciousness of desire "in the air." These shot-reverse-shots—abstracted, almost jarring, certainly

Celia senses Mark's gaze . . .

" . . . a current flowing" between them, "warm and sweet . . ."

. . . in an exchange of reciprocal desire.

(*Secret beyond the Door*)

awkward by any standards of continuity—in fact provide no spatial or perspectival orientation (of a visual sort). Rather, they function here very much like images that are marked as part of a character's memory: cameoed, set off from real space, they highlight the narrative moment that the female voice-off privileges—a moment of reciprocal desire. (Indeed, the shot of Stefan, which, according to Susan White, was only included reluctantly by Ophüls at the last minute, is also a near-perfect reprise of the photograph he signs for a fan in Lisa's presence "earlier" in the film. Is Lisa, then, "imagining" his face in this moment rather than seeing it?)[45]

Celia and Mark, then, first "meet" via a pre-visible "felt" gaze, reminding of Lacan's description of the gaze as somehow sensed rather than seen.[46] Celia says, "There was a current flowing between us, warm and sweet. Frightening too, because he saw behind my makeup something no one had ever seen. Something I didn't know was there." The "current" she describes, articulating their mutually felt desire, flows "between"— between their eyes, now locked across space, between sweetness and fear, warmth and cold, between the visible (her makeup) and the hidden, between the conscious and the unconscious (what she did not know was there). But above all, *between,* belonging to neither and to both simultaneously, born of difference.

Point of view in this scene emerges *as* this "between." Celia's voice-off, at the onset of the sequence, provokes our sense of her internal and subjective emotions: we see the scene through her eyes. And, as earlier, we understand the voice we hear represents her thought process. But in the moment she expresses the feeling of being watched, point of view complicates. If we are aligned with her, then we are watched, as well— though, clearly, as spectators, we are also aligned with whomever is, in fact, watching, whomever is offscreen, where the camera would be. Thus, even before the image of Mark arrives to render visually obvious what is happening to Celia's point of view, the split has already occurred. The voice-off articulates that split but also provides its simultaneous suspension, its abeyance—for indeed, we share both Celia's and Mark's points of view as image and voice "look" at each other. They look at each other, but not as they do a moment later, within the visual perspectival refraction that the shot-reverse-shot sets into motion. It might be more descriptive, in fact, to use Celia's poetically expressed sense of what is happening, and to likewise think here of point of view "flowing between" them.

This fusional point of view is brought out even more vividly in the scene that follows. Celia gets rid of her friend, wanting the now inevitable meeting with Mark to take place "on her own ground." Shot from a slightly high angle, point of view is again split. The voice conjures her anticipatory staging of the scene, as the image suggests a sense of the invisible Mark "watching" her from above. When he walks in frame, this mutual control over perspective persists: Celia's contrivance of the meeting is underscored by the theatrical mise-en-scène as Mark, on cue, enters stage right—but Mark remains "above her," aligned with the high angle of the camera.[47]

This scene acts to solidify the heterogeneous nature of Celia's point of view and the way in which her voice-off inscribes a perspective that moves between her and Mark. Their repartee is instructive. Mark teases her about the wallet she's bought for Bob, saying, "If R.D.'s anything like me, he won't like that wallet." She responds, dryly, "He's not a bit like you." He rallies back, "You're not a bit like you." This dialogue underscores an identity between them, each sentence coming to replace one for the other by means of Jakobsonian shifts.[48] Mark proposes himself as a replacement for Bob, which Celia rejects, making clear that Mark is no substitute, but an original—pulling the term "Mark" out of an imaginary dyad with poor R.D. Mark's final sentence neatly reinscribes couple A (Celia + R.D.) with couple B (Celia + Mark): for, if Celia is "not a bit like" herself, she belongs with a man who, like her, is not a bit like another. This "not being like" establishes their mirror-like relation: only *they* reflect meaningfully back onto each other. Moreover, upping the stakes of this sudden recognition of self in other, Mark here defines Celia's problem: she does not know herself (but, apparently, he does). If we look to the story for an explanation of his clairvoyance, his next sentence provides a rationale ("you're not what you seem to be, anyway"). The lover's instinct about the essence of the beloved provides him with a special sensitivity to the false demeanor she shows the world. But if we look to the symbolic structuration of identity here, and specifically point of view, it seems that Mark's knowledge comes from literally having access to her point of view, as it is identical to his. That she does not know herself, by extension, implies, that neither does he. If he can know her in this way (by knowing she has a self beyond her knowledge), she can know him in the same way. In many respects, this conversation marks out one of the primary narrative arcs of the film. Celia's search for herself will be conducted through her investigation of Mark's self, of Mark's secret. The puzzle is only to be solved between them.

Mark is adamantly "marked" by the film as Mr. Right for Celia, who we know is waiting for someone like her, like her brother. She and Mark share the same morbid fascination for the fight, the imaginary space of their true first meeting, speaking first of its outcome before even introducing themselves. Among the many factors that come to link them in this scene, it is the fact that Mark talks like Celia that strikes the auditor most powerfully. The exaggerated, musical intonation of his voice and the "poetic" mannerisms of his speech, that is, sonorously mirror her way of expressing herself, as she does, explicitly, in her voice-off. It is the peculiar melodic vocalization and representation of Celia's interior consciousness that Mark's voice reflects and recalls—her lyrical, internal voice as only she (and the spectator) hears it. For, in ordinary synch dialogue, Celia's manner of speaking is, in contrast, quite prosaic, delivered in a dry, flat intonation. Mark's voice, then, in a way, can be said to exteriorize the internality associated with Celia's voice-off. The mellifluous, poetic charge that emerges originally from within her head, representing her thoughts, desires, and fears, now echoes "outside" the inner domain of her specific subjective consciousness, ricocheting back to her in the silvery words of Mark's speech. Yet another "between," this seeming fusion, or confusion of consciousnesses where Celia's thoughts materialize into Mark's utterances, signals, again, a kind of identity between them.

They seem absorbed in a metaphysical flirtation wherein they can read each other's thoughts, look into the other's soul. Mark launches into a rhapsodic description of "who she is," describing her in swelling, mystical terms—"a force of nature . . . turbulent . . . a cyclone about to hit a quiet meadow . . . a strange hush about to be broken," etc. Celia's voice-off, however, suddenly "interrupts" his dialogue, speaking "over" him. Mark's voice, in fact, is still "there" (we see that he is still talking, his lips move, though the sound of his speech has faded entirely) beneath Celia's voice-off in this scene. Her inner thoughts rise in volume to dominate an otherwise hushed sound track, "I heard his voice, and then I didn't hear it anymore. The beating of my blood was louder . . . I knew before I knew his name, or touched his hand. And, for an endless moment, I seemed to float like a feather blown to a place where time had stopped. Strange, I thought then of daffodils."

Thus, despite a strong representation of fusion between them here on the level of dialogue, formally, a separation seems effected between them as Celia's voice "blocks" Mark's from being heard.[49] At first glance, one might assume that she preempts him in enunciatory status: we hear her voice and align ourselves with her point of view; Mark's voice is silenced, and hence his point of view suppressed.

On the contrary, the functioning of the voice-off in this scene strongly expresses both their points of view. Celia's voice-off takes over, it is true, but the sense of alliance between their voices is marked. On one hand, the transitions easing us in and out of the inner recesses of her voice-off here are smooth, imperceptible, inviting. Like elements in a musical composition (which, in their mellifluousness, both these voices very much resemble), their aural interaction is harmonious, inviting no recognition of contrapuntal opposition, dissonance, or other auditory conflict. In fact, the choreography of voices in this scene is carefully orchestrated to highlight each at the proper moment for an overall effect of lyrical speech shared between them.

As in the earlier "wedding" scene, we are told that her heartbeat has drowned out all sound, but the drowning, in both scenes, arrives in the form of silence. "I heard his voice, and then I didn't hear it anymore." Crucial here is the slippage from one to the other, from voice to silence. Just as important, it is Mark's *voice,* rather than his words, that Celia singles out as the source of her pleasure, as the trigger of the silence that follows. Without Mark's voice, so fascinating in its perfect mirroring of her own, so poetic in its style and resonant in its grain, Celia could not access what is behind the words—the silence. What falls away, here, then, is not really Mark's voice, but his words—and what Celia hears is the silence that is the other side of the voice.[50] His voice affects her in the same way that her voice-off affects the spectator: detaching her from a real space and plunging her into an imaginary one that is marked as subjective, filtered through a heightened identification with an expressed consciousness. Her "point of audition," here, radically ambiguous, simulates ours. It is a perspective peculiar to the voice, in that it abolishes distance and difference. Mark's voice is "in" her head, just as her voice is "in" ours. The fact that we no longer hear Mark's voice points not to his elision from the scene, to the suppression of his voice, but to the representation of his voice qua voice for Celia. For if, as Poizat notes relative to opera, " . . . silence is what best presents the object-voice, as paradoxical as this may seem," Mark's silence here presents his voice as such, as the object of her desire and the mark of his own.[51] Mark's silence, really, is an ecstatic excess, internalized by her: moreover, her own voice sets off this silence, renders it acute. Two sides of the same coin, voice and silence, come to "represent" Celia's point of view here in a new light. Having evolved from hallucinatory subjectivity to subjective thought, the voice now represents two voices, two thoughts, two consciousnesses "collapsed" into one. This collapse, however, should not be confused with a fusion where perspective and point of view are lost altogether, or with a battle in which one collapses into the other, at its own expense. Rather, here, the spectator can recognize Mark's "voice" *in* Celia's. The silence bears as much weight as the voice: their difference sustains a kind of union. The point of view evoked here belongs to neither Celia nor Mark exclusively, but emerges between them. For, though Celia is "listening" to Mark's voice only to find herself blanketed in the silence "on the other side of" the words, she is also listening to her own voice, to her own silence. The spectator is aligned with her consciousness, but this consciousness is rapt in communion with another.

Thinking in Circles: Sliding down the Dark Side of the Voice

This collusion, however, evolves into a problem: Celia's difference, her separation from Mark is brought into question. The beginning of the film dedicates itself to defining Celia's problem, specifically, as *not knowing herself.* Mark suggests that she does not know who she is, just as the larger narrative sets her up as "asleep," "dreaming," "unconscious," "drowning"—in a word: ambivalent. (The voice-off, however, works to counter-indicate this problem: she speaks from a place of knowledge to come.) In the fight scene where she "feels" his troubling consciousness in the cool air at the nape of her neck, the *idea* of a gaze levied at her invites her to discover her own look. She casts a look back to see Mark, but this returned gaze is also a look within, a new consciousness of herself via a mediator that deepens and doubles her own point of view.[52] In that she gazes at herself, her gaze might be described as narcissistic. But neither the gaze nor the object of that gaze is in the least reducible to Celia's fascination with her own image. Rather, the gaze is a look inward—the object, the truth of "who she is," her "self."

The question of a woman's trouble in discovering her own identity, in knowing herself, then, serves to launch this narrative. But Celia's identity and consciousness, by the close of this first spiral turn, are conflated with Mark's. Specifically, the film redefines Celia's problem *as Mark's mind.* Indeed, the bulk of the rest of the film is dedicated to this detour through Mark to herself. She can solve the riddle of her self, the film implies, only through the unlocking of *his* secret. We "return" to the wedding scene (B) which links the first spiral to the second: in this transition, the shift of emphasis from Celia to Mark is evident. Starting out in present tense, Celia's "stream of consciousness" voice-off stresses her fear at "marrying a stranger," fantasizing about running away (as she has done before). But, giving in to social convention ("it just isn't done"), her voice-off slides into a past tense, "narrating" mode, musing, (now, apparently after the fact), that maybe she *should have* followed the "dark voice" in her head. The voice-off then recedes even more emphatically from the problem of her own desire, moving into an explanation of the legend of the hacienda's fountain, as the image circles the courtyard, coming to rest on the sleeping couple. This progression from Celia's "interiority" out into the space of the couple is underscored moments later, when Mark opens his eyes and an identical tracking shot re-spirals across the space, with his "voice-off" (offscreen dialogue) taking the place of Celia's to comment on the "felicitous" character of the architecture.[53] Mark's point of view is thus inscribed as doubling Celia's, and underscored as the point of an elaborate transition from the first part of the film to the second. This shift emphasizes that point of view is complicating here to account for Mark—moving from Celia's self-absorption to her obsession with her husband (an obsession, however, that is still very much about her).

This second spiral turn engages the second third of the film, which can be split into two halves or phases: the "early phase" of their marriage, in which Celia's ambivalence towards her husband develops into overt fear, and the "mature phase," where Celia openly challenges her fear and

"I'm marrying a stranger."

(*Secret beyond the Door*)

Mark's problem. Celia's voice-off, initiating the narrative's second spiral twist, turns obsessively upon Mark, struggling to come to terms with his "strange" behavior, with his sudden distance. Where earlier, her internal ruminations express the immediacy of her desires and fears, the voice-off in this section narrates events with more detachment, divulging a kind of analytic interpretation of events rather than an "experiencing" of them. This slightly more "narrative" quality puts Celia's narration "on the side" of conventional male voice-off, generally speaking, although it still bears many of the audible codes associated with "female voice-off": poeticism, lyricism, obsessive repetition, etc. (One need only think of *Out of the Past, Dark Passage, Murder My Sweet, Double Indemnity,* etc., to appreciate the distinctive "narrating" tonality usually associated to the male voice-off.) In one instance of this "narrating" voice, Celia, furious at Mark for his gloomy indifference, considers going "home" to New York. Then, she "conjures up" Rick, her dead brother. The rest of her voice-off in this scene comprises of "Rick's advice" as she imagines it—admonitions to stand by her man, even when he is moody, "for better, for worse." Celia's inner thoughts, now explicitly mediated by patriarchy, are channeled into the service of preserving her marriage—but also, significantly, of empathizing with her husband, for as she admits to herself (or as Rick "accuses"), she's "no easy dish herself." Referring his strange behavior back to herself, she naturalizes it, a tactic used over and over in the film to augment suspense and appease our fears. Indeed, this whole section of the film vacillates, via Celia's anxiety about her husband, on an interpretive seesaw of meaning. Is Mark mad? Or is Celia paranoid? The film gives us every reason to believe both explanations, before tipping the balance, apparently, in Celia's favor.

At the center of this section, Celia's voice-off "breaks down" in front of David, Mark's son, after David reveals that Mark "killed" his first wife Eleanor. (Fittingly, this sequence immediately follows a brutal argument between David and Mark, who shouts at his son, "Are you deaf?" It is Celia, in fact, who "can't hear" in the next scene.) Paralleling the mutual seduction scene described earlier, Celia again "blocks out" the sound of someone's voice, but this time it is not an ecstatic communion that fires the silence around her. Rather, the isolation of her voice-off here represents her disconnection from "reality," her disorientation and confusion, and implies how deeply she now identifies with Mark and his psychic state. Admitting that she's "thinking in circles," she recycles "clues" to Mark's neurosis ("the gardener said he had the lilacs dug out . . ."), observes her own inability to speak ("David is leaving. I shouldn't have let him go like that. I should have defended Mark"), plunges deeply into her fears about Mark ("Can one kill by purposefully denying love?"), and finally comes to the central question: "What goes on in his mind that he can change so suddenly? He keeps it locked, like this door. I have to open them both—for his sake."

This passage makes Celia's project clear. Appended to the earlier tantalizing prospect Mark's strangeness suggested to her, of seeing something new in herself through him, is this further realization—she must "unlock" the secret of Mark's psyche to reach her own. Generally speaking, the voice-off in this passage is only linked through loose juxtaposition to the image, freely floating over Celia's face to drive home the idea that we hear her thoughts. These moments of the film, however, signify as privileged doublings of voice and image, as strongly amplified alignments of Celia's inner thoughts and her visual perception. Thus, despite the powerful undertow to Mark's consciousness, Celia's point of view is still strongly present here. The present tense that governs throughout this scene, moreover, complicates her point of view in two key moments of purposeful connection between image and sound. She watches David leave and "thinks": "David's leaving . . ."—underscoring her paralysis. So, too, does she "see" the door she must unlock (and we see it with her) as she utters, "He keeps it locked, like this door."

The door she "sees" during this sequence looks like the door from a dream—abstracted from diegetic space, hypersymbolic, Freudian. We associate dream images with Celia's internal vision, but this is "Mark's door," coincidentally, a door that leads into Celia's room, thus a room that "symbolically" represents both their subjectivities as a single (secret) space. The moment then, that Celia's voice utters the words "like this door" and we see the door, represented like an image on some internal screen in her mind, we also perceive that this internal image is *what Celia imagines Mark sees,* and also what he cannot see past.[54] (The door is closed, opaque.) Again, in the very privileging of Celia's subjectivity, her point of view intersects with Mark's.

The uneasy midpoint of the film emerges between two critical eruptions of voice-off; the first accompanies Celia's discovery of Mark's dark secret and her clandestine access to the locked room, the second occurs after Celia flees out into the night, terrorized by the revelation of Mark's murderous desire. In the "bedroom" scene, her voice-off moves from disbelief to compassion to shock as she realizes, "It's my room. It's waiting

"He keeps it locked, like this door."

(*Secret beyond the Door*)

for me." Crucially, her consciousness here is expressly linked to Mark's, as she speaks directly to him, "Oh Mark, darling, you blame yourself—you torture yourself. You think you killed because you couldn't give her love. That's why the room is only a copy. You couldn't kill . . ." Celia thus holds an imaginary conversation with Mark "in her head," conjuring him up, much as she did her dead brother Rick. But with this difference: where formerly she imagines how Rick would chastise her, and "listens" to him via her own voice, this time she talks "to" Mark, and *he* "listens," in her imagination. In both instances, however, it is quite obvious that Celia is in both "places" at once, able to comprehend the other's point of view as well as her own.

It is in the imbalance between the candlesticks that Celia recognizes the truth about Mark, and herself; just as he is her problem, she is his.[55] Where she believes her solution lies in "understanding and helping" him, his evident goal is her eradication, the erasing of her signification of the feminine (conveniently marked by the castrated candle). This mise-en-abîme between them, where identity, desire, and consciousness seem dangerously unstable, culminates in Celia's recognition of a paradox: to "know her self" through Mark, she must abandon her subjectivity, which is "his" problem.[56] Her apparent submission or subjugation to that erasure seems evident in her panicked flight before his implacable stride down the dark corridors and shadowy staircases of Levender Falls, her doomed retreat into the dark, foggy grounds. A man follows her into the shrouded landscape, where we hear her scream and lose her altogether in a fade out.

The Scream: Voice Degree Zero

Mary Ann Doane has described the effect of this scene in strong terms, pointing out that "the blackness together with the scream signify an extraordinary violence—a discursive rather than a physical violence, for this scene marks the end of Celia's voice-over."[57] A discursive shift does indeed take place here, but not as "a forceful and disruptive transfer of the discourse from Celia to Mark."[58] Celia's scream, in fact, opens onto a different interpretation of "what has happened" to Celia's point of view, and, specifically, to her voice-off (which in the next scene is indeed supplaced by Mark's morose voice-off fantasies about the murder trial to come). Her scream, rising out of silence, reminds, for one thing, of those moments where her voice-off is "linked" to silence—to the other side of speech, where meaning falls away, to a "pure voice." The scream of the woman, of course, is a compulsory fixture in certain film genres, particularly suspense and horror films, as well as melodrama. A woman's scream, an auditory excess, points, in a general sense, to a violence done the woman's body/image on-screen or off—it comes to stand, like a strange synecdoche, "for" the woman's body, to which something frightful has been done. Similarly, Poizat notes that in opera, the "art of the voice," "the cry" is frequently associated with the death of a woman protagonist, the soprano. He also notes how rarely such a cry occurs in relation to a male hero. With one exception—the male hero who "is projected from 'spaces/places' (*lieux*) of characters who have something to do with what one might call a feminine position, but in the sense where the position of The Woman established in operatic fantasies . . . is not the position 'of' woman, but a position 'outside-sex' (*horsexe*)."[59] The cry or scream, then, is linked either to the female voice or to a voice that is neither strictly speaking female nor male, but something "outside" (and between) the two. This "sexually indeterminate" cry, as Poizat describes it, is "high"—soprano.[60] Could then, this scream of Celia's, a soprano moment of "pure voice" lanced out against silence and breaking with speech as such, be of this order—a scream "of" the voice "between" her and Mark? (The only other scream in the film, that of the gypsy woman, is, in a sense, "how they met," again, a linking of their subjectivities through voice-off. Significantly,

that scream's denotation of fear quickly converts [retroactively] to a suggestion of eroticism. Both these connotations follow to the scream here,
where Celia "meets" Mark's desire.)

For, as indicated above, there is a confusion of identity between Celia
and Mark—not only a blurring of their subjective positions and boundaries, but also, crucially, their characters' points of view. The scream is
connected to both of them, connected to an expression of fear that both
characters embody in this narrative, a fear of their own desire. Significantly, too, the scream marks a moment in which we imagine they have
finally come together in offscreen space—a rare event in this part of the
narrative, which rather repeatedly articulates their separation and distance. Moreover, both Celia and Mark "disappear" at this moment: it is
frightening precisely because we cannot see either of them, cannot place
them visually at all. Where earlier we sense Celia's voice-off is the "origin" of the images we see, here this orienting point of view "disappears"
(along with Celia with/into Mark) and we do not know where to attribute
perspective. The loss of the visual referent to the guiding consciousness
"behind" the scene suggests a point of view in crisis. Unable to read the
image, or "see" what is happening, we however do (powerfully) perceive
a kind of "zero hour" of subjectivity brought out by the scream and the
unseeable image. This perception of a turning point of subjectivity is the
focalization here, and no wonder that it is "attached" to neither Celia nor
Mark specifically, for it concerns them both. That this urgent moment is
punctuated by a blackout seems fitting. Where Doane describes this fade
to black as "a void in the image track," there really is no such thing.[61]
Rather, the blackness here represents and signifies a kind of *blindness* for
the spectator, and for the characters as well. A loss of consciousness (such
as the famous blackouts in *Dark Passage* and *Murder My Sweet*)—but here,
with a twist: two consciousnesses getting "lost" in each other.

Significantly, the "unseeing" view proposed by the image that ends in
this scene arrives not through a literal "subjective" point of view shot, but
a rather long shot expressing nobody's view in particular. As Branigan has
rightly pointed out, relative to *Lady in the Lake,* the famous effort to limit
point of view and hence to create an impression of subjective alignment
with the character failed precisely because the filmmakers confused the
representation of point of view with the point-of-view *shot* per se.[62] Subjective limitation of a consciousness represented for a character cannot
translate mechanically into the literal cinching in of frame lines to simu-
late circumscribed vision. The long shot, then, of the garden, where both

characters have drifted into dark and mist and become indistinguishable, invisible, in fact provides both a representation and an internal focalization of their mutual point of view at this junction: a point of view in climax, as expressed through the cry emerging from an image no one sees. As to the question "Who is seeing that they are not seeing?" it may be relevant to recall Nick Browne's "nobody's" shot (in relation to a scene in *Stagecoach*) and his reminder that the film subject, "is like a dreamer . . . a plural subject: in his reading he is and is not himself."[63] The shot "no one" sees here, too, expresses a plurality of positions, but a plurality in crisis, collapsing into itself: where Celia and Mark are and are not themselves. Hence, a crisis not only for the characters but for the viewer who tries to "be in several places at once"—places, that, it would seem, are evaporating before her/his eyes.

Hallucinations, Collapsed Limits, and "Shared" Voices

The resolution of this crisis seems to be the loss of Celia's subjectivity, as witnessed by Mark's sudden usurpation of the voice-off in the next scene. Where, formerly, Celia inhabits every scene, suddenly she has been "eliminated," and Mark's presence and importance are now constrastingly highlighted by the narrative. Mark tortures himself with paranoid images (as both verbalized graphically in his voice-off and literally rendered on screen in fantastic Kafkaesque abstractions reminiscent of the Dali dream/hallucination sequences in *Spellbound*) of the trial scene "in his head," where he will be called upon to declare "whether the murder was premeditated."[64] The spectator can only presume that Celia *was* murdered in the garden. And yet there is a nagging suspicion throughout Mark's masochistic self-flagellation that perhaps we should not jump to conclusions: this scene is too over-the-top to be reliable (its overwrought stylization makes it less realistic, more "fantastic" and hence less credible, than the rest of the film). If this is finally Mark's point of view, that is, we now perceive how warped that point of view really is—and we do not trust it.

In fact, Celia's point of view and her voice-off are still very much "present" in the scene, despite her seeming elision. If we understand the project of this part of the film as an attempt—and specifically Celia's attempt—to interpret Mark, then this voice-off responds directly to this effort, finally getting "inside" Mark's head and showing us what he's thinking. His voice here responds to her desire, and to the powerful mechanism of her investigatory drive. Indeed, what would Celia's voice "be" if, in fact, she could speak for/as Mark? In the scene leading up to the crisis of their reciprocal desire, she speaks to him in her head. Now he speaks, not to her, but to an imagined judge and jury: but his response is a confession, a revelation of his secret—the very expression she so desires to make him pronounce. (In fact, this scene in Mark's room could be construed as the "reverse shot" of Celia's interior gaze into the locked chamber which embodies Mark's consciousness, as we see him stage and perform her insights into his psychology: "Oh, darling, you torture yourself," etc.) Moreover, Mark's thoughts here are clearly mad, as he imagines killing Celia, or rather having killed her, just as she imagines him desiring to do. Neither hers nor his, this voice belongs to no one. It is, like a "madman's" or a schizophrenic's speaking the voice "heard" in the head. An inverse scenario of *Psycho,* where the mother's voice in Perkins' head speaks psychosis, here the man's voice expresses madness most directly. But in both cases, madness is suggested because a confusion reigns in the voice: is it male or female? Herein lies its troubling message, its suggestion of a collapsed limit.

Thus, this part of the film, where we see Mark without Celia present and hear his voice-off take over where hers left off, only superficially implies her textual suppression. For it does not only respond to Celia's project to "get inside his head." Mark's voice-off, that is, functions as an extension of Celia's. The "voice" we have come to connect with her character (specifically voice-off) now emanates from him. The strong alignment of offscreen space and an orienting perspective with Celia, that is, inflects the voice-off that comes to "replace" hers. Thus, in a way, his voice-off is both *his* voice (literally) and *her* voice (figuratively and structurally), inasmuch as it represents her desire—the pronouncing of Mark's desire—at the same time as it represents the admission of his internal fantasy. The fact, also, that the surface shift in point of view is not borne out by a concurrent displacement of the narrative interest confirms the thesis that we are still following Celia's train of thought here. This scene in no way upsets, overturns, or derails her/the narrative's drive to get to the bottom of Mark's riddle: rather, it extends this movement, logically, in a deepening point of view.

This "shared" voice-off would have had an intriguing formal precedent in Celia's originary voice-off itself, if Fritz Lang had been free to construct the sound track according to his inclinations. Lang originally recorded a different actress' voice (Colleen Collins's) to serve as Joan Bennett's voice-off, a radical experiment in "thought voice" that executive producer William Goetz finessed out of the final film. Lang was deeply committed to this "thought voice" technique, in which the character's interior monologue would have been delivered in the voice of another person (strikingly similar, in fact, to the shared/split voice-off that Mark's thought-voice suggests)—and Bennett's recording of her character's voice-off sealed the ill will between the partners of Diana Productions.[65] Since Lang was "enthusiastic" about the original script's incorporation of this "new method of narration," it seems likely that his later repudiation of the film as his "worst" reflects his resentment at the frustration of this formal innovation.[66] However, Lang (whether intentionally or not) creates a comparable (if, perhaps, even more radical) instance of "thought-voice" in the scene discussed above: Celia's "voice" speaks as/in Mark's as he contemplates the repercussions of his desire. In this respect, the voice-off here represents, on yet another level, a paradox, such as occurs in self-consciousness: "a fusion of subject and object . . . a two-in-one . . . [a] splitting up of the knowing side and the known side, but the known and the knower are patently identical." "[A] unity-in-difference . . . self consciousness makes possible *a fusion of mental entities* which would be judged merely contradictory by the standards of ordinary logic."[67] Celia's and Mark's desires can be seen thus, as "opposites . . . [brought together] . . . in such a way that they are no longer opposite in their former and univocal sense."[68] They speak their difference, their desire, as this voice-paradox.

Mark's desire, coincidentally, is to kill Celia, and if the voice of madness here is as much hers as his, then this desire must be, in a sense, mutual. Celia's initial "problem," invoked in Mexico, finds its response here—she is drawn to a man's potential violence to a woman. Her desire, on one level at least, is to be like the gypsy, "proud," the centerpiece of a murderous circle of passion. We (and Celia, since the fight is filtered through her) first perceive a woman in danger (through her scream) and only later realize that she is not the object of violence but its Object. The men do not want to hurt her, but to claim her, as booty, as proof of their superior manhood. Mark, in fact, acknowledges this objectification of the gypsy when he tries to pick up Celia, quipping, "to the victor the spoils." Celia responds to his objectification with élan: she wants objectification (of sorts, for she also want subjectivity within it) and Mark seduces her with his interpretation of her desire.

It is hardly cheering, from a feminist perspective, to understand Celia's point of view as married, perforce, to the point of view that objectifies and threatens her, but there is some consolation in the fact that Celia's subjectivity is still at stake in this scene, indeed, in the film overall. In an ironic respect, the scene in Mark's tortured "room" captures her subjective point of view best of all—this is a dark glance at a woman's desire to inspire desire. There is a level, certainly, on which the story can be read much more allegorically (in terms of a woman's "point of view" over all). Her desire to be desired, her fear of "drowning" in her husband's identity (taking his name/losing her self), and her fear that marriage is a death sentence for her subjectivity[69] all contribute to a fatalistic view of the implications of mirrored reciprocity in love. This scene, then, ironically "centered" on Mark, reveals metaphysical—even existential—fears women feel in a patriarchal bond.

This is also a paradoxical scene, for Celia is not dead, and Mark's fantasy is just that. She returns to her mad husband, no longer afraid (on the other side of her fear, now that she's looked into Mark's [twisted] heart.) The tables have turned: now Mark is afraid of himself and determined to leave. He comes to her room, and in a wide shot shrouded in ominous shadows, their figures silhouetted, barely visible, he tells her he's going to New York. She responds that she will miss him, and he urges her to go to Levender Falls (the city) for the night. She claims she is not afraid, he says he loves her, and she replies, "I know." This scene, in terms of voice-off, is quite remarkable—their dialogue is rendered in an ambiguous sound strata "between" synch and voice-off.

Mark and Celia speak via voice-off to each other.

(*Secret beyond the Door*)

It is unclear if they are speaking in voice-off or badly dubbed synch (the frame's darkness makes it hard to tell, indeed, if their lips move at all). Gently disembodied, their words seem to float over their image, next to their moving lips, but slightly askew, slightly "off." The uncanny effect, surely calculated (the sound in Lang's films, like everything else, is notoriously precise), works in a number of directions. It renders the scene "dream-like," unreal: are they speaking to each other or communicating transpersonally "through" thought? The spectator, in a sense, is doubly a voyeur, as he or she merely "overhears" this conversation (an impression underscored by dim lighting here), halfway between dialogue and voiceoff, only uneasily attached to the story proper, and no longer expressly directed to our privileged ear as the secret recipient of the voice-off. A rare instance of what Kozloff has termed a "voice-over conversation," this communication differs sharply from a conversation rendered in clear synch dialogue, by virtue of the strong suggestion of subjectivity implied by the voice-off that, shared "between" the two characters, points to their identity-in-difference.[70] Now the idea that they both speak "in" (the) voiceoff, suggested above in relation to Mark's paranoid fantasy, is rendered obvious as they speak via voice-off to each other. Again, too, the voice-off is connected here to a representation of silence—for if these voices are voices-off, then they need not speak to be heard, they speak, in a sense, through the very silence beneath the words. This interior bi-logue here, again, stresses a kind of shared consciousness.

Indeed, in a sense, it is in the barely perceptible "distance" between them (implied by the miniscule gap "between" the voice-off and the body here) where we can locate the point of view offered for/of our characters. They are literally "in" this gap, in this blind nearness to each other, in this "between" that the voice-off articulates so plainly here. What we "see" represented here is the voice-off itself, rendered visible through the simultaneous detached wide angle long-shot framing (underscoring the remoteness of the characters and the volume of offscreen space from which the voice-off usually speaks), the shadowy figures through which the voiceoff speaks "doubled," the blurred limit between them, the suggestion of a heterogeneous consciousness communicating, in a sense, to itself.[71] It is a "blind" image, similar to the darkness under Celia's scream but no longer in crisis: rather, in this instance, the simultaneous signification of the two characters' perceptions seems harmonic, like the playing of a chord. Thus, though this is not a subjective "image" per se, in the sense that it denotes a subjective physical emplacement of a body that "is" seeing, this is nonetheless a highly subjective point of view, shared here by Celia, Mark, and the spectator who perceives their shared consciousness. The voice-off creates this triangle, which, unlike a visual three-way refraction, links rather than splits, elaborates a point of view that is *thought* rather than seen. The place of listening and speaking, as this scene confirms, the place of the ear, is not a single "point," as is so often imagined relative to the image, but an alignment with a flow of points, places, consciousnesses.[72] This place, this "point of view" detaches from purely visual metaphors, suggesting the synthetic perception of difference. It is the space of the "middle" voice discussed above, a place *between.* Expressed and represented here by the subtle dislocation the voice-off instigates for the spectator between a perception of image and one of consciousness, between two desires that are one, theirs is still a troubled union; but here, the characters sustain it, perceiving each other through it (rather than as their obliteration).

Progressive, Deepening Ripples: The Wake of the Voice

The conclusion of this film follows with the exorcism of Mark's demons. Staged by Celia, who takes possession of "her" locked room (the copy of her bedroom Mark has prepared, anticipating her murder), the couple together discover the dark secrets which separate/bind them: symbolic flowers (Celia-daffodils/Mark-lilacs), dead parents, and, above all, repression (the locked door). Significantly, this scene plays like an inquisition (or therapy session), Celia extracting the "truth" from Mark in order to heal him. Significant, because Celia's questions, though not delivered in "voice-off," still bear its weight: delivered from offscreen, they probe his image, seek his thoughts. The most heightened of these moments, a protracted closeup of Mark's face, is accompanied by Celia's voice, insisting, "you're keeping something locked up in your mind, Mark." Laughably trite, perhaps, this moment nevertheless triggers an avalanche of self-understanding from Mark, a torrent of interior connections he was unable to make previously. Due to the integration, so to speak, of voice-off with the character's diegetic space, Celia's voice works like a voice-off here, even if it is not overtly coded as such by the film. Just as the point of view suggested by the voice-off has mutated, transformed through the course of the narrative, from signifying Celia's deeply internal subjectivity to include and sustain that of Mark, the "representation" of voice-off itself has been inflected, moving from radical alterity from the image and the diegesis to radical nearness. Offscreen space itself has both narrowed (the gulf between the voice-off and the image is less trenchant than it was when a strange woman's voice began speaking of daffodils), and widened (the subjective point of view it provides now expands beyond a representation of one character's interiority to include two). Such heterogeneity sustained as a kind of union (of consciousness, of difference, of space) constitutes the voice-off. In a sense, then, Celia no longer "needs" the voice-off for her subjectivity to be read in her voice as it sallies from offscreen space in this film, but not merely because, as common sense might dictate, she remains an implied narrator by virtue of once having spoken.[73] Rather, Celia's voice-off has, throughout the course of the film, been progressively structured into her diegetic voice, and into the narrative per se. This should not be construed as a work of embodiment, such as Silverman has described—a forcible pinning of her voice to her body that deprives her of any subjectivity or point of view. Rather, it represents a process of condensation, where the different voices signified by Celia's voice-off coincide powerfully. This moment, in fact, profoundly links Celia, the diegetic character who speaks, with Celia, the disembodied voice-off, representing an integration and intensification of these two voices coming together. The voice-off, that is, slipping imperceptibly here between non-diegetic space to diegetic space, "also" speaks here, in this shared voice between the "two Celias." It moreover brings a point of view to bear on the scene, one that is, coincidentally, fully amplified by the close-up of Mark. We "look" at Mark here through the character Celia's eyes, in a literal point-of-view shot, but this point-of-view shot is associated expressly with her voice, which retains its association to offscreen space and (through concomitant implications) a shared consciousness with him. Thus the "voice-off Celia" finally can "see" with the "character Celia's" eyes, inhabiting her body in a diegetic, spatial sense. She sees Mark in the clarity of a concert of consciousness between them.

Ironically, it is with the locking, not the unlocking, of the door that the secrets are revealed. Moreover, it is a *sound* that triggers Mark's memory, as it does Celia's, his mind reaching back "to childhood," hers reaching back, with the spectator, to where we heard this sound before—"in Mexico." The original locking of the door, Celia's "childish prank," opens a long detour through a masculine psyche, one being unraveled. A second locking finally initiates a return to the space of the hacienda, a feminine space. The lockings both belong, also, to Celia's desire—the first letting out the "evil" that Mark says was in him, the second locking it back in (like Pandora, Celia's temptation to see what's inside dooms her to seeing the truth). Stephen Heath has described how the narrative in *Touch of Evil* is triggered by a kiss: its interruption provides the explosive drive for a chain of causality that leads, inevitably, back to the resumption of the kiss, now conclusive.[74] The "locked door" in this film does not work on the same principle of causality: not only does it not initiate the narrative per se, but it is constantly returned to throughout the film, an obsessive repetition that allows for one digression after another as the narrative circles in its helical movement. It should be noted that the sound of the locking is as important as the "action" of locking, if not more so. This acoustic effect, its importance, is linked to the consciousnesses of the characters, who come together in recognizing the sound as both past and present. We do not see "Mrs. Robie" herself turn the key—rather, we see a woman's hand, dissociated from space and reminding, in fact, of a similar shot of the door that emerges during Celia's internal monologue earlier in the film. Connected thus to her internal consciousness on two levels, the locking sound and the image of the hand that springs originally from her internal point of view bring us back to Celia herself, as a reminder that her subjectivity is still at stake in this film.

Indeed, if there is something slightly unconvincing about their blissful reunion at the hacienda, it's not only because the "Freudian" explanation rings a mite hollow to our post-50s ears. If this is a story "about" a certain feminine subjectivity, that is, a story of a woman who wants to know her self but quickly misunderstands herself as her lover, it is also a story of her balking once she sees the truth. The locking of the door serves to "lock in" Mark's narrative, the one that overwhelms Celia's for much of the movie (though, as I have shown, this narrative serves merely to *displace* her own—in psychoanalytic terms, a case of secondary revision of a wish, perhaps, that cannot be told under patriarchy). It also "locks" the narrative as a whole, halting the investigation of her subjectivity so compellingly posed in the opening sequences. Hence, the hidden meaning of the final two lines of dialogue, where Mark admits, "I have a long way to go." Celia reminds, "We have a long way to go." Mark can conceive of a subjective trajectory on his own: Celia cannot. The film's use of voice-off, however, represents *Celia's* view, not Mark's, eliciting and articulating this heterogeneous point of view and the shared consciousness *she* desires, for the viewer.

Reversing the Case: All about Eve

It is notable, in itself, that most films elect either a male voice-off or a female voice-off; there are relatively few texts from the 1940s in which overt "shared" voice-off comes into play. Outside of *Secret beyond the Door,* the most well-known and oft-cited instance of such apparent point-of-view "transfers" occurs in *All about Eve.*[75] In relation to *Secret beyond the Door,* the shift from Celia's voice to that of Mark's is invariably read by film theorists as a suppression of her voice and subjectivity, under the logic that the disappearance of a voice-off = the suppression of narratological authority or subjective presence of the "first" voice-off. Contrastingly, in *All about Eve,* where Addison's voice-off gives way (first to Karen's, and then to Margo's voice-off), no such "obvious" conclusion is generally drawn. Rather, as Kozloff suggests and as other critics usually agree, Addison retains control of the point of view, despite his voice's disappearance. (Addison's voice, it should be noted, does return briefly within the diegesis after Karen and Margo narrate.) Kozloff attributes Addison's domination of the film's point of view to his initial command of speech, his direct address to the spectator and his apparent dictation of the image and sound track. He "freezes" the image to dwell on his thoughts about Eve, himself, and the other characters in the film, and he "silences" other dialogue so that he may be heard. She goes on to describe what she calls the "unequal status" of the character-narrators in this film, claiming that Addison is "the most powerful," where Karen's and Margo's voices-off respond to his "unspoken command to reveal [their] secrets."[76] The rest of Kozloff's discussion stresses repeatedly that, despite a certain amount of character revelation provided by the female voices-off in this film (Karen's expressing her "tender heart . . . [and] naiveté" while Margo's displays "generous . . . self-indulgence"), Addison remains "the frame narrator," privileged and implicitly present throughout.[77] As the representative of patriarchy, Addison's point of view overwhelms those of the other characters. But are Karen's and Margo's voices-off really so marginalized in this film? Is their point of view subservient in being "embedded" within his?

Kozloff herself notes that Mankiewicz originally intended for the film to "return" to the space of the banquet, so that the characters could pass along "the baton" of voice-off explicitly.[78] This suggests, certainly, that, in the historical author's mind at least, the character's voices all held equal weight.[79] However, even looking at the film in the truncated version, one can offer a reading of the voice-off that suggests that the point of view of the two women finds strong articulation here. Indeed, as in *Secret beyond the Door,* the point of view is "shared" by these three voices-off—and by the multiple consciousness of the characters with access to this formal element.

The overall structure of *All about Eve* works similarly to that of *Secret beyond the Door,* in that its temporal/spatial arrangement operates via a spiraling movement inward. We begin at the end, but within moments even the beginning is interrupted, "held up" by a voice that halts "linear" narrative movement, stopping time's flow. Addison indeed introduces the story with a flourish, and the "freezing" of the image implies that we are hearing his thoughts, which pour out in a rush as "time stands still." He turns his gaze onto the other characters, and we perceive that much of this initial scene is playing out, in a sense, through his eyes. Important, too, Addison's voice-off here functions as a digression, a detour from the linearity of plot (and the speech being delivered on-screen that Addison "decides" we do not need to hear). When Addison allows synch sound to take over again, we hear the droning of the "oldest" actor delivering a paean to Eve's youth and beauty. Significantly, the only image cut during the "actor's" speech occurs as a moment of voice-off (of offscreen dialogue) as the speaker refers to Eve's hands "over" a closeup view of this part of her anatomy. Kozloff implies that this moment is the only one *not* controlled by Addison: but, in fact, this is a shot that could be said to convey Addison's desire, which we have already heard in the grain of his voice, as he caresses Eve's name.[80] The image itself strongly evokes Eve's offscreen presence, as it is literally from her implied physical point of view. Thus, point of view, already in this first scene, seems complex, shared between two offscreen consciousnesses, and linked to desire ("for" Eve, but, as made clear in Addison's narcissism, really for the "self"). In any event, we know that Addison is not only a strong voice-off presence here, but we understand him as constituting a strongly voyeuristic gaze. It makes as much sense to attribute this shot to his roving eye as it does to understand the elaborate pans traversing the cast of characters in the previous sequence as authorized by him.

Interestingly—and paradoxically, perhaps—an argument can be made that the stress on Addison's point of view as so explicitly linked to the "objectifying" gaze of the voyeur limits him in his relationship to the voice-off "authority" he bears. That is, despite the markings of "subjectivity," Addison's voice-off strongly signifies "exteriority"—he is not "inside" the story but outside it, looking on. Beyond ironic detachment, for example, we cannot guess what Addison is "feeling," and the voice-off betrays nothing of his potential vulnerabilities here, such as his diegetic behavior towards the close of the film reveals, being in love with Eve but having to blackmail her to keep her near. (Except, of course, for the subtle "grain" of desire remarked on above.) Addison's voice-off hits the image to bring out subtleties we read in the faces of Karen, Margo, Lloyd, and Bill, but it remains outside himself, his voice-off here functioning like a mask between us and his consciousness. Where Karen's and Margo's voices-off contrastingly draw us "in" to a subjectivistic consciousness, Addison gazes out: in this way, his voice-off reflects a less internal bent. One may object that, in this case, Addison is indeed "more powerful" than the others, but only if a hierarchical systemization of narrational levels is assumed. Certainly, Addison has a kind of point of view here, but his point of view is limited, in that he cannot access certain levels of the story. His point of view is lacking, needs the deepening perspective provided by the others. He articulates as much, if we read against the grain of patriarchal complacency he connotes, for his bemused query, "What can there be to know that you don't know?" suggests, in fact, that he is talking to himself as well as to the audience. (In fact, Addison is later revealed *not* to know everything about Eve.) Instead of telling us himself "what we don't know," he turns his gaze to Karen, almost in appeal. Karen, significantly, does not return the gaze, absorbed in her own point of view, following her own train of thought. Kozloff insists that Addison "commands" Karen's voice-off to begin. The relationship is rather one of deferral. Addison's point of view defers to Karen's, which picks up the story, goes where he cannot go. Where he cannot go, precisely, is into the spiraling narrative of a "feminine" time and space that marks this text. On a par with the male spectator, perhaps, he thinks himself "above" the emotionality the others will display, until he loses what is (in his case) a marker of distance from the text, his voice-off. A more subjective point of view is revealed for his character near the end of the film—inspired, fittingly, by the disturbing expression of desire spoken by Eve.

Karen's voice-off bears all the traditional attributes of a female voice-off—slightly breathy and quieter than Addison's, it represents a stream of consciousness rather than a polished discourse. Karen's voice-off signifies as thought, reverie, a lapsing into the preconscious; she triggers memory/a flashback. (In contrast, Addison's voice-off registers as performance—the refined elocution of a finely crafted written text.) Karen muses, "I remember I asked the taxi to wait. Where was she? Strange, I'd become so accustomed to seeing her there night after night . . . looking for a girl I'd never spoken to." Her voice slips imperceptibly from the space of the banquet (speaking off from a future time) to the space of the drizzly street (speaking off from a present tense as she looks for Eve, thinking of the girl she's never spoken to). Her reverie is interrupted by Eve's offscreen voice, bringing her into the past/present, calling: "Mrs. Richards . . ."[81]

In the scenes that follow, Karen's point of view and status as the bearer of the voice-off slips imperceptibly into Margo's. Karen, in fact, leaves after introducing Margo, Bill, and Eve, musing again, in voice-off, "where were we going that night, Lloyd and I? Funny, the things you remember, and the things you don't." The scene that follows, it would seem, are the things Karen did not and could not possibly remember, not having been there, diegetically speaking. Yet, it is not inconceivable to associate the point of view here with her voice-off, with her remembering (not-remembering) from the banquet hall. She could be said to bear a privileged knowledge and power greater than Addison's, for example, in her ability to see and remember what she did not herself experience. But this may be stretching the impact of her voice-off over the images here. For, in fact, the next irruption of voice-off might be said to retroactively structure this scene as a "shared" point of view between Karen and Margo (and Addison, by extension). After Bill leaves, Margo's voice-off, without any segue at all, launches in, declaring, "That very night, we sent for Eve's things, her few pitiful possessions." Then, over what is a remarkably economical scene (it is really a single shot, but is "coded" as a montage sequence through its lack of diegetic sound, to-and-fros of Eve being "helpful," Birdy casting multiple disapproving glances, Margo eating/lolling), the voice-off suggests at a passage of time during which "the honeymoon was on."

The ironical stance of these words as Margo pronounces them, and of the point of view "on" Eve, here, reminds of Karen, whose voice-off has already implied at a radical disjunction between what we "see" (Eve's sweetness-and-light personality) and what we "know" (via voice-off—the signifier of consciousness). It also recalls Addison, extending his point of view via these feminine emissaries into the space of the story, but thus deepening his voyeuristic detachment into a strong identification with and against Eve. Margo gets "closest" to Eve, her would-be "sister" who desires, specifically, to be Margo. Margo's desire, on one level, reflects Eve's. She wants to be what Eve is, young and desirable. Thus, Margo's point of view is the most deeply "embedded" here. (We have no formal introduction to her as new narrator, and we are almost surprised to recognize that she, not Karen, is now speaking. Moreover, she has only one instance of voice-off in the film, whereas Karen and Addison both speak in voice-off three times.) The most deeply embedded, her voice-off is also the most subjectivistic. The explicit doubling between her and Eve implicates her as "another Eve." Moreover, Margo perceives Eve's duplicity before anyone else. Margo recognizes her desire in Eve. Margo's point of view, that is, clarifies the irony Addison introduces and redefines it in terms of a feminine desire to be an Other.

Margo's (and Eve's) desire for Bill here represents, incidentally, a perfect example of what René Girard calls "triangular desire," wherein the object is not "the object" at all: it is rather a *mediator* who possesses that object, and who represents an "essence" or "being" that the subject lacks and desires.[82] Margo and Eve really desire each other, not Bill. Without getting sidetracked into a discussion of "desire" here, it is yet crucial in reminding that this film centers on the female subject—her being, her desire, her fears, and the point of view these engender.[83] Margo's voice-off and our consciousness of her point of view emerge at the vortex point of the spirals that constitute this narrative. Her voice-off contributes strongly to our understanding of her character's point of view (her subjectivity is split by the mirror Eve holds up to her) but also refracts backward and forward to reconstruct Karen's and Addison's points of view. Addison's ironic distance still "works" here through Margo, but it shows us something different: Eve's desire rather than his. Moreover, Margo's point of view continues to structure how we read this film, undermining Karen's point of view when *she* next speaks in voice-off, plotting to teach Margo a lesson through a "harmless joke." Again rendered in stream of consciousness, Karen's subjectivity, brought out here by her voice-off and by her de-embeddedness (she is "closer" to Addison, the male "exterior" to the woman's story—not able to see "inside" Eve yet, as Margo does) now signals her *lack* of perspective, compared to the perspective Margo's point of view embodies. Thus we read Karen's point of view here *along with* Margo's, but now in an inverse direction, Margo's voice-off having opened onto an evocation of subjectivity that now exposes Karen's view as superficial. Ironically, however, in Karen's de-embeddedness, she is doubly embedded—for, in being aligned to a degree with Addison, the limits of this more distant, detached perception of Eve are stressed. Later, when she employs voice-off to express her feelings of rejection, watching her husband Lloyd cater to Eve's every whim, she has finally traversed from an Addisonian-type point of view (narrator/external consciousness) to a Margoesque-type point of view (consciousness/internal knowledge). That is, her voice-off functions as an evocation of her subjectivity and a point of view she *shares* with Margo and the spectator.

But what of Addison? For one thing, Addison's status as the voice of male patriarchy seems questionable at best. Surely, he plays with language, wields the power of the word. But he is on the side of linguistic excess, a far cry from the taciturn macho voices-off of film noir. Though ironic about others, Addison takes himself very seriously; he suffers a little from the "sincerity" of a female voice-off in this respect.[84] Addison loves to hear himself talk, or rather, loves the sound of his own voice. His voice qua voice, that is, also operates powerfully here, as powerfully as the words he pronounces. But in both respects, he is on the side of the feminine, on the side of the voice per se: the side of excess, of grain, of difference. The voluptuous tonality and linguistic extravagance marking Addison can be said to be a kind of "writing aloud," which is "nothing like speech," according to Barthes. "Vocal writing . . . is carried not by dramatic inflections . . . but by the *grain* of the voice."[85] Like a caricature of both female and male voice-off stereotypes, Addison pushes signification to the limit. Sanders's notoriously "effete" and "feminine" persona, moreover, is strongly emphasized here, as if Mankiewicz encouraged him to milk his trademark queeniness. Further, the character of Addison never denies the drama of the personal, as Bill and Lloyd invariably do. Rather, he revels in the emotional theater of melodrama, the allure of gossip, the reality of sexual politics, and he perceives the validity of the feminine perspective (a perspective with which, one could argue, he would like to identify). He is "the dandy," a woman's man, scarcely believable when he stakes claim to Eve. (Significantly, there is no physical relationship established between them, just a master-slave psychological relation.) Notably, the more "masculine" men of *All about Eve,* Bill and Lloyd, have no access to voice-off here. They, it should be pointed out, are the most deeply embedded of the characters, and they are routinely manipulated and outclassed by the women that surround them.

Addison's voice-off, then, signifies, as it were, "between" a male and a female voice-off, in bearing the attributes of both: speech, detachment, and distance on one "side," grain, excess, and shared consciousness on the "other." These two "sides" to his voice, moreover, get played out *between* the characters as they speak from offscreen space. Addison's voice, by the end of the film, has lost much of its power and clairvoyance, which were in fact attributes arising from its excess, proximity, and grain. I would argue that Addison's voice-off, by the end of the film, "caps" the tale in a most perfunctory way, as he gives a brief docu-like rundown on the history of the Schubert theater and proclaims that Eve gave the performance of her life. His voice-off seems, again, distant from the story, a literal spectator who perceives a performance but is no longer "backstage" as the voices-off have been throughout the film. But Addison's loss is Karen's gain, for she successfully integrates Margo's deeply identified point of view with Addison's distance. It is Karen's consciousness and point of view that dominate the last third of the film. This statement is misleading, though, for Karen's voice-off really represents a shared consciousness between Addison, Margo, herself, and Eve: a point of view that emerges through the difference that voice sustains.

3

discourse, enunciation, and contradiction

What is so perilous, then, in the fact people speak, and that their speech proliferates? What is the danger in that?

Michel Foucault, "Orders of Discourse"

I carry revenges in my throat.

George Eliot's heroine, Armgart

Drowning in Music: "Beyond" Dissonance

At the conclusion of *Humoresque* (1946), a melancholy John Garfield (Paul Boray), in shock at his fiancée's sudden and tragic suicide, looks down at the city from his penthouse and reminisces to a friend how she "once asked [him] what it was like to live up here—the Boray point-of-view." He continues, "It's lonely. . . . It all seemed so simple once . . . you find out it's not that easy. Nothing comes free. One way or another, you pay for what you are." His statement is ambiguous, referring, perhaps to his "paying" for his involvement with a married woman, Helen—or of "paying" for his selfish absorption with his music at the expense of her needs. Perhaps, also, he is referring to Helen, who has "paid" for being pragmatic, rather than romantic, about marriage and divorce, for being a woman of ambition, for desiring more than being desired. Significantly, we are offered no "point-of-view" shot that might tell us something of the "Boray point-of-view." Rather, Paul gazes inward, toward himself and his past, completing the spiral flashback that has returned us to the "beginning" of the film. His inward look also inscribes a retroactive connection to a strongly subjective point-of-view shot that Helen herself possesses in the previous scene. What is "lacking" from Paul's perspective (both formally and symbolically) here is, specifically, the view that Helen provides.

Drunk and tormented by the "impossibility" of their marriage, Helen paces her beach house, as she listens to Paul's live musical performance from Carnegie Hall on the radio. Two voices-off suddenly emerge to counterpose with the aural dominance of Paul's offscreen violin here—acting as "voices in her head," they strongly represent Helen's thinking consciousness, lost in morbid contemplation. One voice, that of her soon-to-be-divorced husband, gently admonishes her that neither she nor Paul will ever "change," and that Paul only cares about his music. The second voice-off (Paul's) echoes his selfish whining on the telephone moments before, when, upset that she is not at the performance, he accuses her of trying to ruin his concert, ruin his career, ruin "everything." In representing Helen's thoughts, these voices are "alien"—Helen does not want to hear them. She rejects them, smashing her glass against a window, cutting the voices-off short in the shattering sound. The internality they evoke—of Helen's mind—displaces now onto the "other" voice that continues to sound in the room—Paul's music. Indeed, the dissonance between "Paul the man" and "Paul the musician" is stressed here. Helen prefers "the voice" of the second, and it amplifies as she walks outside the house, subtly shifting from its status as "offscreen sound" emanating from a radio into a powerful aural connection between them that plays "in Helen's head" but which seems supernaturally to fill the very space of the universe between and around these characters as the scene progresses.

Thus the "voice" of his violin follows her as she wanders along the beach, swelling in ecstatic crescendos, filling the screen with his aural presence. But this is not just Paul's "voice": it is also Helen's—her internality produces it and "plays" it as surely as his fingers draw the bow miles away. We hear it as they do—a sound created between their two figures, speaking for both of them. Shared in this way between them, this "voice" draws her to the ocean's edge. It illustrates her passion with/as this elemental force. Massive waves pound the shore, terrifying and intimate, linked to her body through deliberate pans, tracking shots that isolate her against the water and the shimmering of light that plays off its liquid surface and her black sequined gown. Helen faces the water, and a series of reverse shots frame her face ever more closely, juxtaposed with the encroaching waves that rise in height as the violin reaches a fever pitch. She moves toward the water/camera, blurring out of focus. In the final, eerie "point-of-view" shot, taken as she "goes under," the ocean waves tumble "over" her perception, giving way to the inky depths beneath and the bubbles that tell us her breath is giving out. This point of view, excessively excessive, aligns us solidly with Helen in her last moments, as it aligns her with Paul, whose rendition of *Tristan and Isolde* follows (or leads) her to her grave. But it also shows that she sees something he does not—"the impossible." Rather, Helen internalizes, becomes one with an impossibility that Paul externalizes and renders perceptible. Helen's suicidal gesture, and what she sees underwater, represent differently the emotions Paul evokes and experiences as he plays his instrument. Here music—the voice between them—expresses an interior condition that is valid for both of them, but which is performed in different ways, through different gestures, "heard" differently "through" them. This voice not only links them but articulates their difference, for it "speaks" of the divide between them: it bridges and opens a yawning chasm of misunderstanding; it expresses the perception of mutual loss for the viewer.

Paul's performance of this condition, as violinist, connects him to Helen's emotional state, one he gives expression for her. It also reminds of his professional status—of the choices that he, as a man of talent, possesses. The music testifies to his right to stand on stage in a concert hall, to be a success, to make it in the world. Moreover, the pain he describes, though emanating from the vibrations his body instigates, remains a *representation* for him (at this point)—it is something he "paints" sonorously and experiences only unconsciously. Helen's performance is in part a tribute to the beauty and power of his, a response to the "truth" that she hears in what he plays (love is doomed), as well as an effort to escape its signification (for she blocks her ears as she paces the deserted beach, trying to get his music out of her head). For Helen, moreover, the tragedy expressed in the music relates to her experience—it "plays" out her life in a way she appreciates with acute self-consciousness. Her magnificent gesture of self-annihilation also has a social meaning connected to the "choices" available to her as a woman. Helen, that is, has two options: marriage or death. In the sense that Helen is Paul's patroness, she has midwifed his music. The music, "his" voice, is her music as well, as she has provided the means for the voice to be heard. She is the listening subject, like the spectator: the voice is both hers and not hers. Helen, who has "created" Paul Boray, cannot create herself. To retain what little power she has in the world (power to support/create artists, rather than to be one herself)—she rejects the role of wife. Thus, the distinction between their respective experiences should not be confused. Paul's is aesthetic, the absorption of man with his work, while Helen's is political, a free fall out of an intolerable social reality.

A highly charged "point-of-view" shot, in conjunction with the highly sub-jective "voice-off" of the music, thus slips from a description of character consciousness(es) (inviting us to understand and identify with these two characters simultaneously) to perform a discursive function in the film. This moment foregrounds the question of "I" on both the image and sound track, exhibiting itself as a site of enunciation.[1] This discourse is radically heterogeneous, pointing to a contradiction between two subjectivities even as it unites them, articulating strongly a host of ideological frictions that characterize the film as a whole—frictions between feminine and masculine discourse. That this moment is one of *drowning* points not only to death but also to desire. Awash in music, swept away by the oceanic beyond, her dress glittering like the sky and water around her, Helen's death expresses a dissolution into longing and sensuality, an ecstatic culmination rather than a mortal end. This is no ordinary, depressing suicide but an oper-atic flourish that reduces Paul's subjective significance (playing the vio-lin) to *score*. Helen and Paul at this moment are both in a state of desire, expressed between them in distinct performances. Their subjectivities, in a sense, signify desire *between* them, offscreen sound coming to express them simultaneously. This scene represents their desire as transcendent and sacrificial (which can be read ideologically as both bourgeois [love = the sublime] and radical [marriage = death]). The "impossible look" at the beyond, moreover, as Helen drowns, bears witness to her subjective power: for "the representation of desire is often embedded in the formal act of enunciation."[2] Crawford's character's subjectivity is a force that speaks in this film, to the point where the narrative is lost without her. After her apotheosis, Garfield's character's problems cease to interest us. We real-ize the film, which initially presented itself as his story, was really "about" her. A feminine discourse finds expression alongside that of an apparently strongly entrenched masculine one, in the very "silencing" of the female protagonist most strongly aligned with a subjective point of view.

Listening for "What a Woman Wants"

Christine Gledhill has pointed out that "discourse . . . [can be] distin-guished from point of view in that the latter is attached to a particular character or authorial position, while a discourse stretches across the text through a variety of different articulations of which character is only one; it need not be coherent but can be broken by a number of shorter or longer gaps or silences."[3] Her stress on the "gaps and silences" that may characterize a discourse is particularly pertinent in looking at the discourses "stretching" across the film texts analyzed in this chapter, all of which are incoherent in the sense that the positions of enunciation which produce them are fragmentary in nature and linked to an unstable (sometimes because they are unknown, other times because they are silenced or displaced) character source. The tracing of discursive movement in films bearing female voice-off represents a challenge, because of the fluidity and ambiguity of the voice's "authoriality" in the text. The "status" of the voice-off is constantly changing, metamorphosing, and there are a number of factors to keep in mind while trying to chart its course: fluctuations in "grain," its evolving relationship to the image, mutating perspectives as different characters "speak" as voice-off, etc. Discourse, that is, is not a static "position" outside the text, a monolithic structure enveloping it. Rather, discourse "speaks" through the film, "through" the female voice-off—not "as" it. This chapter explores the emergence, via the female voice-off, of a feminine discourse that coexists in contradiction to the patriarchal in a formative dynamic. Throughout, the connections between feminine discursive empowerment (such as is expressed through female voice-off, speech generally, writing, or other forms of discursive production) and female desire raise central and absorbing questions. What do/did women want—the women represented in the films and the women watching them—and how are such desires articulated within the texts where these figures intersect? Moreover, if, as J. P. Telotte has suggested, discourse is "privileged over sexuality and revealed as the true route of desire," what can we learn from films in which sexuality itself is a powerful discursive force?[4] What is the nature of enunciation in films in which formal disjunction, conflicting desires, disparate discourses, and contradictory will-to-meanings surface? Finally, how may the spectatorial address of women (in the 1940s and more recently) by and in these films deploy a politics of speech and voice that opens onto a subjective experience of contradiction? In these films, in fact, the female voice-off signifies an effort to address the spectator who relates her own experiences to those she sees on screen. But it also speaks of heterogeneous consciousness, an awareness of a paradoxical discursive "place," of a self that is also other, eliciting recognition of the subjectivity of women *in a plurality*.

Ultimately, this plurality becomes political. These films strikingly romanti-
cize and resurrect a female experience that excludes men, and they evoke
a shared feminine politic that exists in dynamic tension with "dominant"
ideology. The voice-off, then, exacerbates not merely our consciousness
of the constructive force of difference between voice and image, but provokes a recognition of the different, plural subjects who speak, despite
and through contradiction, in patriarchy.

The Click of a Camera: Sound (and Words) of Desire

In his famous evocation of the classical Hollywood cinema's simultaneous
exhibitionist and "secretive" relationship to the spectator, Christian Metz
cites Émile Benveniste to describe the double movement by which cinema presents itself simultaneously as both discourse and as story. Metz
links the problem of cinema's ideological contract to the symbolic positioning of the spectator and the subject's desire, stressing that while the
" . . . traditional film is presented as story . . . it is discourse: . . . the very
principle of [its] effectiveness . . . is precisely that it obliterates all traces
of the enunciation, and masquerades as story."[5] In Metz's terms, "story"
and "discourse" are really the same thing in a classically constructed film,
"story" being an alias, a mask that hides the discourse from us. "Story,"
thus, works as an ideological Trojan horse of discourse, acting as its apparently innocent, "transparent" representation.

Metz's understanding of story/discourse links their production explicitly
to the camera, and, within the film text (and the spectator's experience
of that text), to the image. Metz is not alone in this regard: Kaja Silverman
notes the "surprising unanimity" with which writers like Metz, Geoffrey
Nowell-Smith, Jean-Louis Baudry, Laura Mulvey, Jean-Pierre Oudart, and
others have "identified cinema's discursive function with the visual axis."[6]
Metz, specifically, insists on the visible and on the gaze as the loci of discursive production in cinema, with a number of telling metaphors. Referring to processes of reflexivity that structure identification in relation to
the primal scene, for example, he alludes only to the visual register of the
child's experience in the dark. This is a scenario in which, as Guy Rosolato has noted, the question of sound is already foregrounded in Freud's
description.[7] Freud's female patient fantasizes the "click" of a camera while
lovemaking; this acoustic detail leads Rosolato to reinterpret the primal
scene in terms of sound—the "click" representing/recalling the sound the
parents make, as well as the sound that would give the hidden child away.

Thus the position of the voyeur, so central to the question of the spectator's desire, entails an awareness both of sound and a consciousness of contradiction, of being both "here" and "there," "object" and "subject." Metz also stresses the image's confinement to the screen, and the fundamental disavowal beneath the apparent exhibitionism of the image, which "make[s] it (at best) a beautiful closed object which must remain unaware of the pleasure it gives us . . . whose contours remain intact and which cannot therefore be torn open into an inside and an outside, into a subject capable of saying, 'Yes!'"[8] He sees a voyeuristic paralysis in the "spectator-fish, taking in everything with their eyes, nothing with their bodies . . . [a spectator who,] hooked up to himself by the invisible thread of sight . . . [identified with] . . . a self filtered out into pure vision . . . , [preliminarily] identif[ies] with the (invisible) seeing agency of the film itself as discourse, as the agency which *puts forward* the story and shows it to us."[9]

Thus, within this discussion of discourse emerges a second discourse, within film theory, one that heralds the primacy of the image in cinema, the "pure"-ness of all-seeing-ness, and the reduction (and confinement) of enunciation to a story that is apprehended solely through the eyes.[10] The slippage here, gliding between the phenomenon of the image and its strikingly suggestive metapsychological relationship to a viewer, the processes of narration, and the enunciation of discourse is both elegant, rhetorically, and truly misleading. For if, as Silverman has pointed out, it is not at all obvious "who is speaking" in the cinema (as a discursive enunciator), then it is still less obvious that the image is "all" that "speaks."[11] As we have seen, the spectator of the sound film cannot be accurately described as in "a state of . . . pure visual capacity," as Metz suggests.[12] Doane has noted that not only is sound not necessarily "subordinate" to the image, but "it is doubtful that any image (in the sound film) is uninflected by sound."[13] If the image produces discourse, then, so does sound. Or, perhaps more accurately, the image and sound track produce discourse(s) together, between them.

Yet Metz's main point here remains trenchant, in his insistence on the ideological "transparency" of the story—its will-to-meaning that keeps the spectator happily unaware of the production process, the institutional face of the cinema, or the enunciation of discourse. To account for sound, and, specifically, the discursive function of speech (which is highlighted through voice-off in the cinema), then, is it simply a matter of extending the analogy, of blending these signifiers into the image as elements of that infamous exhibitionism that courts the spectator's eye (and also) ear, only

to pretend it is not "speaking" at all? The seductive simplicity of this resolution should be questioned on (at least) two counts. First, the exhibitionist nature of a "speaker" (a voice bearing speech in the cinema) is very
different from that of an image: it hails the subject, often quite explicitly,
rather than via the disavowal Metz describes relative to the image, especially in cases of voice-off that distinctly underscore their direct address
to the viewer. Just as those moments when a character looks at the camera are generally considered to "break the frame" and to draw attention
to the place and process of enunciation, the voice-off acknowledges the
viewer directly, and articulates an "I-you" relationship audibly, betraying
itself without dissimulation. Speech, in fact, as Foucault describes it, has
a privileged relationship to discourse. "In appearance, speech may well
be of little account, but the prohibitions surrounding it soon reveal its
links with desire and power. This should not be very surprising, for psychoanalysis has already shown us that speech is not merely the medium
which manifests—or dissembles—desire; it is also *the object of desire.*
Similarly, historians have constantly impressed upon us that speech is no
mere verbalization of conflicts and systems of domination, but that it is
the very object of man's conflicts."[14] Foucault also notes, "we are not free
to say just anything"; moreover, he warns that the rules of exclusion and
prohibition can tell us as much about discourse (and speech) as what is
pronounced.[15] Looked at this way, the explicit foregrounding of speech
within a film seems a crucial signpost in tracing the discursive operations of a film. What is said and what is left *unsaid* bear equal weight in
Foucault's theory: thus the discourse "expressed" through speech in the
cinema may be apprehended not only through what characters say but
how speech is used and defined within the film, whose speech is valorized
and whose is restricted, how silence "works," and how different "voices"
intersect, commingle, or compete. In looking for "who is speaking" in the
cinema, then, one needs to look not only at the image but at its relationship to sound and to the relative status of speech and voices within the
sound track. All these factors count, not in isolation but in their interaction and contradistinction.

Second, voice and speech, in contributing to the production of discourse
of and in a film, may also "speak" differently from the discourse produced
by the image, thus producing an occasion of contradiction. Such contradiction should not be understood as simply the effect of authorial strategies or of an alternative textual reading imposed by a spectator, but as a
fundamental movement traceable in all discursive forms. As regards the

cinema, contradictory discourses can be observed in classical films as
well as in those with alternative signifying practices. The nonpatriarchal
discourse, far from being "contained" and visible only at moments of rupture or aberration, is a formative enunciatory element, fundamental to
the structure of representation. Kaja Silverman argues persuasively for
the need to think of dominant cinema in other than "monolithically phallic" terms. She ultimately suggests, however, that "authorial voices that
speak against the operations of dominant meaning [are] . . . much likelier
to manifest themselves through isolated formal and diegetic irregularities
than through formal systematicity," echoing a familiar strain of feminist
theory which sees the ideological movement of the classical film as virtually unassailable, except in "weak" spots, such as those produced by
excess.[16] However, transgression can be seen as not only part of narrative
movement per se (the introduction of heterogeneity inspiring the forward
drive) but as part of the pleasure of texts, even (or especially) some of
those we normally think of as "conventional." The introduction of a female
voice-off indicates an explicit surplus of contradiction, foregrounding the
pleasure of heterogeneity—one that capitalizes on the nature of sound film
in both marking the gap between sound and image, and fully exploiting it.
The principle of ideological "containment" (of difference, for example, or
of the feminine, in classical films) has, moreover, become a dangerously
inhibiting discourse itself. In the well-meaning attempt to articulate how
women have been "suppressed" by texts, another suppression takes place
on the level of theory, wherein we are forced into corners "defending" the
impossibility of our own subjectivity.

One of the most pernicious of such descriptions relates to the frequent
observation that feminine discourse or subjectivity is often associated
with "interiority" and/or "space" in the diegesis. This "interiority" has been
invariably represented as necessarily translating into a *negative* value—
resulting in the containment and repression of the feminine. (A parallel
alignment with "exteriority" and "narrative linearity" translates into a positive affirmation of the masculine subject.) In part, such assumptions have
been drawn from narratological theories that identify agency and forward
narrative movement with the male hero, so that a non-"forward" narrative
inflection associated with a female character translates into "stasis" or
"regression" by default.[17] Signs of feminine subjectivity that "only exist at
the expense of the forward trajectory of the narrative" are interpreted as
necessarily rebounding back into signs of objectification.[18] The description of a vertical or "backward" (flashback) movement of a narrative as

"static," or "regressive," especially in cinema, where time contributes to our experience of story in a direct way, should be questioned. In another direction, this negative value placed on interiority derives from psychoanalytic models that confuse the interior of the diegesis with the unknowable nether regions of the pre-Symbolic. The viability of transposing psychoanalytic metaphors, as Silverman has, onto textual movements per se seems a questionable enterprise. Though the subject's experience of the body as self indisputably brings up the descriptive categories of interiority and exteriority, the spatiality involved—a psychic one in many respects—differs significantly from the represented "spatiality" of or within narrative movement. Moreover, as described at length in Chapter 1, the association of the voice-off with interiority carries with it the simultaneous recognition of difference (exteriority, within this paradigm). These terms, "interior" and "exterior," then, have been brilliantly extended from a psychoanalytic domain, as well as, to a degree, from phenomenological debates, and brought to bear on the problem of discursive enunciation in classical (and other) films. They have been compellingly described by feminists in theories that have severely compromised the possibility for woman's speech—and for feminine discourse—to be "heard" in most classical Hollywood films. The definitions of these terms themselves ("interior" and "exterior"), not at all self-evident, however, need clarification, as they are deployed differently in different theories, particularly in the two most influential—those developed by Doane and Silverman. Few critics have taken issue with the depressing scenarios associated with the paradigms outlined below. However, they deserve close inspection—for on them turns the possibility of the articulation and recognition of feminine discourse within representation produced in patriarchy.

Spatial Realms and Enunciation: Body as Text

Mary Ann Doane explores the voice's relationship to the body via a spatial metaphor. She suggests different spatial descriptions for several possible relations: the synch voice (anchored to a body); voice-off (belonging to a body, but "deepening the diegesis," and heterogeneous to the image); the voice-over interior monologue (turning the body "inside-out," representing its "inner lining"); and voice-over documentary commentary (disembodied—traditionally male). Thus Doane's spatial/sound scheme works according to a certain progression from "inside" to "outside," with the voice-over commentary dwelling, since it is "not localizable . . . [or] yoked to a body

. . . in a radical otherness with respect to the diegesis which endows this voice with a certain *authority . . . outside* [diegetic] *space.*"[19] The vocabulary she uses is revealing, betraying a phobia about voices "yoked" to bodies, and a localization of power and authority with the "exterior." As discussed earlier in this book, this lexicon portrays voice as bearing subjectivity *only* if disassociated from the body, appealing to a mode of thinking that equates distance with knowledge. Such distance coincides more comfortably with a visual articulation of character relations and diegetic space than with an aural one. The "discourse of distance," in fact, is another "problem" perhaps for feminists to begin to question. For, despite the leftist-seeming model of distantiation that is Bertolt Brecht's legacy, this "position" relative to a text seems analogous to a patriarchal "viewing" position—certainly, it is very similar to the subjective transcendence Baudry has suggested is part and parcel of an ideological placement.[20] Within Doane's analysis, however, the strict correlation of the "internal" to a feminine space and the "external" to the masculine one is not manifest, except in her observation that most voice-over commentaries are male voices-off. (It is significant, moreover, that she allows for a truly "disembodied" voice-over only with respect to documentary: does Doane mean to suggest that it is generic convention that moves the voice to the outside? In this case, the discussion may turn not on voice, but on the relationship of fiction to reality as brought out by generic conventions.)[21]

Silverman's work extends Doane's spatial taxonomy into a complicated hierarchy of progressive and relative embodiments, and explicitly maps the "interior" of the diegesis onto the feminine and the "exterior" onto the masculine. She claims that a "rule of synchronization" exists within classical cinema that invariably brings a voice "back" to its body, and she suggests that this rule is more emphatically pursued with regard to the female than to the male voice, because the male subject (to whom all Hollywood texts, in her view, are dedicated) projects his own lack onto the female image/voice as a kind of protective distantiation. Silverman's view of discourse and enunciation is deeply entrenched in her complex psychoanalytic preamble, especially as regards the elaboration of diegetic spatiality. Generally speaking, Silverman falls in line with the view that equates diegetic power with disembodiment: " . . . the voice-over is privileged to the degree that *it transcends the body.* Conversely, it loses power and authority with every corporeal encroachment, from a regional accent or idiosyncratic 'grain' to definitive localization in the image."[22] Synchronization, a complete "embodiment" within her theory, is a strong nail in the coffin barring characters from discursive authority. Although she acknowledges that complete dis-embodiment is rare for *either* a male or a female voice-off in Hollywood cinema, she asserts that "nevertheless, in his most exemplary guise, classic cinema's male subject sees without being seen, and speaks from an inaccessible vantage point."[23] How a "rare" condition can be assumed to be "exemplary" is left unexplained, as she moves on immediately to discuss the "embodied" male voice-over, suggesting that the characters bearing it are by no means invariably "invisible," "powerful," or unconstrained by or within narrative. Indeed, Silverman describes these embodied male voice-overs in terms that she will later conflate with "femininity," saying that the voice-overs of films like *Sunset Boulevard, Out of the Past, D. O. A.,* etc., because they introduce flashbacks, "anchor [the voice] to the order of the spectacle and the gaze, suggest[ing] that its regressive journey carries it to the heart of the diegesis, rather than to the latter's outer edges."[24] This statement, looked at retroactively in relation to remarks Silverman makes later in her book, is provocative in that Silverman here acknowledges that diegetic "interiority" *can* be the province of the male as well as the female subject (something subsequent chapters are apt to disallow). It also reveals a tendency to generalize about the functioning of voice-off to image, as she implies that all these voices-off "work" the same way, to simply "accompany . . . [the] flashback."[25] Not only are the aural and narrative characteristics of these voices-off rather different in the various films she mentions (in terms of grain, performance, tonality, frequency, etc.) but even *within the same film* the voice-off often operates differently at different moments. In *Out of the Past,* for example, Robert Mitchum's voice-off speaks first in synch, "drifting" back into a flashback, the voice "accompanying" the image for a while, as Silverman describes. A little later, however, the voice sometimes takes up without a return to Mitchum's face (and, significantly, these sections bring us closer to his desire). Thus one must question the accuracy of her description of these voices-off as merely "translating" what they say *into images*—since the voice in these instances does not merely give way to the visual register to have the image "tell all." Rather, it operates simultaneous to it. Mitchum's voice-off intersects with the image and thus *inflects* the meaning. Silverman's theoretical point becomes clear, though, with this determined conflation of flashback ("regressive journey") with the image and with an "interior" diegetic space she associates to "the order of the spectacle and the gaze."[26] Her rhetoric, that is, stresses an identification between an "interior" flashback space and the feminine—both of which she posits as discursively "impotent" in the classical cinema.

Direct/Indirect Auditory Mastery: "Raping" the Voice-off

When Silverman turns from a general discussion of "embodied voice-over" to consider its incarnation as "internal monologue" in films, she subtly turns the screw of her argument. She slides almost imperceptibly from a discussion of "embodied *male* voice-over" to "embodied *female* voice-over" (without drawing our attention explicitly to this shift in emphasis), characterizing them in negative terms of involuntary "constraint." The fact that she does not mention or account for male voice-over examples of "internal monologue" (the type of male "embodied voice-over" found in *Dark Passage* or *All about Eve,* for example) implies that "interior monologue" is more characteristic of female voice-off (a fair generalization). But it also suggests that the "involuntary" or constrained quality she notes in embodied voice-over has particularly to do with these *female* voices (and, in fact, she only first mentions this "involuntary" attribute once she turns to the female voices-off in *The Beguiled* and *Bonjour Tristesse*). Her description of these voices as "constrained" rests on a reasoning that describes female voice-off as subjected, in these instances, to a kind of metaphorical rape. Borrowing from Doane, she notes that the internal monologue, "turn[s] the body 'inside out' . . . like a searchlight suddenly turned upon a character's thoughts: it makes audible what is ostensibly inaudible, transforming the private into public."[27] She continues, "On these occasions the discursive mode is direct rather than indirect. No distance separates teller from tale; instead, the voice-over is stripped of temporal protection and thrust into diegetic immediacy. Thus deprived of enunciatory pretense, it is no longer in a position to masquerade as the point of textual origin. Moreover, since this voice-over derives from an interior rather than an exterior register (in other words, since it represents thought rather than speech) the listener's access to it is unlicensed by the character from whom it derives, and so clearly constitutes a form of auditory mastery."[28]

Where the embodied male voice-over, in Silverman's account, suffers from a little specularity, the embodied female voice-over sustains a much more aggressive intrusion—it is the victim/object of the discursive invasion and "unlicensed listening" of the spectator/subject, and it cannot pretend to enunciate itself. Silverman sees the female voice-off as vulnerable in this way, because it is more direct. "Unprotected" by the factor that might keep it intact—a temporal disjunction from the image that provides "distance"—the (female) interior monologue is stuck "inside" the image, inside the diegesis.

Silverman does not mention any films with male voice-off that can be said to suffer from the same contaminating "immediacy" that makes what is more "direct" (surprisingly) *less* expressive of subjectivity than what is mediated. Most views of the interior monologue, as demonstrated in the previous chapter, are in fact at odds with Silverman's view that such directness constitutes an objectification. The very marking of directness by any formal attribute in the cinema is usually associated with enunciatory privilege, and with the apparatus (here, imagined to include sound recording). To a degree, Silverman's logic seems inflected by a similar, but often contradictory, mistrust of "directness" evident also in Doane's work. Doane suggests that the "voice-over" commentary is the form of greatest directness in auditory "address" in that it "speaks without mediation to the audience, bypassing the 'characters' and establishing a complicity between itself and the spectator—together they understand and thus *place* the image."[29] "Directness," in her account, seems to denote intimacy and the sharing of knowledge (understanding). Later, in extending this analogy to what she calls the "voice-off" category, Doane suggests that the intervention of the character presence makes the relationship *less direct* and thus situates the spectator in the eavesdropper's position, a position she likens to voyeurism.[30] The use of the word "direct" in the two theorists' work ultimately becomes confusing and seemingly arbitrary, when compared to one another. Ironically, Doane sees the most "exterior" voice as the most "direct" and the most intimate (complicit), while Silverman sees the more "interior" voice as most direct. Unlike Doane, Silverman understands directness of address to be a sign not of complicity but of radical separation or mediation (one that is aggressive).

Interior = Inferior: The Fated Place of the Woman's Voice

Whereas Doane's explication links all the voices she discusses in pointing out their universal appeal to the invocatory drive, Silverman's analysis works to single out the female voice-off and to establish its particular objectification within classical cinema. She thus slips the question from degrees of "embodiment" onto an implicit "voyeurism," ironically using the same psychoanalytic model Metz employs when writing about the filmic image to describe the voice, a nonvisual signifier. This "voyeurism," as the spectator "spies" on the character's inner thoughts, she claims, is routinely exploited in the "direct" expression of the interior monologue so often adopted by the female voice-off. Her shift from the body to the image here, moreover, stages a second leap of logic, one that pins the problem of "interiority" and non-discursivity to the female voice-off (and the female character) even more resolutely.

While concluding her remarks on the embodied voice-over, Silverman claims that it "designates not only psychological but diegetic interiority . . . it emanates from the center of the story, rather than from some radically other time and place."[31] The displacement of the psychological onto the diegetic, which she considers obvious at this point, however, is really still a tenuous point. It depends, for one thing, on a visual narrative structuration—the flashback—which, though often *associated* to the voice-off, is not exactly the same thing. Moreover, it seems Silverman assumes that the image determines the "fate" of the sound here. She sees the flashbacks as determinant of meaning in conscribing the voice to diegetic interiority, rather than, for example, entertaining the notion that the intrusion of voice-off into a flashback can suggest a contradictory temporality in a dynamic fashion (past/present–forward/backward signifying simultaneously). Further, her conclusion depends on an idiosyncratic reading of a certain kind of "directness" of speech/thought, one representing "indirectness" and objectification (as described above). Paradoxically, the spectator's "direct" relationship to the interior monologue allows (him) both the distanced protection of the eavesdropper *and* the violent "subjectivity" of the rapist. Finally, the paradigms of "directness" vs. "interiority" become increasingly confused and cross-referenced until they seem synonymous not only with each other but also with non-discursivity in Silverman's theory. Both these tropes (interiority/directness) are frequently invoked in much film theory (and in other sections of Silverman's book itself) as "signs" of subjectivity. It seems, however, that Silverman equates discursive enunciation with a position of diegetic, "externally-coded" authority and power alone. Indeed, there is, in her book, a surprising lack of any search for a representation of "subjectivity" in these films, beyond those described in metaphors of distanced patriarchal projection on the part of a male subject. Attempting to find forms of female subjectivity represented *in the same way* that male subjectivity is constructed in these films may be a vain pursuit. Should one applaud, for example, the female character's transposition onto or ascension to a place of patriarchal "power and authority" or "exteriority" to the diegesis as such, if it were "possible"? Female subjectivity is something Silverman seems to be searching for elsewhere in *The Acoustic Mirror,* (and feminine subjectivity is something she argues persuasively to "exist" within both patriarchy and psychoanalysis). However, in the Hollywood cinema, she maintains, a vise-like discursive grip on the female character is absolute, constraining her to the interior, "inferior" position.[32]

Silverman implies that this equation should be taken *literally* with respect to Hollywood films, discounting a strong symbolic heritage in Western culture which equates interiority with centrality, consciousness, depth, and primacy, through its metaphorical relationship to the mind and the heart. Viewed in this light, female voices-off that emerge exclusively from the center of the text, as is the case in *The Locket, The Enchanted Cottage,* and *The Barefoot Contessa* may well reflect the narrative primacy of these characters rather than their subordination. Each speaks, for one thing, quite literally of her desire. In each of these films, moreover, "embeddedness" does not necessarily translate into increased specularity. In *The Locket* (1946), Nancy relates a traumatic experience from her childhood in a non-eroticizing sequence in which her subjective resistance is pitted against the capitalist/patriarchal law that falsely marks her desire as perverse.[33] In *The Enchanted Cottage* (1945), Dorothy McGuire's character attains (an imagined) specular beauty within the scene she co-voices with Robert Young, a loveliness that the film renders a *spiritual* quality, one specifically critical of the objectifying gaze. In *The Barefoot Contessa* (1954), Ava Gardner finally has her say in one of the only sequences to privilege her feelings and thoughts over the enigma and statuesque allure that obsesses the male voices-off in her regard. It should be noted that she is struggling to understand her husband, though, just as the Bogart character is hoping to share her point of view: these three consciousnesses provide for the spectator/auditor's view *between.* In any event, these seemingly frail female voices-off, which, after long silence, suddenly speak from deep "within" the text, rather than from its "outer edges," cut to the heart of what is at stake in these films: the contradictory experience of subjectivity for a woman in patriarchy.

Although Silverman acknowledges that diegetic interiority is also inhabited by male characters, she suggests that certain mechanisms (the "systematization" of the Hollywood machine) "displac[e] the privileged attributes of the disembodied voice-over onto the *synchronized* male voice . . . [re-inscribe] the opposition between the diegetic and the extradiegetic" within the fiction itself. As a result of these mechanisms, interiority and exteriority are redefined as areas within the narrative rather than as indicators of the great divide separating the diegesis from the enunciation. 'Inside' comes to designate a recessed space within the story while 'outside' refers to those elements of the story which seem in one way or another to frame that recessed space. Woman is confined to the former, and man to the latter."[34] In this account, the female character with voice-off bears a double burden of impotence—not only is she associated with the image per se through her specularity, but the "recessed" space from which her voice-off emanates "folds her in" to the diegesis, smothering any vestige of enunciatory sassiness. In the meantime, the male voice, even synchronized, enjoys more discursive power. The diegetic "containment" of female voice-off, Silverman suggests, can be traced to three operations—via "doubly diegeticized" representations of voice (where it is "performed" by the character or overheard by both spectator and a fictional "eavesdropper"), "talking cures" (where she speaks "involuntarily"), and through the insertion of "grain" into her voice (standing in for her body).[35] Adrienne L. McLean convincingly argues, however, that the inscription of "performance," rather than entrenching a doubly "representational" constraint, emphasizes the female character's enunciative capacity, in her direct address to the spectator, her "auto-eroticism," and her "resistance" through the ironic self-awareness of herself as an object of the gaze as she "flaunts her castration" openly. McLean, significantly, points to sound (music and singing in *Gilda*) as an alternate, "competing" discursive formation to that of the image, stressing, however, that, "music alone cannot be the great alternative; it matters what is done with it."[36]

Another notable weakness in Silverman's argument lies in the ease of its "fit" with theories of spectatorship and enunciation that have been conducted relative to the image alone. It seems, in many respects, the result of an effort to force the voice-off into the service of what is implicitly assumed to "rule" discourse in a film anyway—the image. As noted above, much of Silverman's argument here rests on rhetorical slidings and shiftings whereby she maps the "interior" onto the feminine and vice versa. She conflates "psychological" interiority with diegetic interiority. But, interestingly, she reverses the values one normally would expect to find expressed there, suggesting that if we "hear thought," we are not complicit with a character or "being spoken to" (except by a phallocentric monolith of male subjectivity), but rather we are forcing ourselves on her, in an objectifying way. She argues against the possibility that, for example, the represented "thought" a voice-off expresses can also designate speech (which it "is" on one level at least, as a voice bearing words to our ear), consciousness (as a representation of a vital mind's awareness of and communication of itself), poetry (as the "inside" of an "outside" suggested by the image, or a differing or contradictory expression to what we see), or really *anything* but the "inside" of a body (if it is associated with a female character), because, she claims, Hollywood cinema "sees" the woman's psyche this way. This argumentation forecloses the discursive (im)possibilities of the female voice-off because of the ideological and psychoanalytic assumptions drawn regarding the classical cinema prior to analysis. In this respect, *The Acoustic Mirror* falls prey to what David Bordwell calls contemporary film theory's " . . . [neglect] of what 1960s semiology took as a primary task: the explication of the intersubjective but tacit conventions whereby we 'make sense' of texts at a literal, denotative level"—as witnessed in the lack of analysis of the (classical) films themselves, as Silverman's book pursues a globalizing theory.[37] Crucially, moreover, the terminology that she painstakingly sets out eventually becomes misleading, for she "types" voices according to the hierarchical schema of embodiments she devises, and she evaluates their relative interior/exterior placement within the diegesis as if the voice predictably and invariably functions identically to all other variants of voice-off that share the same technical category of "bodily status." A sweeping generalization, this logic undermines the importance of textual structuration as a process (something Silverman, ironically, stresses at points). Moreover, as Silverman herself notes, these voices are constantly *fluctuating* in their relationship to a represented body and to diegetic interiority, and, thus, never really belong to one or another "category" as such. The relevance of this impressive array of technical strata devised for "fixing" voice relative to the body thus comes into question. The real point is that the voice-off is always threatening to *change*—to escape this relationship to the body; to mobilize another relationship; or to enounce itself at one moment as a "voice-over," the next as "an embodied voice-over," and the next as a "voice-off," "just outside" the frame. In fact, voices-off can quite frequently occupy a number of these strata simultaneously—as in the example Silverman gives from *Kiss Me Deadly,* when Christina's voice is heard panting "over" the credits. Silverman calls this "technically" a voice-over, as it "speaks from a different order from that to which the image belongs."[38] Noting, however, that this voice-off is "thick with body" (Cloris Leachman's throaty gasps, etc.), she concludes that even when granted a "voice-over status," the female voice is thus "embodied."[39] But, since we have seen the character of Christina in the pre-credit sequence, this voice could also be called (in Silverman's terms) an "embodied voice-over" or even a "voice-off" (if we imagine that we are riding in the dark car and she is breathing just offscreen). It is precisely the ambiguity and fluidity of the voice in its relation to the body and to the text that defines it—a quality that, with regard to the classical cinema, Silverman is apt to disallow.[40]

"Nobody's" Voice: The Proliferation of Plurality

Despite Silverman's conviction that the female voice-off always finds itself folded into the diegesis in the classical film, she acknowledges that "both the male and the female subjects are inside meaning, and neither can ever be the punctual source of that meaning."[41] Silverman here is referring to Ideology at large, constraining both male and female characters. Her statement, however, also gives rise to the possibility of competing discourses, or contradictory ones, if, in a sense, "no one" is in "control" of the diegesis. In later chapters, for example, she suggests that female subjectivity and feminine enunciation can be located in films directed by women that were produced within patriarchal culture. She ascribes this possibility not to the conscious intent of the authors (although she comes very near to reactivating auteurism) but to the films' evocation of desires that form and interpolate it.

This logic invites one to imagine that different desires and discourses may also circulate in classical films. If, for example, in the oeuvre of Liliana Cavani, the female director's desires can be represented by male "self-castrating" characters with whom she identifies herself, one wonders why a director like Lang, or Hitchcock, cannot be said to invest certain female characters with a concomitant enunciatory function.[42] Can the "voice" of the male author not find an uncanny "home" in the female voice-off in films that align this voice with subjectivity or marked discursivity? Silverman herself notes with regard to *Rebecca,* that "Rebecca," in her role as "absent one," "stands in for Hitchcock."[43] She attributes this to Rebecca's *invisibility,* however, and not to the express alignment of "Rebecca's/Joan Fontaine's" voice-off (at the beginning of the film) with the apparatus (and by extension Hitchcock). This alignment, however, is conveyed overtly on both the image and sound track. Like the relay of the gaze Raymond Bellour traces in his famous analysis of *Marnie,* a vertical association here marks the spot of self-reflexivity, as the camera dollies "subjectivistically," while the female voice-off directly addresses the viewer and declares her power to transgress the barred spaces and to tell her story (which "began for [her] in the south of France"). The real surrogate here for Hitchcock is not the "absent" Rebecca, except inasmuch as she "is" also Joan Fontaine's character: the studied polish of Fontaine's voice in this opening voice-off underscores that it stands in for not only her character's voice (unnamed, and retroactively associated, remembering Manderley as it was before the fire), but also Rebecca's (both through proximity to the title and in its "cultivated," "ghostly" resonance) *and* Hitchcock's (the Britishness of the grain). These several voices twining into one offer another example of the heterogeneity that the female voice-off sustains so effortlessly. Silverman looks for multiplicity of discourse through the proliferation of multiple unanchored voices in alternative films—we may also look for this pluralism "within" single voices within the classical diegesis, voices which "speak" of a number of subjectivities at once, or who enounce their simultaneous "subjective" and "objectified" relationship to discourse. Thus, discursively, the female voice-off is not necessarily "folded in" to diegetic interiority—it often also "speaks" from the edges, aligned with an authority (with which it may flex in tension).

In the same way, a discursive plurality is inherent in the narrative movement of these films. A forward drive represented as "interior" should not primarily or only be viewed as one of "constraint," especially when it constructs the bulk of the story, both in terms of screen time and screen action. The weighting of the narrative in this lateral direction implies both a discursive primacy (as bearer of meaning) and a strong coefficient of pleasure (as source of interest). Such films, tracking a different narrative course, inward rather than outward, still work as narratives after all. Doane and Silverman find these films deficient because they regard this inward movement as one that fails to emulate the "linear" impulse "to the edges" of the diegesis where they locate the "source" of enunciation. The movement to the interior, in their view, is a paralytic effect that immobilizes rather than empowers agency. Subjectivity/enunciation can only, they suggest, come from "outside." In films such as these, however, in which the "outside" has only a slippery hold on a text, the "inside" moves in powerful, vertiginous cycles to involve the viewer in a drama (usually exploring a character's subjectivity in some way). Surely, that "interior" movement is not devoid of discursive force. The question resurfaces: is "subjectivity" in a film (as a character attribute or as an enunciatory position that character may represent) only to be conceived of within the patriarchal configuration of distance, exteriority, and linearity?

The strongly entrenched bias toward "interior" as "inferior" should be re-evaluated in feminist film theory, as should the conflation of specularity with narrative "stasis"—the view that interruptions to narrative flow (often posed by moments where some kind of feminine subjectivity is at stake) is somehow *negative* or testimony to the woman's discursive impotence. Such "interruptions," "regressive journeys," "recessions," "metaphors," by whatever name, on the contrary, mark strong moments of *discursive contradiction* to the linear discourse that so many theorists identify as "masculine." The "movement" is not to "the edges" but to "the inside"—a significant movement of opposition and of heterogeneity within the text. What to make, indeed, of a narrative that does not go anywhere, that "folds in on itself"? The fact is, it does go somewhere, it moves horizontally as it also moves vertically (through time). Its movement is paradoxical, perhaps, full of contradiction, but no film is literally "stopped" by this vertical folding, this spiraling structure. (It would cease to take place, to be a [narrative] film. As we know from the work of the '60s avant-garde, even the experience of light and shadow relative to time eventually "becomes" narrative.) Rather, it goes somewhere else, taking a detour through what is often a female-centered story, just as often "deviating" from the male-centered story that opens the film. This long digression away from the male-centered narrative puts two temporalities into play, forward and lateral, creating narrative structures that, as described earlier, emerge as circular, vortexical. This digressiveness also mobilizes contradictory discourses that speak from "different" places within the film simultaneously. Such discursive forms are not only a form of "power that lets itself be invaded by the pleasure it is pursuing . . . [but are also its] opposite . . . power asserting itself in the pleasure of showing off, scandalizing, or resisting . . . [T]hese evasions, these circular incitements have traced around bodies and sexes, not boundaries not to be crossed, but *perpetual spirals of power and pleasure*."[44] Discourses take winding, excessive, spiraling paths in films bearing voice-off. The heterogeneous signification of voice foregrounds contradiction, puts it more obviously into play throughout the text, buckling against constraint and coherence.

"Un-muzzling" Contradiction: The Myth of Coherence

In *The Archeology of Knowledge*, Foucault traces the analytical interest of coherence, explaining it as a principle that organizes discourse and restores it to unity. Coherence, he claims, is the production of a work exercised on a text; it is, in fact, *sought out* by the speaking subject.[45] Moreover, Foucault expressly singles out analysis (and thus, by extension, the *analyst*) as "suppress[ing] contradiction as best it can."[46] He goes on to describe the fundamental paradox that contradiction poses to coherence, stating that "contradiction, far from being an appearance or accident of discourse, far from being that from which it must be freed if its truth is at last to be revealed, constitutes the very law of its existence: it is on the basis of such a contradiction that discourse emerges, and it is in order both to translate it and to overcome it that discourse begins to speak; it is in order to escape that contradiction, whereas contradiction is ceaselessly reborn through discourse, that discourse endlessly pursues itself and endlessly begins again."[47]

Thus, contradiction and coherence structure each other, incite and elicit each other, co-exist in a dynamic relation that never abates in its productive movement. The desire for coherence, for intelligibility itself, bears the traces of this relationship—the structuring out of that which is illogical, that which signifies differently, that which is incoherent (this is perhaps of special interest for feminist theory, as the feminine is so often represented in exactly this way).

The analogic relationship between Foucault's description of contradiction and the workings of the Hegelian notion of self-consciousness as described in previous chapters is striking (as is a correspondence with the psychoanalytic subject's heterogeneous relation to voice-off). Foucault in fact has warned, "We have to determine the extent to which our anti-Hegelianism is possibly one of his tricks directed against us, at the end of which he stands, motionless, waiting for us."[48] A concept common to both writers' work, in fact, brings the notions of self-consciousness and discursive contradiction together: the formative contribution of paradox. Paradox represents a dynamic, one that, in Hegel's description of subject/object relations "brings identity and difference together" and one that, as an act of enunciation, Foucault has shown to be constitutive of discourse itself.[49] Foucault describes, moreover, the paradoxical enunciation of the sophists as a form of discourse that permitted more room *between* thought and words, something Western thought has "muzzled." This "muzzling," he implies, makes meaning more obvious. Paradox, then "un-muzzles" meaning, rendering it less transparent, less coherent.[50]

Paradox as invoked by these writers reveals a route toward dislodging the pessimistic assumption that patriarchal discourse always has the last word. Feminine discourse contradicts the patriarchal formatively and cannot be "contained" as such. The very impulse to view the patriarchal as a monolith that "contains" difference imposes an analytic coherence that should be questioned, and, ultimately, rejected. Of course, the kinds of studies that have investigated the mapping of power and desire in patriarchal discursive forms have undertaken a work of the greatest importance. However, there is something to be gained in looking away from models of coherence (even those critical of coherence in pointing it out) to bring forward possibilities of contradiction, of difference sustained, of dynamic paradox.

That Obscure Subject of Discourse

Feminist film theory and criticism has a strong tradition of searching within texts for feminine discourse, locating and tracing its enunciation, only to (usually) resignedly bring it back under the shadow of the patriarchal at the last minute. Claire Johnston's work, as Janet Bergstrom has pointed out, inaugurated a strong feminist tradition of searching for "progressive classical texts," such as films made within the Hollywood system by women directors like Ida Lupino and Dorothy Arzner, which in Johnston's view offered a kind of resistance to patriarchy through moments of strong rupture from prevailing ideology. As Bergstrom describes it, Johnston's "rupture thesis" envisioned progressive texts as ones which both foregrounded the discourse of the woman "while at the same time rendering the dominant discourse of the male fragmented and incoherent."[51] Bergstrom points out, however, that Johnston's work reflects a "reified" use of ideology and notes that the very ruptures Johnston points out as "progressive" are discussed by Stephen Heath as *fundamental* to the construction of the classical text.[52] Bergstrom's comments are provocative in suggesting that not only is contradiction within a text not necessarily anti-patriarchal or "progressive," but that it may not necessarily be found only in films made by women. Further, she suggests, moments of "rupture" may not adequately demonstrate the workings of a text overall: there is a need, she insists, for filmic analyses to look at "narrative movement as a whole," to study the "process" by which film "produc[es] meaning."[53] Although Bergstrom's essay indicates, at points, that the classical text ultimately smoothes out contradiction through its exploitation of redundant tropes, her final paragraph hints at a more optimistic view of such films. She argues, "Textual analyses of the most classical of films . . . have shown consistently how women function in different but equally crucial ways to insure narrative, to position the enunciation."[54]

In an article that responds to Bergstrom's call for a sustained analysis of textual movement, rather than solely of moments of rupture, Jacquelyn Suter maps out the feminine discourse she sees at work in *Christopher Strong* and comes to a more pessimistic view of this "progressive" Arzner film than does Johnston. Suter sees the feminine voice in this film as having "an organization of its own which is interwoven with/into the patriarchal."[55] She goes on to note, however, that ultimately, "because the feminine discourse is a part of the narrative structure and not ec-centric to it, it is liable to eventual usurpation by the meta-discourse" (of realist narrative coherence).[56] She suggests that an "intervention into the patriarchal order by generating a text which foregrounds contradiction and by positioning the spectator in such a way that throws into question his/her voyeuristic relation to the image" is necessary for a forceful expression of the feminine.[57] Like Mulvey and Silverman, she implies that such contradiction must emerge out of alternative film practices. Unlike Mulvey, Suter does not despair of narrative itself as ontologically occlusive of the feminine: she cites Chantal Akerman's *Jeanne Dielman* as an example of narrative that strongly articulates feminine discourse.

Whereas Suter and Mulvey do conceive of the *possibility* of feminine subjectivity in classical cinema, Raymond Bellour's groundbreaking work on enunciation in the films of Hitchcock suggests that the structuring work of the patriarchal forecloses the possibility of such an expression altogether.[58] Bergstrom notes, with respect to Bellour's work, a "totalistic and deterministic . . . picture of the classical cinema . . . [of] a logically consistent, complete and closed system."[59] Significantly, Bellour's analyses heavily favor an image-centered elaboration of enunciatory structuration, one that looks to the gaze as *the* locus of subjectivity and power in film. As his vision-oriented understanding of identificatory processes neatly underwrites the enunciatory work he describes, in being driven by a (sadistic/voyeuristic) staving off of sexual difference by a male spectator prototype, he concludes that all classical Hollywood cinema reworks Oedipal conflicts in order to contain/eliminate the (unbearable/castrated) figure of the woman.[60] Bellour's preferred *auteurs;* Hitchcock and Lang, however, while indisputably "masters" of teasing, luring, representing, and refracting the eye, were both enthusiastic pioneers in the development of a strongly dynamic use of sound. One need only think of the radical sound experiments of *Blackmail* and *M.*[61] On this count alone it seems that Bellour's analyses of their films are only half-finished, or, at the very least, that they betray a familiar bias to the visual (and thus, according to his own logic, the masculine subject). When Bellour does account for the workings of sound, it is as a code, one "present" in the image or not.[62] Where in relation to the image, innumerable such codes are devised for tracking the enunciatory progress of the film, sound (to quote Bellour's own phraseology) comes off as "obvious," a pure content, not meriting the meticulous subtleties that characterize his interest in the workings of image (angle, movement, composition, etc.). Rarely, for example, does Bellour ever draw attention to whether a sound or a voice emanates from on-screen or off, much less elaborate sound's dynamic relationship to the image, its grain, the acoustic "hierarchies" established in the mix, etc. Rather, his analysis falls into a critical camp that looks at sound as little more than "added value" to an image that reigns supreme.

Effacing Effacement: Tracking the "Other" Axis of Enunciation

Despite Bellour's lack of interest in sound's or voice's discursive functions in film, he does expressly link the subject of enunciation to *speech*. He writes, "The term 'enunciator' as I use it marks both the person who possesses the right of speech within the film, and the source (*instance*) toward which the series of representations is logically channeled back."[63] Bellour's understanding of "the right of speech," in fact, seems ironically linked to the possession of the gaze in a film, and its relay from author to character and on to (male) spectator. He does not ever really explain this rather sudden and remarkable leap in his logic. (His conclusion is tautological, deriving from his assumption that the subject of desire is masculine and that the image determines enunciation in film.)[64] If we displace his model onto speech and voice, it would seem, however, as logical to attribute "the right of speech" to a character bearing voice-off as it would to a character possessing the gaze—for the voice-off is a more than adequate "marker" of privileged speech.

Doane and Silverman, in fact, note that there is always some self-referentiality to the voice-off. Silverman remarks that "insofar as the voice-over asserts its independence from the visual track, it presents itself as an enunciator."[65] For Silverman, however, the degree of "independence" required is so stringent that few voices meet her criteria. The second half of her sentence, however, reminds us that part of the mark of the enunciator is its "self-presentation," its drawing attention to itself. Many voices-off force their recognition on the viewer in this way. Doane adds to this the intriguing observation that, "As soon as the sound is detached from its source, no longer anchored by a represented body, its potential work as a signifier is revealed. There is always something uncanny about a voice which emanates from a source outside the frame."[66] Doane goes on to point to ways that voices are "anchored" against this "uncanny" signifying power, but the suggestion remains that even a voice coming from offscreen space (and not particularly "coded" as a "voice-over") is noticeable in its difference from the image, marks an enunciatory potential.

Provisionally, at least, one can conclude that a central narrating character may function as an enunciator, even in Bellour's system, inasmuch as voice-off draws attention to itself as an act of enunciation (speech). The second definition of "enunciator" that Bellour provides, "the source towards which the series of representations is logically channeled back," could, if we follow Bellour's schema, represent the author (Hitchcock) or what he represents (patriarchal authority). However, this second "enunciator," I argue, must also be defined as the desiring subject, a subject "constructed by" the "first" enunciator. If the "first" enunciator, then, possesses a right of speech "marked" as feminine (such as a highly "visible" female voice-off), then this second enunciator conceivably responds to the desire implicit in the discourse "she/it" expresses.

Predictably, when one defines enunciation through images, all the "enunciative loci" Bellour describes conform to a masculine prototype. The mere postulate that sound works to construct an enunciator throws the tidy arrangement into disarray. All the assumptions that govern his argument, predicated on defining "speech" as "look," begin to topple. There may be room, that is, within an enunciatory model that disrupts the "pure" visual paradigm (and along with it "the holy Trinity" of author, character, and spectator/subject brought together by the gaze) for feminine discourse, a feminine subject, desire of a different order. This desire, and the subject assumed through it, thus cannot be understood as relating to the visual axis of film alone, or even primarily. For, according to this model, sound/voice/speech can also "mark" the character, her desire, and the subject who hears.

One last look at Bellour's understanding of enunciation is instructive in this regard—instructive, because he points to a strong contradiction at the heart of enunciation, one which rephrases, in a sense, the contradiction implicit in Foucault's description of the formative structuration of discourse cited earlier. It is a double contradiction, as we shall see. After remarking on the strong structuring presence of the enunciator in the film systems he analyzes, Bellour recalls Metz' distinction/collapse of story and discourse, and the effacement by which the fiction film conceals its own marks of enunciation. Bellour suggests that " . . . this effacement . . . is precisely the means, at once subtle and powerful, whereby a very strongly marked process of enunciation manifests itself, which defines and structures a certain subject of desire."[67] The bulk of his work stresses the apparent collusion of a strongly signified enunciator with a discourse that contains and effaces sexual difference/the feminine. But here Bellour's argument suggests a simultaneous *effacement of effacement.* Bellour's view of classical cinema seems torn. On one hand, he privileges the (Hitchcockian) texts that foreground enunciation, enunciation of a discourse of containment. On the other hand, he claims the "less extraordinary" texts of classical cinema efface the marks of enunciation (the marks that work to eradicate the feminine) and through this "other" effacement enunciate a certain "subject of desire."[68] Though it is clear Bellour himself does not entertain the possibility that this desire is anything but masculine, the question arises: if the masculine subject's desire is at stake in the visual nexus of marked enunciation that Bellour describes, whose desire is at stake in the effacement of those markers? No matter what the answer (for I hardly wish to define feminine or masculine desire in this way), contradiction is at the heart of the process, a contradiction that speaks not simply of containment and coherence, but of the simultaneous activation of difference.

Before turning to a more concrete explication of these ideas through a sustained examination of discursive paradox in *A Letter to Three Wives,* a final definition is in order. "What," indeed, is feminine discourse? Suter describes discourse generally as "an ideological position from which a subject 'speaks' (acts/interacts) with the social order": she defines the "feminine" part of the equation through her analysis, as *what differs,* in a sense, from the patriarchal.[69] She looks for what she calls "the feminine voice."[70] Taking a different approach, this book does not accept, as a given, that patriarchy "contains" the feminine—that a "meta-discourse," as Suter describes, always has the last word in classical cinema.[71] Moreover, by focusing on sound (specifically the female voice-off), the analyses offered in this chapter offer a way to read "against" the woman's "iconic" status within the image track. The female voice-off, as a feminine discourse, speaks beyond the character to which it is assigned in the diegesis— articulating the experience of other more visible, "looked-at" women in the text. Finally, though the question of voice (in its expression of non-speech) remains vital, the problem of speech (as manifested and emphasized by voice-off) emerges as a crucial arena within which to approach a discussion of feminine discourse. These voices-off speak as represented "women," articulate their/a desire, assume subjectivity, and seize power within the text. Their speech occurs in a discursive context—where language, knowledge, desire, and power intersect—a context, moreover, that the voice-off also helps to construct. There is no "outside" to "inside" relationship in discourse. To paraphrase Foucault, speech both manifests desire and is its object. Moreover, he warns, the "danger spots" (to the "controlling" features of discourse) are precisely "those dealing with politics and sexuality."[72] The female voice-off, enunciating the subjectivity of the "objectified" other in patriarchy, is dangerous indeed.

Complicit Consciousness: The "Hailing" of Other Women

The female voice-off thus not only "draws attention to itself" (to itself as both speech *and* as voice) but also evokes a source of enunciation. By "hailing" the spectator, the female voice-off differs notably from the image of the woman. Where, as Mulvey, Doane, Silverman, Bellour, and others have noted, the image of the woman "exhibits" itself as the *clandestine* object offered to a voyeur's gaze, as "passive" spectacle, the female voice-off asserts itself quite openly as a subject. Not only does the female voice-off invariably take a first person stance toward the story/spectator, but, more often than not, it implicates the viewer in a "direct-address" relationship, invoking a discourse of "speaking to" as well as of "speaking."[73] The voice-off of Addie Ross in Joseph Mankiewicz's *A Letter to Three Wives* (1949), for example, opens the film by establishing a strong direct relationship to the spectator, reminding that, "to begin with, any persons in this story might be fictitious—and any resemblance to you or me might be purely coincidental." Not only is Addie's status as some kind of "author" implied here, but she refers directly to the viewer's presence and implication within the "story" that is about to follow. Addie's suggestion, in fact, that the viewer is *not* "at stake" here, is a joke: the voice-off points to itself *and* at the supposedly "concealed" voyeur, rather than effacing these discursive sites.[74] Other examples abound of this implication of the spectator in the discourse of the film that "is speaking."[75] At the opening of *Rebecca*, Fontaine's voice-off, like Addie's, invokes the spectator, reminding, "*We* can never go back to Manderley again. . . ." (She could also be speaking of all the other voices implicit in her own, as mentioned above.) In other films, the "direct," inclusive quality of the female voice-off arrives via the spectator's implied alliance with another character to whom the female

voice-off is addressing itself in the diegesis, as, for example, when a letter is read (Lisa's voice speaking "to" Stefan in *Letter from an Unknown
Woman*); when imaginary conversations are held in her mind (Claudette
Colbert's "talks" with her absent husband in *Since You Went Away*); or
when real conversations with interested diegetic "audiences" lead into
confessions or stories of some kind (*Mildred Pierce, All This and Heaven,
Too, Now Voyager,* and *So Proudly We Hail*). Finally, the "directness" of
the female voice-off is highlighted in other films by its representation
as thought or consciousness eliciting the spectator's recognition (*Secret
beyond the Door*).

This vigorously marked "subjective" consciousness is also often foregrounded by the *kinds* of reflections the female voice-off shares with the
viewer. They are nearly always rendered in a poetical, highly personal
and affective speech, and frequently underwritten by "subjective" camera
tropes. In *No Man of Her Own,* (Mitchell Leisen's 1950 version) Barbara
Stanwyck's character introduces us to the town of "Corfield" in a direct
address uncannily similar (on the image track) to that of Addie Ross (*A
Letter to Three Wives*). In both films the camera simultaneously dollies in a
highly stylized "omniscient" tracking movement down a small city's streets
to rest finally on an upper-class home—a home the female voice-off wishes
were hers. (In *No Man of Her Own,* Stanwyck lives in the house under a
"false" identity, having pretended to be a dead man's "wife"; in *A Letter to
Three Wives,* Addie is describing the home of her childhood beau, Brad,
a house usurped from Addie by Brad's unexpected new wife, Deborah.)
The omniscient camera, however, refracted through the voice, is not really
the "godlike" view we would ascribe to it in isolation from sound: here, it
"speaks" of a particular organizing consciousness, a subjectivity enounced
most directly by the voice, a feminine desire (interestingly associated to
the entitlement to occupy the house rather than to possess the man.)[76]

The number of films with female voice-off that open in this way, in fact,
suggest a kind of trope associated with female voice-off in general. In addition to the two films mentioned, *Since You Went Away* opens with a similar
tracking in on the home accompanied by Colbert's voice. Joan Crawford's
voice-off in *Mildred Pierce* "starts" in just such a way, as we dissolve from
the police station where she is giving her statement to end up at the modest home where she lives with her (soon to be estranged) husband. The
heroine of *I Walked with a Zombie* stares via a subjective tracking gaze
through a grilled gate at her mysterious, seductive new home. In *Raw
Deal,* the "home" that the opening voice-off leads us toward is, ironically,

a prison. And, of course, *Rebecca*'s opening tracking shot/voice-off pairing, ending in the imagining of Manderley's decay, is legendary. In addition to *underscoring* the enunciatory subjectivity of the voice (the dolly shot miming it on the image track), the linking of the female voice-off to a discourse of subjectivity related to the home, origins, class, and family is obvious. The female voice-off's expressed *relationship* to this discourse is often a problem, in fact, that the narrative will take up: Mildred Pierce's first home is too *modest* (for Joan Crawford), Colbert's home is too *empty,* Brad and Deborah's house *excludes* Addie (who was "supposed" to have been Brad's wife), Manderley is a phantom paradise, always already lost.

The problem, moreover, is revealed to the spectator as a kind of secret, a confidence entrusted to her by the female voice-off who shares her most personal inner thoughts. Thus, in *No Man of Her Own,* Stanwyck's voice becomes increasingly "subjective" as we move from the streets into the house itself. Out on the quiet Corfield avenue, she describes, in lyrical tones, the general ambiance of the garden and house, "the fragrance of the heliotropes . . . the dazzling white of the porch supports," and repeats that it is "a pleasant life in Corfield." Then, shifting timbre, she confesses, "But not for us, not for us," acknowledging the dark side of this tranquil world.[77] Since the spectator does not yet know who "us" is, she is subtly hailed, implicated in this discourse. Inside the house, the voice continues over a mix of silence and music as we reach an inner room: Stanwyck sits on the couch "thinking" and looking at her husband pensively, a quiet aura of tragedy linking them. She tells us, "I love him, and he loves me, I know he does," but she insists he will leave her before long. Then, in another subtle shift, she assumes direct discourse with him/us, saying, "*You* believed our love could save *us* . . . ," etc. Thus, the spectator is hailed first as the recipient of a story (the indirect address outside the house) and also as a listening subject (direct discourse via a second character—her husband).

Such shifting from one enunciative "pole" to another, moreover (from third person to first and back again in rhetorical fluctuations from "narrating" to "stream of consciousness" to "imaginary conversation" etc.), is typical of female voice-off. (Male voices-off more typically remain fairly "consistent" in the kind of enunciatory "position" the voice speaks [to and of]. In fact, a "stream of consciousness" is rarely employed in male voice-off—unless "bracketed" by a narrational "distance," as is the case in *Murder My Sweet.*) We have observed the many fluctuations, positions, "tenses"—in short, enunciative powers taken up by Celia's voice-off in

Secret beyond the Door. Similarly, in *Now Voyager* (1942), Charlotte's voice-off, when describing her adolescent love affair to Dr. Jacquith, takes a narrating enunciatory stance of indirect past tense as we watch the flashback transpire. Later, after meeting Jerry on the boat, she gazes at her reflection in a window, her voice-off whispering her direct present tense inner thoughts, " . . . *he* wishes [he understood me better]." The heroine of *Raw Deal*, Pat, also bears a free-ranging voice-off—one minute describing "extra-diegetically" the tricks of fate that have conspired to rob her of the man she's helped to escape from prison (and for whom she's sacrificed everything), the next vocalizing her tortured inner thoughts *within* the diegesis.[78] In *Brief Encounter*, Celia Johnson's voice-off sweeps from a tortured inner monologue that serves to "block out" a gossipy woman's chatter on the train to an imaginary "conversation" in which she tries to explain her love affair to her oblivious husband, who sits absorbed with his crossword puzzle. Frances Dee's voice-off in *I Walked with a Zombie*, too, drifts from a "narrating third person" to "interior monologue" and back again. (Other voices-off surface in *Zombie*—male voices-off that serve to deepen her awareness of the racial tensions in the culture she now inhabits, and, further, audibly figure the contradictions her new consciousness brings into relief. These voices-off work not to "replace" her voice-off, but, in a condensation similar to that described in relation to *Secret beyond the Door,* represent extensions of her point of view that amplify a plurality of subjectivities.) This fluidity, this multiplicity, serves to highlight the process of enunciation itself: to draw out its vicissitudes, potentialities, powers. Moreover, this expressly mutable and plural discourse is that marked as a feminine discourse, expressly aligned with the female voice-off. Feminine discourse is represented thus as enunciating more than one "place" for a subject, who "speaks" from many different positions in the text, elaborating multiple perspectives. This fluidity of subjectivity and plurality of enunciation should not be mistaken for what might seem to be its corollary on the image track—the "omniscient subjectivity" of a male-coded gaze that aligns with the mobile (and often "overhead") camera and effortlessly transcends difference for an illusion of centrality and coherence. Rather, this "vocal subject" speaks *through* difference, enunciating a plurality of voices in one.

One could, metaphorically speaking, "read" this discursive subject, as Michael Renov does, as "possess[ing] that grand skepticism [of the woman] . . . that makes of [the character of Pat in *Raw Deal*] . . . the distant voice who speaks for both women [the two "rivals" for the man in the film], *for all women.*"[79] Renov harkens this analogy back to Nietzsche and Derrida, in positing that "woman is . . . constituted as a subject whose multiplicity of positions . . . produces a knowledge effect. . . ."[80] He claims, moreover, that the "will-to-knowledge" of the female character is "most clearly expressed through her enunciative power" (a power which he ascribes directly to her character's possession and deployment of voice-off).[81] Renov's linking of a female voice-off to a will-to-knowledge and the enunciation of plurality (even though he does not mark out this aspect of his argument in terms of voice per se) provides several intriguing points of departure for a discussion of feminine discourse in films with female voice-off. The "knowledge" he describes compares strikingly with the paradoxical "self-consciousness" outlined earlier in this book, in that it allows for a recognition of self and other simultaneously—a recognition of self in the other. The question of desire, too, is implied in Renov's description, for the knowledge arrives via the "will." Pat's character, like Celia's in *Secret,* wants to understand the other, desires the truth that, even in its apparent obliteration of her as object of desire, allows her to take action, to be a subject through her sacrifice. Finally, there is the question of to whom and for whom this discourse speaks, the question of "women" at large. For although Renov does not exploit the metaphor he brings up earlier, in suggesting Pat "speaks for all women," its repercussions are provocative. Is there a sense in which the female voice-off "speaks" to and for "all women"? Or, to rephrase his analogy, does the plurality of discursive positions enunciated by the female voice-off elaborate difference that can be sustained, affirmed, or even celebrated "within" patriarchal discourse itself? In an attempt to further tackle these questions, and with the hopes of elaborating more fully the relations of female voice-off to speech, desire and power, let us take a close look at *A Letter to Three Wives.*

Detached Attachment: The Ambivalent "Author"

As noted above, Addie Ross's voice-off inaugurates the narrative of *A Letter to Three Wives,* her authorial prestige underscored by her claim to knowledge/judgment. She claims, "the name of the town isn't important," stressing her ironic detachment as she sneers at "plain Main Street" and "those horrible chain stores that breed like rabbits." These authorial markers are aggravated by her direct address to the spectator ("any resemblance to you or me *might* be fictitious") and her haughty tone, as well as by the "omniscient" tracking shot described above. She both observes the images along with us and suggests that she is *producing* them (implying that she is the arbiter of what is or is not fiction). Addie Ross's voice-off, in some respects, represents an anomaly of sorts in her strident striking of enunciatory power, with respect to the majority of other female voices-off in classic cinema. Her voice-off, that is, seems to lack all sincerity in its utter embrace of a cool, even cruel, ironic detachment, one that reminds of the noir male voices-off of any number of films. Unlike the caustic narrators of *Murder My Sweet* and *Out of the Past,* however, Addie's irony lacks any real humor or self-deprecation. This egotism makes her doubly villainous (an immodest woman—a scandal to patriarchy!) and her voice-off doubly interesting (for as we shall see, she also speaks *for* patriarchy). Her nearest counterpart in the voice-off world is probably Addison DeWitt in *All about Eve.* (Mankiewicz may be sneaking in a joke in giving them such similar first names, as if they're two siblings from a singularly snobbish family.) Addie's voice-off bears none of the fatalism inherent in most noirish evocations of sardonic voice-off. Rather than being subject to fate, she *is* Fate: she controls the narrative itself (or so it seems). Her irony would seem to give her, on one hand, a "distance" from the story that aligns her with the immunity of the patriarchal enunciator. But her sarcasm, paradoxically, simultaneously implies a lack of distance—for she is *too* ironic, not really detached from the scene she describes: she *hates.* Her sneering tone betrays an *interest* that renders her irony suspect. Part of this interest in fact, is explicitly ideological: her first target of disdain is none other than Smalltown, USA.

Her scorn reaches Capitalism, too, embodied in the "horrible" chain stores that "breed like rabbits." This metaphor "speaks" both of the polluting activity of mechanical reproduction (a strong thematic in the film's denunciation of, among other things, the dissemination of popular culture via radio), and of reproduction itself. The second jab cuts both ways, "against" and "for" sex: "women" can be mapped onto "rabbits" as breeders cursed to have sex for biological purposes (one suspects Addie Ross has no children). This is a town where women are subjected to a biological role, something Addie explicitly critiques. (Addie is the first to "speak" of sex here, and, as we shall see, she actively castrates others for her own pleasure). Her attitude suggests that sex for biological purposes is repugnant, implying a preference for another, perhaps opposite purpose of sex for women—pleasure.

But she swiftly moves on from a general disdain for the town to jeer the "upper" class. As the camera moves into the Bishop's mansion, Addie reminisces, "[Brad] gave me my first black eye . . . and my first kiss," her scornful tone giving way, for a moment, to wistful desire. That Addie's desire entails both being beaten and being kissed is certainly telling: it introduces an ambivalence towards men that snakes through the film. It should be noted, moreover, that Addie's "ironic detachment" falters at this statement. The discourse of romantic fatalism, implicit in her invocation of a shared past with Brad, is at odds with her declared disinterest in Small-town and its inhabitants. No longer "looking down," she is now "looking in," and conveniently, the camera obliges by bringing us inside the house. What is inside, the image Addie's desire conjures up, however, is not Brad. Addie's attention here, enunciated doubly as the camera comes to rest on Deborah, and as Addie's voice-off pronounces the word "wife," is not on the character Deborah, but her *social* function, her marital relation. Addie's desire is/was to "be" in Deborah's place, the wife of Brad, rather than a desire for Brad himself. Coincidentally, this is also how Deborah appears to define herself (of the three "wives" she is the least independent and the most troubled about how to sustain her identity in the shadow of marriage). Most emphatically, however, Deborah's image takes the place of the voice-off, which "disappears" after introducing her. Deborah is thus preliminarily "marked" as taking up enunciation in its wake.

The "Model" Woman: Internalizing the Enemy

Within the scene that plays out between Deborah and Brad, moreover, an identification of sorts is established between Deborah and Addie. Just as Addie desires to "be" where/what Deborah is, Deborah desires to be (like) Addie (as demonstrated in her obsessive envy).[82] On one hand, Deborah is represented as Addie's "opposite": where Addie is "sophisticated" (we know it from her cultivated voice, and learn more about her "exquisite taste" later), Deborah is gauche (she does not know how to manipulate her own husband, for one thing). But the two women are also linked in impor-tant ways: they have the same dress (a reminder of her own non-unique-ness Deborah finds painful), they both "want" to be Brad's wife, etc. Addie, moreover, is introduced here as an "idea" of femininity to which Deborah compares herself, an "ideal" to which she is held, and found lacking. She accuses Brad of "setting her up" against Addie, saying, "Addie used to be a kind of ideal for you, didn't she?" When Brad rejoins, "How did Addie get into this conversation?" the discursive lines begin to come into focus. Most obviously, if Addie represents a "paragon" for the masculine subject, her voice-off must "speak," on one level, for patriarchy. This alignment with patriarchal discourse explains her omnipresence (they can't *not* talk about her) and her transparency—she is everywhere and nowhere. It also explains her threat. As the denizen of an ideology that seeks to control and contain women, she endangers the expression of feminine discourse, imperils feminine subjectivity.

This preliminary enunciation of patriarchal discourse via Addie's voice-off, however, is already troubled, and contradictory.[83] Addie, in introducing this scene, designates Deborah as her discursive emissary, not Brad, the male character bearing the gaze. Deborah is identified with the "position" of Addie, the enunciator. Despite the fact that they "are" different characters, Addie's voice-off points to Deborah as the figure within the diegesis that will play out the desire she articulates. It is a desire also represented as ambivalence, expressed in the anxiety and fear that plague the wives as they reflect upon the triangular relationship between them, their husbands, and Addie. In this sense, Addie represents the "internalization" of the patriarchal ideal for the women in the story: she is the model of femininity that robs them of their subjecthood. Her voice-off, thus, functions as an expression of contradiction, enunciating the patriarchal discourse of suppressing the feminine *along with* a feminine discourse about the experience of being suppressed, and the contradictions of being a female subject within patriarchy.

This process of internalization, this movement of the voice-off "into" the "minds" of the wives, a process by which the voice becomes "their own" inner voices (and yet, always the voice of another), is first stressed by the tracking shot into Deborah's home as Addie's voice-off slips from sardonic asides into desiring subjectivity. When the voice-off next emerges, it is explicitly associated with Deborah's inner thoughts. Deborah, driving away from her house after the quarrel with Brad (a quarrel "about" Addie, but really about Deborah's recognition that his desire entails her subjugation to an oppressive ideal), is deep in contemplation. Addie's voice breaks in, as if watching the film with us, to comment, in a snotty voice, "She won't stay mad at him long. She's too much in love. Pretty soon, she'll be full of self-reproach. Women are so silly." Addie's words function to underscore a patriarchal dismissal of a woman's anger—reducing it to childishness and irrationality. But if we imagine for a moment that the voice-off here also represents an internalized feminine discourse, another meaning is expressed, one that is not "buried" but which is actually as clearly enunciated as the first. That is, the voice literally suggests that it is silly to be full of self-reproach and implies, moreover, that Deborah's anger is justified, if untenable under the role assigned a woman "in love." That the voice-off accompanies a close-up of Deborah's face is not insignificant. It adds to our association of this voice with her thoughts, which we thus perceive as a contradiction. Deborah's subjectivity enunciated in this way expresses both the patriarchal discourse and the feminine discourse that critiques and undercuts it. Neither discourse, moreover, "dominates" the scene, but a sympathy for Deborah is established that joins with the feminine discourse in countermanding the work of the patriarchal. Addie's voice here is persecutory, and Deborah's subjectivity profits from Addie's loss. We find ourselves on Deborah's "side." (This "preference" for Deborah over Addie, however, means nothing in itself, as they enunciate contradiction *between* them. The subjectivity we attribute to Deborah is a function of Addie's voice.) Finally, Addie's enunciatory mobility is again emphasized, in that she is both producer of discourse and a spectator, "watching" Deborah. She thus "collapses one of the divisions upon which classic cinema is predicated—the division . . . between the site of enunciation and that of spectatorship."[84] Addie also "posits an implicit reversibility between the positions of director and viewer, or speaking and spoken subjects."[85] Addie functions here as a powerful reminder of the plurality of discourse and its many origins and expressions. The "reversibility" she brings into relief, moreover, triggers the spectator's recognition of the apparatus, but not through the discomfiture of a look at the camera. Rather, it is as speaking subject that Addie thrusts the viewer into a self-aware "place" in the narrative. She is not only in control, but she flaunts it and points to her alliance with us offscreen.

Veiled Threats: The Secret Life of Men

Addie "introduces" the second "wife" of the second couple in the story: Rita and George Phipps—middle class, "on their way up." Addie attributes the Phippses' potential class mobility entirely to Rita's ambition, foreshadowing the "problem" that will plague this couple (the emasculation of her husband through their role-reversal, and the success Rita desires and achieves). Subtly, at this moment, Addie's voice-off also undergoes a "shift" to directly enounce Deborah's inner thoughts, as she says, "There she is now, ready, waiting, that's Rita!" Thus Addie's voice-off, with characteristic fluidity, drifts from its narrating capacity to "become" Deborah's "internal monologue" as she/they reflect(s) on the punctuality of this capable friend.

As a later scene demonstrates as well, it is not in the least surprising that Deborah's inner thoughts should "sound" like Addie Ross: deeply insecure, Deborah ruthlessly rails against her own inadequacies as a woman, set up against a standard Addie Ross represents.[86] Addie's voice thus comes to stand in for self-loathing of a very particular sort, one brought about by the internalization of an impossible conceptualization of the self as a flawless image. It is not accidental, in this sense, that Mankiewicz never shows us what Addie looks like—*no one* can look like Addie. (Maybe, as with Medusa, no one can look *at* her either.)

Moreover, Deborah begins to *talk like* Addie when Rita gets in the car, wondering aloud why George is "being so mysterious." Rita does not know what her friend is talking about until Deborah points out that George "isn't going fishing" on his day off, and is wearing a blue suit. Like Addie, Deborah "knows" all about George and Rita and their daily life: she can predict their actions. But she also functions as an extension of Addie's "voice" here in planting a seed of anxiety in Rita, who, coincidentally, has also had some sort of marital dispute that morning. As in the scene between Brad and Deborah earlier, an embedded question about male autonomy arises and is associated to the quarrels with an aura of mystery and vague threat. Neither Rita nor Deborah really knows where their husbands are going that day or why (Brad, like George, evades his wife's questions on this subject). The comings and goings of the women, on the other hand, have been clearly mapped out (they are volunteers at a picnic with a nebulous group of picnicking "kids"). Thus, Deborah articulates a fear the women share—a nagging suspicion that, despite the bonds of marriage, their husbands are "free," while they are not. She spreads a kind of contagion of anxiety, alerting Rita that her husband has "another life" of which she knows nothing. In this sense, then, the internalization of a feminine discourse that expresses a need for vigilance over a potentially straying mate becomes disseminated among the women characters. The root of this discourse, Addie's voice-off, slides from offscreen to "on," now reaching the level of "ordinary" dialog. Moreover, it is expressed like a community project, as one wife helping another keep an eye on her hubby.

In the car, Rita admits that her time-consuming work for the radio has kept her from knowing what George is up to, but she defends herself by quoting Addie. She works for "one hundred pieces of what Addie Ross calls the most restful shade of green in the world. Unquote." Deborah, sighing, wonders aloud why they always end up talking about Addie. Addie, apparently still eavesdropping from above, breaks in to answer Deborah's question: "Because maybe if you girls didn't talk about me, you wouldn't talk about anything at all. That's right, I'm Addie. I'm the one they just can't help talking about. My very dearest friends, too." This strange "conversation" continues as Deborah wonders if Addie knows "how they feel about her." Addie replies, "I know, believe me I do." The voice-off continues, "But it doesn't matter . . . as much as what all of you don't know—yet."

Addie's voice-off clearly restates its enunciative privilege here, implying that they cannot talk without "her." She is, in a sense, the "subject" of their conversations, of their speech itself. She is the drive behind what they express. Possessing the right of speech, she claims to possess the right of knowledge (she "knows how they feel") as well as the right of power. Clearly, as we have seen, she is on the side of the "author," in knowing "more" than the characters and speaking directly, here, to the audience by finally introducing herself. This introduction, of course, puts her more squarely in the diegesis than before: she is now a character, like the others. She enounces, moreover, the Gordian knot that this narrative will work to untangle; what is important is not what she knows, but what they do not know, what is hidden. She implies that in her all-powerful capacity, she knows what they do not, a suggestion underscored by her invisibility to the spectator, who attributes omniscience to noncorporeal beings. Yet, even as she enounces her power, she speaks her constraint. For, unlike some voices-off that reach the literal space of the character to whom it speaks (like Lisa's in *Letter from an Unknown Woman*), Addie's voice-off here is not heard by Rita and Deborah in this scene, only by us. Her lack of a body is both a form of power and a limit. And thus the question could be raised: if Addie has no body and no image, (or only the tiniest fragment of one), how can she possibly compete with women who do? If Addie poses a threat to them, it is, literally, as this voice—a voice enouncing the contradictory discourses that constitute the feminine in patriarchy, a voice that they internalize and experience as subjectivity. The body, in fact, is a battleground between these women, a privilege that gives the diegetic characters some advantages over Addie. Indeed, Lora Mae, the third "wife," in particular capitalizes on her possession of specular leverage, as we shall see.

Bombshell: When a Woman Writes Desire

Lora Mae is brought into the story without the ceremonious introduction Addie has provided for everyone else, a departure from custom that marks Lora Mae as different. Seeing her at the ferry, Deborah (Addie's designated driver within the film) "names" Lora Mae, who immediately brings up Addie's "disappearance." She declares sardonically, "Addie left town this morning, for good." Though it is unthinkable (since *we* know how much Addie would hate it), apparently Addie was originally doomed to the kid's picnic along with the other wives. The three women shrug off her absence as in-character (Addie is mysterious, secretive, like their husbands). When a letter suddenly arrives, "special delivery," they raise their brows, then, despite Deborah's sixth sense that whatever is in the note will ruin their day, they read it together—but not aloud or to each other. It is Addie's voice-off that speaks the words on the page, with characteristic ironic relish. Her voice-off now serves as internal "thought-voice" for all three wives.[87] The letter, moreover, is shown in closeup on the screen. An embossed linen paper bearing an elegant feminine script, the letter stands in for Addie's body, imagined as "perfect," beautiful, refined, etc. (and also repeats the opening title sequence, reminding of the extra-diegetic). Along with her voice, thus, the letter re-inscribes her status as enunciator, the producer of discourse. Both image and sound track, that is, figure Addie as voice-off.

This pivotal moment displays Addie's power over them (she can "take" one of their husbands with her as a "memento," a husband they apparently cannot control the same way). It also provides the hermeneutic that will drive the rest of the narrative (which husband?). In her representation of "the voice of patriarchy," Addie presents her threat: one of the wives has been negligent and will be punished (lose her husband). But Addie's voice also expresses an idea pretty disturbing for patriarchy as well: the men here are objects of exchange among the women, pawns in a catfight where the reward of victory is subjective power, rather than the man himself. (It is a somewhat "patriarchal" articulation of feminine discourse, to be sure, but reversing the usual subject/object relations between the sexes, at least.) This letter cuts both ways, displaying the discursive contradiction openly, "speaking" both the patriarchal agenda that will be played out as a kind of pleasure (the narrativization of bringing these uppity, postwar women down a peg, getting them to shape up and remember their place) and the feminine discourse that makes it possible and defies it (women have power over men, a fact Addie's voice and letter brandish with glee), also for the sake of pleasure. (Where is the fun in bringing them down, that is, if their subjectivity is an idle threat?)

Dissolving Voices: Identity-in-the-Mix

The subjectivity of these women and the nature of their "problem" (ways they have been negligent wives and ways they have resisted objectification) in fact is the primary narrative and ideological concern of this film. When the voice-off next surfaces, it begins to blur the distinctions between "Addie's" subjectivity and Deborah's even more explicitly than before. The women, after casting a longing look at the telephone, the sole means of communicating with their husbands for the rest of the day, get on a boat with the kids, and sail to an island.[88] Rita and Lora Mae pretend to shrug off their anxiety (try to pretend they do not hear the voice "inside their heads": Addie who now speaks "as" their thought). Rita jokes, "This is like some movie about a women's prison."[89] But Deborah, already established as the most paranoid of the three, and over-identified with Addie as we've seen, "hears" Addie's voice taunting her. Another enunciatory shift thus takes place: where first, Addie spoke "off" as a narrator, then "inhabited" Deborah's (and later the other wives') thoughts, here Deborah seems to literally perceive the voice-off. It "possesses her," or, as a character describes later relative to radio, "she's being penetrated." (The radio's "penetration" is figured by the film to be an ideological act. As we have seen, in one respect, Addie's voice-off possession functions the same way.) This vocal/auditory possession is, in fact, a typical trope of female voice-off, especially in cases like this, where a hallucination of speech tortures a thinking subject.[90] The line is blurred between thought and perception; we perceive that the character hears the voice as if it is *real,* not in her head. Addie speaks to her, asking directly, "Do you remember your first Saturday in town? That was in May, too. Is it Brad? Is it Brad? Is it Brad?" With each "Is it Brad?" however, Addie's voice slips again, becomes less distinguishably her own: it begins, in fact, to sound more like Deborah's voice, an effect highlighted by reverberation and an audio dissolve from Addie's to Deborah's voice. The voice is also "echoed" by the rhythmical sound of the boat chugging, as if the boat's voice were also taunting, "Is it Brad? (This is an auditory moment that seems highly "self-reflexive" in pointing to the mechanical reproduction of the apparatus through this distorted repetition, revealing, as the French would say, *le dispositif.*) The slippage "from" Addie "to" Deborah, however, is not clearly marked or audible: rather, the voice-off here gives a vague impression of being both women's voices *simultaneously.* Addie's voice-off, metamorphosed in this way, is also Deborah's voice-off. Moreover, this voice-off introduces a flashback that tells us Deborah's side of the story. Partly "enounced" by Addie, partly by Deborah, the flashback reflects (at least) two discourses. One could put it this way: Deborah "within" the flashback now represents that "feminine discourse" implicit in Addie's voice. Her desires, speech, and difficulty "being" an image express her subjectivity, just as Addie's voice-off (in the role of patriarchy) subliminally continues to enounce a contradictory discourse, through *her* alliance with offscreen space.

Subjectivity Run Amok: The Impossibility of Being (an Image)

Deborah's flashback, as mentioned earlier, relates her newlywed anxiety about meeting Brad's upper-class friends. She drinks too many martinis, depressed about her hair and awful dress. Brad, a "typical man," does not see what is the matter with her, but then neither does his gaze tell her she looks desirable. When Deborah meets Rita and George (a schoolteacher) they have just finished looking at her portrait on a mantlepiece: the conversation turns on her youthful prettiness. The discussion rotates to Addie (they *have* to talk about her), but this time Deborah preempts Addie's domination of discourse; she makes her appearance, interrupts the talk. Her value as image is "worth more" in this scene than Addie's (no longer heard) voice. But this moment also shows us where the patriarchal discourse now "speaks": in Deborah's body/image "problem." Deborah, that is, speaks of the patriarchal place of woman (as image, she halts the narrative for a moment, makes us look at her). But she also speaks incessantly about the impossibility of being that image. She disrupts its "good-object" status, shows us her paradox: she is actually *not* that image but an ungainly, obvious, subjectivity trying/failing to be it.

This excessive subjectivity expresses itself in a number of ways throughout the flashback: her actions (she continues to drink like a fish, spills things, etc.), her speech (her voice slurs, she mispronounces the last name that is [not] her own, she says the wrong things), and, in a highly marked moment, her vision. In an emphatically "subjective" to-and-fro camera movement that blurs to mime her dizzy difficulty as she tries to dance with Brad, the film's style departs from its usual "realist" objectivism and allies itself with Deborah alone.[91] Subjectivity is "localized" with/in Deborah through optical devices that Doane suggests are not only privileged in the cinema (as specific to it), but "disrupt" spatiotemporal continuity and "initiate . . . a stylized violence against a unitary image."[92] Although the narrative flow is in no way profoundly "disrupted" here, these dance-like zooms and blurs do represent a break from a "unitary image." Thus Deborah's subjectivity is strongly foregrounded as a subjectivity in trouble, a subjectivity under siege, a subjectivity blurred/distorted even within itself. (Subjected to the patriarchal, she cannot see straight.) It is a subjectivity, moreover, in competition with another subjectivity, that attributed to the seemingly invincible, ideal Addie Ross by her companions throughout the dinner.

For Addie is still "there," getting people to talk about her by sending a bottle of champagne.[93] (Deborah, not "woman enough" to command full attention, will even have to share the toast with their "absentee hostess.") Addie, aligned with the patriarchal and the "objectifying" image track here, seems to be the invisible (and Machiavellian) hand that plucks the garish flower frou-frou off Deborah's dress, exposing the gaping hole in the fabric underneath. (Just when we see Deborah *see,* we also see that she is seen/castrated.) Addie's discursive complexity still comes across in this scene: through Deborah, the subject of feminine discourse who "plays out" resistance to the patriarchal, *and* through her own "invisible presence," rendered here both through her directorial machinations and her association to offscreen space. (George whistles at the champagne, as if at an offscreen "babe"—Addie, and Deborah and Brad both rise staring into offscreen space to try to catch a glimpse of her.)

Addie Ross's fragmented moment of objectified glory

(*A Letter to Three Wives*)

In fact, when Deborah emerges from the bathroom, having humiliated herself and Brad (or so, at least, she fears), she spies Brad talking to a woman we assume is Addie. The fragmented woman *par excellence,* Addie here "is" nothing more than an alluring shoulder blade and slender arm. We "recognize" her, moreover, from her voice, as she laughs, in her unmistakably affected tone, at something Brad has apparently said. This is the only moment when Addie inhabits the screen as image in the film. Addie never comes closer to being "seen" than at this moment—and there is a marked effort here to "embody" her thus as the object of the male gaze. (As competing image, indeed, the fragmented woman "beats out" Deborah: Brad never turns his rapt gaze from Addie's shoulder to see Deborah's return.) But this effort fails before it really begins, for even in her fragmented moment of objectified glory, Addie signifies her privilege in offscreen space, her knowledge of her feminine power, in her voice-off laugh. Heard through Deborah's, our designated enunciator's, ears, this is a laugh of triumph, the laugh of the subject who has beaten out the other woman and annexed the man (who is nothing more than a dupe). But Addie's laugh also tells us that her subjectivity chooses self-objectification as its weapon. Not only does Addie's body conform perfectly to the fragmented fetish, her laugh reflects an abdication of speech and refracts Brad's subjectivity back to him. Our powerful voice-off plays to/with his ego. She not only laughs at what he says, but she says nothing herself. Interestingly, her voice, the laugh, speaks "like" an image—but *articulates* her silence, her silencing of herself. And so the vertiginous paradox created by two discourses continues indefatigably—Addie's laugh representing her will-to-power and her will-to-powerlessness, the ideal of femininity that patriarchy demands Deborah to embody (and which she cannot), a powerful evocation of feminine desire and subjectivity that castrates and is castrated. Similarly, the establishment of her character as a "mystery," a source of powerful mythology, both alludes to an elusive subjectivity that cannot be limited and named, and that is simultaneously and ceaselessly "objectified" though the others' obsessive naming. The men deem her "a class act," having "the natural equipment of good taste," saying she's "generous to a fault," while the women echo, "to a fault, that's Addie," comparing her to a well-trussed car and pointing out her glaring lack (no husband).

Listening to Static: Estranging Discourse

"Rita's" flashback, in the second spiral of the film, is triggered by Deborah, who reminds her friend helpfully of George's "strange" behavior that morning. Rita loses herself in thought, and a voice in her head asks, "Why didn't George go fishing? Why was George wearing the blue suit?" The blurring of whose voice-off this is—Addie's? Deborah's? Rita's?—is pronounced. It sounds like all three, vaguely. This indistinct voice is rendered bizarre, moreover, by its subjection to a soft, trumpet-like musical echo. It sounds like a distorted refraction of a voice rather than a voice pronounced directly, an impression aggravated by its lower tone overall and its loss of elocutionary distinctness. On one hand, then, Addie's voice-off seems more distant here; she is less powerful than before, less subjectively present (we cannot even tell if this is her voice ringing in Rita's head). On the other hand, Addie may be said to be more deeply internalized than before, for recognition is a form of distanciation, and differentiation. Moreover, the voice-off here *represents its own function* all the more clearly through this mutation: as a less "pure" signifier of Addie per se, it makes for a "purer" signifier of Addie as contradiction. One can read this voice, for example, as the patriarchal discourse hinting at the particular nature of Rita's "crime" against George (which revolves around his preference for classical records over radiophonic reproduction).[94] In this sense, the voice-off, too, still bears the stamp of Addie, who remembers George's birthday, which Rita has forgotten, in her preoccupation with a "pretentious" dinner party meant to impress her boss. Addie's gift this time is a record of classical music (a rare Brahms, very "classy"). The bugle sound, that is, foreshadows the dispute to follow, paves the way for the record that will cause marital discord. But one can also see the feminine discourse expressing itself in this scene, in the emphasis of the uncanny "strangeness" of the voice, its distortion, its inhabiting of Rita's thoughts like a foreign body. This voice is both Rita's and alien to her. The implication is strong, moreover, that the women are, in a sense, infecting one another with their own fear. Addie infects Deborah, who infects Rita, who will infect Lora Mae.[95] As feminine discourse, the voice-off speaks of women's self-subjugation, and the contagion of a discourse that pits them against each other instead of bringing them into solidarity.

Radio is the interference in the marriage between Rita and George. Her writing, her production of discourse, puts her on the side of power (monetary and enunciatory) as *her* speech is disseminated and the language

George represents (traditional literature, etc.) has been disempowered by popular culture's embrace of the banal.[96] (We do not really know what Rita writes, though, only that her boss keeps "murdering her brain children.") Rita, however, actively expresses her desire to continue writing, and her sense of satisfaction at earning money is clear. George professes to be supportive of his wife's new power, but the change in their roles causes ceaseless friction between them. At the climax of a heated argument between them, he shouts, "I want my wife back!"

The film's "response" to George's complaint arrives with Addie's gift, and a handwritten note attached to it. Addie's voice-off reads (over George's ecstatic face): "If music be the food of love—play on! Addie." For the first time since the triggering of Deborah's flashback, some twenty minutes earlier in the film, we hear our old friend's voice clear as a bell, back in the driver's seat. Again, her enunciative prerogative is marked on both the image and the sound track, and again she marshals a staging of a "problem" for the film to play out: marital discord for the Phippses. Both the present she sends (notably, a present of "good" sound as opposed to Rita's "trashy" radio) and the suspicion she provokes (for Rita and for the spectator) jeopardize the precarious stability of their marriage. For Mrs. Manly breaks the precious disk, "radio" again symbolically ruining a good thing. Addie's note speaks of "love," a word of seduction, suggesting to Rita and to us that she may have designs on George. Addie's discourse here again functions as a patriarchal "reminder" to Rita (to remember George, to put him first, to be "womanly").[97] But Addie also represents Rita's assumption of discourse and all the "love stories" she writes, in that her production of a discourse of love is not convincing. Addie, as we know her from the film, has nothing to do with "love": the note she writes is yet another bid for *power* over a man. So, too, is Rita's writing equally cynical, an emblem of her power. Addie's voice thus condenses the discursive contradiction between Rita and George, a struggle for the power of speech. It is a struggle in process, persistent (they are "not speaking" at the beginning of the film). When Rita brings up Addie as part of the problem, and George yells, "Let's try to keep Addie out of this," the two currents are clear. Rita knows that Addie (discourse) is the root of the problem, for Addie represents *Rita's own desire*—a discursive power. George even complains that the influence of the discourse she has taken up (its "drooling pap") has changed her from the "independent woman . . . who once thought the same thing about everything" as he does. And as George puts it, he does not want a female subject in the conversation or in the house: he wants a *wife,* an object.

The Voice behind the Curtain: Uncovering the Sound of the "Machine"

The third spiral flashback "belongs" to Lora Mae and is marshaled into play by the "troublemaking" discursive power that has relayed from Addie to Deborah and now on to Rita. Rita finds Lora Mae in the locker room: she is the only one of the three women who thus far has "resisted" Addie's voice and remained active all day—hiking, playing softball, etc. Just as Deborah needles Rita earlier, planting doubts and fears in her mind about George, now Rita works on Lora Mae, suggesting that now that Hollingsway is a corporate "giant," he might go looking for some of that "class" he's always admired in Addie Ross. But Lora Mae continues to "resist" the patriarchal message sifted down from Addie's voice-off–*off,* declaring defiantly that she has "got everything she wants." Rita, who "sees through" Lora Mae's bravado, warns her friend, "I think you're just as worried as the rest of us" (a strange phraseology that seems to include many more women than just Rita and Deborah). When Rita leaves, Lora Mae's offhand air ruffles visibly in response to the distraction of a sound—a noise that has been sublimi-nally present from the beginning of the scene but is brought up in the mix at this moment. We do not know yet what the sound is either, but it has a rhythmical, pattering, echoey tonality suggestive of water or tapping. The effect of the sound over her worried face is to highlight her isolation and to suggest that what she normally "blots out" becomes manifest to her consciousness in this moment of quiet solitude. In this way, the discrep-ancy becomes obvious (via the acoustic distraction) between what she says and what she really feels/thinks. Responding to her (and our) curios-ity, the camera tilts down just past her body to reveal the source: water is dripping noisily from a leaky pipe under a faucet into a metal pail.

Rick Altman has noted the "tendency to move the camera to a sound, to point it at the area from which the sound is coming," and suggests that the impulse in cinema to "locate" the source of the sound derives from the "question" that sound poses. He claims, quoting Robert Bresson, that "sound always evokes an image; an image never evokes a sound."[98] He further contends that the "source" the image track provides is always a *lie* (sound and image, lying together about their unity, conceal their source[lessness]). But, in contrast to this assumption that the pan to the source of the sound responds to an effort to efface "the truth" of hetero-geneity, the result of the camera movement and the tracing of sound's "source" in this scene rather opens up and reveals "the lie," and the dif-

Lora Mae "hears herself hearing."

"Maybe you haven't got everything that you wanted after all."

(*A Letter to Three Wives*)

ficulty of locating an *origin* (not just to sound, but to discourse, and to ideology).

Cutting back from the faucet to a tighter shot of Lora Mae's face, we see her expression grow increasingly grave, as if she is only now fully "internalizing" the threat behind Rita's words. At this moment, Addie's voice-off emerges, but again somewhat indistinctly, suggesting (like a hypnotist), "Maybe you haven't got everything you wanted after all."[99] Reverse shot to the pail, from Lora Mae's point of view, with an added "subjective" impetus: the camera dollies in to the dripping water. Simultaneously, the sound of the water begins to metamorphose Addie's voice, rendering it "through" the echoey sound of the pail. Within seconds, very little, if any, vestige of "human-ness" remains in the strange chanting/dripping voice-off here, and even less "female-ness."[100] Rather, like a robot mechanically repeating his master's command, the voice-off here implies simultaneously that it comes from "within" Lora Mae's mind, *and* that this voice is not her own.

Thus, as this scene progresses, the "question" of *source* becomes quite complex. Lora Mae (and the spectator), having pinpointed the source of the dripping, seems to identify it next as the source of another sound that "follows," Addie's voice. (The water comes first and Addie's voice seems to emerge in response to what it suggests.) She thus identifies the "origin" of Addie's voice "in" the dripping water, only to next perceive that the voice and the drops are "one" in a machine-like distortion. She seems, that is, to be casting about for the source of the *question the sound raises,* rather than the actual sound, for clearly Addie's voice does not "come from" the faucet. Rather, it was always already there—she just did not pay attention to it before. In this sense, Lora Mae's sudden awareness of the dripping also underscores the listening subject's own funneling of sounds in "real life," where he or she pays attention to only those sounds that seem "important." In a film, as Alan Williams has pointed out, such discretionary, focusing tasks are taken up by the recordist, mixer, director, etc.[101] Still the idea is represented: this character suddenly perceives "background" noise as foregrounded sound. The film works moreover to emphasize her and our recognition of this transition in value as a shift in consciousness. Lora Mae, that is, "hears herself hearing." This moment suggests her recognition that the sound/question involves distortion and mediation, two processes brought out by the crazy effects placed on the sound/voice and the represented idea that the voice in her head emerges *under pressure,* much like water leaks from this unreliable pipe. It is Addie's voice—but also *not* "Addie's," in that now its patriarchal tenor is rendered obvious: part "male," part "machine," part "nature," this is the voice of Ideology, which subliminally encourages her to doubt herself.

This is a moment, perhaps, when *histoire* grows quiet, in which *discours*'s whisper can be "heard" more clearly.[102] The "strangeness" of this voice keeps it at a remove from Lora Mae's subjectivity. That is, though this voice is clearly "in Lora Mae's head," we hear that it is alien to her, strangely Other. When it addresses her as "you," it enounces a certain separation rather than suggesting that she is "talking to herself." At the same time, the voice opens onto Lora Mae's subjectivity in interesting ways. It speaks directly of and to Lora Mae's desire, implying that she is *not* satisfied, that she does *not* have "everything," that she *wants more.* It in fact encourages her to desire, to stir up and trouble the marriage contract she has finessed, to make a demand. In this respect, it differs markedly from the voices-off that lead into Rita's and Deborah's flashbacks, which speak much more directly to internalized anxiety about the loss of their mate to a rival. Lora Mae's "anxiety" here reaches far beyond Hollingsway; in fact, in another contrast to the other voice-off flashbacks, her husband's name is not even mentioned. We do not, as yet, know "what" she wants; for the "problem" is not enounced in terms of a plaguing question about her husband's "secret" subjectivity. If Lora Mae has a problem, it has to do with her own dissatisfaction, rather than her husband's. The implication arises that Hollingsway has not given her what *she* wants. Indeed, though the contrary "message" also comes through (she'll lose her husband because he does not know she loves him), the film strongly suggests here that it is Hollingsway who may lose Lora Mae. The "responsibility" for Addie's interference (in her role of patriarchal marriage counselor) in this case rests on the male subject's failure to please, rather than the woman's. Lora Mae's "story" thus becomes privileged in the narrative in a number of ways; not only is she the most superficially "resistant" to Addie, but her subjectivity is foregrounded as a problem the film will explore. Her subjectivity, her desire, and her contentment in marriage, this time, are at issue, rather than the man's. In fact, this voice sets up and leads into the longest flashback of the film, wherein Lora Mae's desires are traced, culminating in her calculated seduction of Hollingsway.

The Demanding Body: Routing the Image

We already know a great deal about this couple from the other flashbacks, in which salient features of their unhappy marriage emerge. Lora Mae and Hollingsway have communication problems: they disparage each other openly, and they particularly try to control or criticize each other's speech. Hollingsway, for example, repeatedly tells Lora Mae to "shut up" (she ignores him), and Lora Mae routinely dismisses whatever he says as the unreliable excesses of a drunk (he ignores her). In this final "example" of marriage, then, the story takes us beyond the pale of Deborah's emergent recognition of disappointment marring her idealistic dream, and Rita's more jaundiced, but still chastened, efforts to break the mold of traditional sex roles. Here is no pretense of romantic love, no ideological illusion to soften the reality of a sexual and social contract that both parties accept for their own, apparently cynical, reasons. Here too is the emergence of a discourse that equates frank speech with "truth," only to later recast such "truth" as a distortion that keeps the couple from harmonious communication.

Lora Mae, a working class girl, lives literally "on the wrong side of the tracks" (as emphasized by the locomotive that rolls by and shakes the crummy apartment she shares with her bingo-playing mom and shrill sister). Hollingsway, her boss, is represented as higher class by virtue of income (which is why she wants to land him). But, importantly, the social distance between them collapses because of the similarity of the way they speak. Both use the direct, straight-shooting type of language associated with "lower class" standing in the cinema, in contrast to both other couples. Thus, their "common language" stresses, despite their constant bickering, a good fit. But the trouble between them also relates to their speech: they are too frank, too direct. They do not know how to lie convincingly enough to believe the lies themselves, how to use the language where the man proposes and the woman pretends not to demand a proposal in return. Unlike the more stable couples in the film, these two know their marriage is based on a "lie" that is too much the truth to sustain within bourgeois marital self-representation: Hollingsway and Lora Mae have struck a bargain.

Lora Mae tells him early on that she has "definite ideas" (no sex without the price tag—marriage). Later, spying Addie's picture in a silver frame on Hollingsway's piano, she lets him know that's "where" she wants to be. A stereotyped commitment-phobe, Hollingsway won't bite, but she traps him, using her body as bait, "playing" the woman in the photograph, the ideal object of desire. Not only does she exploit her sexual power self-consciously, she manipulates him very obviously, manipulation being the point of her actions in the film—and the spectator is alerted to her finesse in controlling the signs of corporeal and imagistic seduction.

There is a strong argument to be made in this film for performative resistance against her own specularity, as Lora Mae "pretends" to be an unconscious object of the gaze, tearing her stocking so as to lift her leg up for Hollingsway to view, assuming the facial "inscrutability" of a pouting

Lora Mae flaunts her body.

(*A Letter to Three Wives*)

model as she waits "helplessly" for him to light her cigarette, arranging her cleavage for him to inadvertently spy, etc. But despite her success in ultimately lassoing Hollingsway, in a sense, Lora Mae renders "the image of woman" too well, too aggressively to be "contained" in the silver frame she claims to want to inhabit. For one thing, she uses not only her image but also her body, her "sexiness"—and the explicit weight of her body keeps her from attaining the abstraction that Addie symbolizes here. Lora Mae, that is, fails as miserably as Deborah does to "be" Addie Ross, but in Lora Mae's case the failure comes from a too parodic and *self-conscious* simulation of the ideal, that, refracted as a mirror image to the male subject's gaze, "ruins" the artlessness of (his) desire. She will not let Hollingsway retain an illusory image of her; rather, she "shows off" her object status at every turn. Lora Mae "fails" because her subjectivity expresses itself as she works to lure the male eye, because *she* has control over her body and her "sexiness" rather than the man; moreover, she *flaunts* her control. Thus, whereas earlier Addie's voice-off laugh gives Brad center stage, stroking his ego but without letting him in on the secret, Lora Mae's imitations of the "self-effacing" woman fall flat: Hollingsway *knows* she's snowing him. Likewise, when she feigns "ladylike" behavior out of keeping with her class upbringing and natural disposition (most noticeably in an affected tone of *voice*), she seeks not to "be like Addie" or the upper class (as Deborah and Rita did) but to control Hollingsway, to make him treat her with respect, and to *make* him desire her. Like Addie, then, Lora Mae is something of a director here, an actor/director who uses her body as her "instrument," "representing" herself as a desirable woman and dictating the man's desire.

This "weightedness" of Lora Mae's image is truly fascinating for the complex discursivity it introduces into the film. It is almost a given in feminist analyses of film to interpret excessive embodiment as a sign of a woman's objectification: Lora Mae, however, in deploying her body through this film, *resists* the objectification that Addie Ross (on one level) represents. Lora Mae's body is her weapon here (and not, perhaps, a surprising weapon for a woman seeking to determine her own destiny within a patriarchal system). As body, then, and as image, within this flashback, Lora Mae successfully "routs" Addie Ross, the idealized absent One, overpowering the attractive abstraction of the photo on the piano, edging Addie out of Hollingsway's life with her more concrete, more powerful sexual bait.[103] Lora Mae also nudges Addie out of the narrative itself. Addie, in her "patriarchal" function as perfect image/ideal–absent woman operates only feebly in this flashback overall: though she is discussed by Hollingsway and Lora Mae at various points, they do not argue "about" her, as the other couples do.[104] She comes up only to have Lora Mae "distract" Hollingsway away from her. In the restaurant, where Addie supposedly is offscreen somewhere, Lora Mae easily brings the conversation and the gaze back to her by asking for a cigarette. (This discursive realignment, centering the problem of desire back onto her despite Addie's offscreen "power," is even noticed by Hollingsway. In fashion typical of this atypical couple, he acknowledges that Lora Mae is smart, underscoring once again their mutual recognition of her discursive power. Her distraction here thus differs markedly from the diversion of the gaze that Deborah poses earlier to Addie's picture, in that Lora Mae's is calculated, not coincidental.) Later, looking at Addie's portrait on the piano (we see it only from behind), Lora Mae again displaces the offscreen abstract image by virtue of her concrete physicality. That is, Hollingsway is not attracted to the photograph, but to Lora Mae—obviously so, by virtue of his disappointment when she again rebuffs his advances. But, like Deborah and Rita, Lora Mae here is also *caught up* by the "idea" that Addie represents—this time, not just an ideal appealing to a man, but an ideal appealing to *her,* expressed here as "being in a frame." Naturally, there is an effort on the part of patriarchal discourse to get Hollingsway and Lora Mae married, to get Lora Mae to wish to be the idealized safe (and bodiless) woman "owned" by the man (an object decorating his home/piano). But once again, "Addie" is a contradictory discourse: whereas the photograph speaks of the male subject's fixation on an absent, ideal woman, it speaks simultaneously of the woman's desire to have power, independence, and entitlement, "to be in a silver frame on her *own* piano in her *own* house."

She desires thus *not* to be "like" Addie, since Addie's photograph, for one thing, is not on Addie's own piano in Addie's own house. (If she desires to be anyone, it would seem she desires to be Deborah, who does preside on her own piano in a framed photograph.) In fact, Lora Mae's desire here is remarkably discursive. She demands—and the demand is what Hollingsway objects to (he has been married before, after all). Addie (the photograph), on the contrary, has not demanded anything, is "content" to let her image reign ("like a queen") in his living room for a year. Lora Mae's insistent kiss after delivering Hollingsway her ultimatum, then, is the "price tag" he speaks of later; he can "own" her and get such kisses for free, if he will cede to her demand. Thus Hollingsway joins George as something of a kept man, for he does give in, capitulate, acknowledge that the woman runs the show. His proposal, singularly unromantic, signals his discursive struggle with her here. Saying, "You win, I'll marry you," he admits defeat. In a shot of the back of her head that can only be described as Godardian, we wait for Lora Mae's response: as she turns, so does the power dynamic. For in getting "what she wanted," Lora Mae does not "get what she wanted after all": him *wanting* to marry her, rather than merely consenting. Lora Mae wants to be the subject, to make demands, but she also wants the "romantic" privilege of a cherished object. Their discursive tango continues: with the next line, Hollingsway makes a new bid for power, re-representing her control as his: "You've made a good deal, Lora Mae." Thus, where the image has failed to objectify her, her own desire, misfiring, turns her into a piece of merchandise. The flip side, of course, is that if Lora Mae has made a "deal," so has Hollingsway—she's bought him. They seal their transaction with a kiss, but the problem of their marriage, unlike the others', needs no further explication through the elaboration of a specific quarrel.

Discursive Lessons: The Diva's Empowerment

Only Lora Mae's flashback "returns" to the present without benefit of voice-off "accompaniment," again marking her as different in some way from the other wives. Their interior "defense" completed, the three women return home to learn their fate. George is waiting for Rita, who, as noted before, now volunteers to assert herself to Mrs. Manley, in accord with her husband's preferences. Significantly, however, she does not give up her job, just refuses to work on the weekend. As cinematic capitulations to patriarchy go, Rita's seems tolerable; she retains her discursive potential, even if she does now sit in her husband's lap. Deborah, however, returns home to find a message left by a "lady" for Brad. A closeup of the note shows feminine writing, and Addie's voice-off murmurs in Deborah's ear, "Mrs. Bishop's husband called to say, he is very sorry. He will not be home tonight."[105] The resurgence of Addie's voice here reminds us of her special "rapport" with Deborah, whose internal thoughts sound like the woman she envies/desires. That she hears Addie's voice-off this way, unencumbered by the machine-like distortions that make the voice's patriarchal agenda more explicit, tells us that where the other wives recognize, to an extent, the insidious "otherness" of Addie's discourse, Deborah still has a long way to go. Still, the *spectator* recognizes this voice as contradictory, as both Addie's and Deborah's voice-off. In fact, the voice-off here acts as a red herring, encouraging us to think Brad has indeed run off with the ubiquitous Other Woman. Addie is back on the side of the director, but this time, instead of telling us how to interpret the image and involving us in snobbish complicity, she tricks us.

When the film makes full circle and returns us to another country club dance, the discursive work of the narrative gels. A contradictory discourse reigns here, speaking both of patriarchy's fantasy of compliant women who "wake up" to save the institution of marriage just in time, and also of the fantasies and fears of women positioned as subjects within the story. Rita, as we have seen, has compromised to save her marriage, but so has her husband. This couple now again represents the stable "median" of the middle class, used to bearing both contradiction and compromise. Rita, moreover, "emulates" Addie here, when, coming off the dance floor, she reprises Addie's voice-off laugh to stroke her husband's ego. As with all imitations of Addie's discursive power, this one cuts both ways: as a sign of the internalization of a patriarchal lesson on "how to be a good wife," and as a sign of cynical and self-reflexive representation of self-objectification designed to placate a male (who is none the wiser and misreads himself as the subject).

Lora Mae and Hollingsway have, on the other hand, reached a crisis point. Their marriage seems threatened, not from without, but from within, because of their inability to declare "love" rather than "war." Oddly enough, the wealthiest couple in the group—and simultaneously the most "working class"—Lora Mae and Hollingsway have not yet made the transition from practicality to romance that patriarchy's view of marriage would seem to demand. As they straddle two classes, they also straddle two views of sex roles. The film implies that they must now finally choose both class alliance and the ideology that goes with it. Hollingsway's "confession" to Deborah sets the wheels in motion. But the final solution requires Lora Mae to redefine her desire, to articulate that when she said she wanted marriage, she really wanted the man. (Coincidentally, this redefinition allows for a collapse between the marriage and the man, which previously were marked as distinct, and radically so.) But this compromise, significantly, only comes about through a highly charged moment wherein Lora Mae's subjectivity is called upon to pronounce itself. Hollingsway, after admitting that he was the one who "ran away with Addie Ross," lets her know she now has all the power; she can fleece him if she wants. Lora Mae responds by telling him, "I stopped listening. Because if you said something, I just didn't hear it." Consistent with this couple, the problem turns on discourse—and also on the nature of the "truth." In this moment, Lora Mae embraces dissimulation, something she has formerly rendered problematic, either by dissimulating too "obviously" or by refusing to play the game the usual way. She thus falls in line with the other wives (lying to keep the man, to keep the peace; "pretending" in order to sustain the fiction of a happy marriage). But she also refigures herself as a listening subject, one who can choose what to hear and what to block out. Paradoxically, she has the last word and uses it to position herself as a subject who cannot/will not hear (the truth). She relinquishes, moreover, the power she has held throughout the film: the power of to extract a price, a sacrifice rendered in the service of a discourse of give and take, wherein "love is a compromise." Lora Mae's subjective choice may be said to be "directed" at placating women with unfaithful husbands, women in rocky marriages, women who feel unloved "for themselves." However, her gesture here, and her vocal declaration of her desire, also articulates a possibility of realigning (this) marriage as something beyond the social contract that has resulted in their mutual objectification and entrapment, refiguring it as a freely willed interdependence. For in this moment, Lora Mae finally gets what she says she really wants earlier in the film—not marriage per se, but a man who "wants to marry her more than anything in the world." Her desire to be desired finally "comes true" only when she admits to her own desire—when she accepts the burden of subjectivity. Where earlier, her subjectivity "expressed itself" through her miming of feminine objectification, in this scene, she enounces the riskier project of declaring reciprocity.

The most dramatic transformation, however, involves Deborah, who, as opposed to the "first" dance, now curbs her excesses (no martinis), behaves like a "lady," dresses perfectly, bears her husband's absence with stoicism. Within the span of the film, Deborah has "learned" to conduct herself according to the internalized standard of Addie Ross with graceful good taste. She's grown up—more independent—questioning George's paternalistic suggestion that she not attend the party without her husband. Deborah has also learned to speak, thanks to Addie. In the wake of the narrative, we now understand that she identifies no longer with her husband, or with herself as "wife," but with Addie: the absence of Brad in this scene underscores her affiliation with the unmarried "independent" voice-off (whose dress, coincidentally, she wears). She speaks of Brad, moreover, as if he were dead, referring to him as "the body under the table": for all narrative purposes, indeed, he has been cast out, buried. His absence foregrounds and perhaps abets her new discursive confidence. For once, Deborah seems whole. Where earlier she only speaks to please and tries to efface herself (failing), she now talks bluntly, expressing her annoyance when George tries to get her to medicate her bad mood with champagne. She even fires a crack at his pretentious use of language, and later, when he tries to interrupt her, ignores him altogether. Moreover, she takes it upon herself to finish "Addie's" work here, mediating between Lora Mae and Hollingsway. Sitting alone with Hollingsway, she sneers at his self-pitying attitude, mocking him openly. Whereas in the opening of the film, Hollingsway is the (somewhat dubious) voice of knowledge, telling Deborah about Brad's relationship with Addie, this time Deborah gives Hollingsway a piece of her mind, pointing out his stupidity to him (in not knowing Lora Mae loves him).[106] She also, against the advice of the others, blurts out the "truth" about Brad and Addie to Hollingsway: as she does so her enunciatory position is heavily underscored. Over the protestations of her friends, she insists on speaking, declaring, "I want to say it out loud." The film cuts to a close up, and Deborah shifts her eyeline deliberately and slowly to look straight in the camera—and then she says, with diva-like melodrama, "My husband's run away with Addie Ross."[107]

In this marked appeal to the spectator, Deborah's alignment with Addie and all other Absent Ones is clear: she articulates not only her discursive subjectivity, but designates that what she says carries beyond the diegetic space into a social space. In this social sense, Deborah speaks to "all the women out there," the postwar spectators who may also be struggling with the specter of Addie Ross, as signifier of the contradictory discursive position of the woman in patriarchy.[108] Important, too, is that Deborah is "wrong": the truth is that she only *imagines* her husband to be with Addie Ross or to prefer Addie to Deborah. This fantasy seems suggested by the film as both something of a nightmare for women (an anxiety that patriarchy fosters to keep them in line) and a secret thrill (in that Addie also represents a woman's discursive power). (Given how well she takes Brad's absence, leads one to wonder, in fact, if the fantasy of freedom from the husband is not another discourse circulating here.) Deborah's announcement, made to the audience as well as to the diegetic circle her friends make here, acknowledges her identification with Addie, her sense of being a subject, speaking aloud what is taboo. It also heralds the sense in which she has been "chosen"—*she,* after all, is thereby held up, "exposed" as the secret, all-important rival, Addie's real object of desire (we know Addie's appetite for their husbands betrays her envy of the women and hence her desire to be like *them*). Deborah, in fact, seems to be enjoying her moment of despair. After her dramatic announcement, she rises, imploring theatrically, "Please, nobody get up," as if they might rise to their feet and applaud. Deborah's pain here provides an opportunity for her to perform, to express her suffering, and to relish the centrality that tragedy bestows upon her character. Although she is relieved of her burden by Hollingsway, who confesses to the crime (and thereby gets the accolades Deborah half expected), Deborah's discursive position in this film has nonetheless undergone a remarkable renaissance. Whereas the others are (to an extent) realigned with matrimony, she finishes the film without the requisite textual confirmation of reconciliation with Brad, leaving the others to dance while she walks happily off alone, returning to offscreen space, Addie's domain.

Circulating, Effervescent Excess: The Up-ending of Closure

Indeed, Addie makes one final "appearance" in the film. Hollingsway and Lora Mae rise to dance with each other, signaling the rebirth of their courtship. A lilting "cha cha cha" picks up on the sound track, and the camera tilts down and moves in to their now-empty table, coming to rest on a champagne goblet. The goblet tips, suspended at an angle for a moment before toppling over and breaking audibly. Addie's voice-off emerges, like the mistress of ceremonies, her tone cheerful, philosophical: "Heigh ho!

Good night, everybody." Whereas Karen Hollinger sees this final remark as expressing Addie's "disdain for the three wives and their dedication to their marriages," this is surely the least openly contemptuous remark "Addie" has made in the course of the film.[109] In fact, Addie's words here operate quite ambiguously (one can well imagine what the snide "husband stealer" *might* have said about the turn of events). We can interpret this enigmatic finish a number of ways. It restores Addie to omniscience (she is realigned with the spectator in privileged communication) and to supernatural power (the glass seems felled by her invisible hand).[110] Of course, her farewell (to "everybody") cannot but implicate the audience offscreen as well as her diegetic "friends": thus in the last moments she wrests authorial credit for the story that has played out. Above all, this odd moment, this seemingly gratuitous flourish of voice-off, reminds us that Addie is "there," watching, but also telling. Retroactively, it seems she must have always "known" that the story would end this way, since she is telling it. Addie, that is, knows that within such a story (a narrative with sympathetic female characters made in 1940s Hollywood), she must be foiled: the happy ending had to happen (just as the spectator knows/knew all along.) Thus the toppled goblet reminds not only of her power, but of her excess. She "authors" this story, but she is also its "trouble," the spilled champagne, the broken glass that triggers a narrative. She is the woman "outside" representation about whom film speaks with pleasure and fascination. The glass topples, and, one senses, her "work" is done, she can move on to other films. Addie's desire, which opens the film, here refuses to "end" it, adamantly rejecting closure on a certain level, reminding of her excess. Her tenacious repossession of discursive power in these final frames also re-articulates the discursive contradiction that drives this narrative over all. The contradiction, however, should not be understood as simply a difference posed by irony in the voice-off that presents "Addie's detached independence" as opposed to a second "female perspective . . . of the devoted wives."[111] Rather, even within Addie's voice-off, discursive contradiction surfaces, pointing simultaneously to a patriarchal agenda to keep women in line, to inspire their recognition of the price they will pay for producing discourse and expressing subjective desire, *while also* speaking clearly and forcefully of those same taboo desires, powers, and subjective expression. The female voice-off in this film points obviously to how discursive contradiction "works" within representational forms produced under patriarchy, to express conflicting truths, paradoxical subjectivities, sustained differences. Such contradiction does not con-

fine itself to films bearing female voice-off but, rather, may be more vigorously foregrounded there for us to perceive. In these films, such contradiction is often "the problem" the narrative seeks to speak, and in speaking,
enounces and affirms. Thus, as Hollinger suggests, the spectator's identification "is split" in a wavering between patriarchy and feminism that
opens up for the female spectator "the space of a reading," because films
with voice-off lead "to a recognition of the social problems underlying
[the] contradictions . . . inherent in [the] roles" (of female characters in
the woman's film).[112] Hollinger's points are well-taken, though perhaps
overly cautious. I see no reason, for example, why a male spectator could
not "read" the film as the female spectator does. The work of the voice-off
does more than "prevent absolute closure around what might appear . . .
an entirely regressive social message."[113] Rather, the discursive contradiction is pervasive and expresses different discourses simultaneously,
speaking of both male and female subjectivity within the contradictory
discursive field that is patriarchy.

Charged with dynamic contradiction, reversals, and paradoxes, and shut-
tling between "embodiment" and "disembodiment" relative to and within
the diegesis, then, the voice-off in this film exhibits a remarkable discursive
mobility and fluidity, as do the voices-off in *Letter from an Unknown Woman*
and *Secret beyond the Door,* as we have seen. The problem of speech, of
feminine discourse, is raised by the female voice-off visibly, but not to be
"identified" with it as the sole bearer of feminine subjectivity (if safely
"detached" from the corrupting influence of a female body). Rather, the
female voice-off floats and transforms, displays the heterogeneity inherent to the voice and to discourse itself. The subjectivity brought up by
the female voice-off cannot be contained even within that voice—hence
the many permutations of voice-off, and explications of subjectivity that
emerge within the rhetorical relationship of sound to image that such a
voice inspires. The flashback structure in this film, rather than folding in
and containing the feminine, "anchoring" it to image, instead problematizes
the contradiction of voice to image in figuring subjectivity and enunciation. As we have seen, it is even possible for a female character "with" a
body to speak her desire more powerfully than the voice-off. The question of whether Addie's most powerfully subjective moments of enunciative expression occur when she is most "authoritatively" disembodied or
structured as "outside" the diegesis, in fact, remains a lively issue. In a
film wherein female subjectivity has so much at stake, perhaps, the clear-
est evocations of female desire and subjectivity come at moments where

the distant authoritative "side" of the voice-off is rendered problematic, exposed as something "other." We cannot conflate enunciation with ideology, that is, and if we seek to understand how women speak, and how their subjectivity is rendered, the heterogeneous flux the female voice-off seems to represent in films bearing this discursive trope offers an audible testimony to speaking difference.

epilogue:
passionate blindness

I make a distinction between an alienating notion of otherness (the Other of man, the Other of the West) and an empowering notion of difference. As long as Difference is not *given* to us, the coast is clear. . . . In a way, a feminist always has at least two gestures at the same time: that of pointing insistently to difference, and that of unsettling every definition of woman arrived at. As a Zen saying goes, "Never take the finger pointing to the moon for the moon itself."

   Trinh T. Minh-Ha, *Framer Framed*

Björk's Selma, in Lars von Trier's *Dancer in the Dark* (2000), is a contemporary melodramatic heroine—a woman who cannot see, but whose voice carries her to an ecstatic inner realm. In the film, Selma is trapped within a patriarchal system that exploits her as a laborer and misjudges her as a criminal (as it has no access to the logic that drives her actions). Taking cues from the musical genre, *Dancer* carves out a metaphysical zone of communication with the viewer through the heightened subjectivity Selma expresses in her passionate singing. It is interesting that these vocal eruptions of Selma's internal consciousness are not introduced until a good thirty minutes of the film have passed. In fact, much of the narrative work up to this point involves establishing Selma's encroaching blindness—and effecting a spectatorial relationship with her that progressively detaches her character, so to speak, from the gaze. This detachment results both in disempowering her (she cannot see, she is vulnerable to the gaze of others) and in dislodging her from the "trap" of vision within the cinematic syntax. Selma seems to float in a space parallel to other characters, her eyes turned inward, her focus on another plane, and her figure posing a riddle to an image that does not serve to represent her. This parallel strata within which Selma's character dwells is underscored by numerous techniques in the film: the handheld style, as rendered in digital video, for example, has an effect of keeping vision off-kilter, stressing a pixilated, fragmented, and unstable vision, making us share a blurry capture of the world. Depth of field is severely racked to create a shallow, and indeed, extremely unstable range of focus within nearly every shot of the film. In short, the image itself is under siege in *Dancer*, emerging as a register where the denizen of sight, the camera, cannot quite grasp what is "there."

The characterization of Selma also contributes to the establishment of her "difference," her inhabitation of some other realm. An odd mix of woman and child, an asexual sprite, a holy fool, a saint, a daydreaming naïf happily at play in her own world, she is regarded with a mix of awe and exasperation by the other characters, who cannot follow her wherever it is she "goes." Indeed, initially, neither can the viewer, though we are told over and over in the first third of the film that she daydreams, a habit that is our first sign of impending peril for this character. In fact, it leads to her distraction at the factory where she works. In these early scenes, Selma constantly seems on the verge of some horrible physical accident. When she is finally injured (during the first song/dance sequence daydream), we realize that the portent of physical peril was a ruse, a narrative strategy to establish a general anxiety for her person. All that happens is a cut finger. Of course, this wound is also the first step toward her eventual execution (and the first narrative event to depict the callousness of the "system" toward someone who is, in the words of the trial lawyer, "handicapped"; whether Selma's handicap is blindness or lack of control over her internality is an interesting question raised by the film).

It is not until Selma sings that we see "inside" her. Coincidentally, she does not sing until her sight has finally completely failed her. Her voice opens onto another realm of perception, which we understand to be triggered by the loss of her outward gaze, and by the creative invocation of an internal vision she summons into acoustic space—a vision that has little to do with *sight*. If elsewhere, in films celebrating the offscreen voice, "blind images," gaps in the image track, represent the internal feminine gaze, here we see into the blindness, grasp what it "looks like." Thus, the musical scenes function as windows into the invisible world of Selma's consciousness.

The sudden eruption of the interior landscape of Selma's mind represents a register of sound, and particularly, of voice that only Selma (and the viewer) can access. A privileged communication, this fantasy serves to link our perception to Selma's, and to establish the limitations imposed by the external vision that rules the consciousness of the other characters. Though the other characters participate in the dancing and singing, they do not seem to perceive what they are doing. This is not their fantasy. They are "directed" by Selma/Björk, doing and saying the things that she would prefer to be real. When the numbers conclude, these characters seem untouched by the experience, while Selma is profoundly affected, as are we. These sequences, moreover, contradict the "image" of Selma that reigns in the rest of the film. Visually, they are shot and timed for a highly saturated color, and they contrast vividly with the drab grays and browns of Selma's "real" world. This is a passionate environment, altered by Selma's subjective perception. Within these scenes, too, Selma, takes on a different persona—the center of attention, a diva with a majestic (rather than "funny") voice. She performs a range of intense and compelling emotions, expresses her sexuality as her body responds pleasurably to the sound she is producing, and projects a sophistication, intelligence, and energy that drains from her elsewhere in the film. The eroticism expressed by Selma in these scenes, however, seems remarkably transgender and is certainly not a response to her delight in her own body (as when Gilda dances). Rather, here, the body, like the mind, is turned inward in pleasure—it vibrates to the voice rather than responding to a sexualized gaze.

In one sense, the musical scenes convey Selma's fantasy that she is *Björk*—drab reality is merely a fatal mistake, and the unassuming factory worker is "really" a charismatic pop superstar. Another repercussion of these sequences is to establish a narrative and discursive paradox to the grim and relentless melodrama that conducts Selma's guttersnipe persona to the gallows. Indeed, there is even a generic conflict here established between the conventions of the musical and those of the melodrama. The film itself continually references musicals and the lyrical escapism of song and dance in the movies. Yet, the use of the voice in *Dancer* might be described as overwhelmingly in the service of pathos, as befits the melodramatic plot per se. In this sense, the film has much more in common with the narrative weight and sublime musical effect of opera than with the slight, silvery worlds inhabited by Fred Astaire, or concocted by Busby Berkeley.

These sequences give access to Selma's ecstatic being, her libidinal self, her desire, her erotic self-image. They cut across the film's more "objective" portrait of her as a timid, closeted wretch, and show the breadth and depth, instead, of a secretly vast experience of life. Suddenly, Selma is a subject, empowered and freed from the alienating objectification that is her working-class persona. Like the lovers in *The Enchanted Cottage*, her "real" inner world, inaccessible to "external" vision, confers a subjective "truth" upon her figure and renders her person as what she *feels* rather than what she *is*—inaugurating an idea of perception as spiritual, rather than biological. The fact that Selma does not need her glasses within these sequences points out the aphysical nature of the vision in sway here—without them, we know, she cannot see—at least not what is physically there. To see what is not visible, that is, glasses are superfluous.

The effect of these sequences is to change how we view Selma in the more linear story from which these sequences spiral. We now "know" that she is never (only/ever) experiencing what we see in the "exterior" world that so abuses her (she is not "there" in the image but drifting in a paradise of sound from which we are temporarily excluded). The image is exposed as lacking, barring access to the internality the voice has opened onto. The singing scenes also inaugurate the vital contradictions that now define her character: she is thereafter weak and powerful, wretched and glorious, trapped and free. She comes, via the sublime refraction of her song, to embody paradox. It is the voicing of her desire within these sequences that alters her character and opens her onto this lively contradiction, which, indeed, comes to fruition in this film as an essential challenge to being that can only be resolved on a spiritual (rather than a physical) level, as we shall see. Selma becomes what her voice expresses about her, metamorphosing into the powerful tragic diva latent in her songs.

These sequences, though coded as fantasy in their referencing of musical film conventions, simultaneously emerge as more "real," in a sense, than the scenes meant to signify "reality" as such within the film—for the musical numbers respond to an extratexual demand for Björk to perform. Björk's voice is the space of cinematic desire here, a desire that arguably works counter to any fetishization of her image. While Björk's body is cloaked under drab, frowsy dresses, and her gaze and that of the viewer are blocked by the impassive, refractive opacity of her lowered lids, her

The asynchronous voice: Selma/Björk as rhapsodic diva

The synchronous voice: Selma in prison

(*Dancer in the Dark*)

voice opens onto freely circulating eros. Moments of digression from the narrative, only apparently structurally "static," these musical sequences in fact drive the pleasure-seeking motor of this particular text. The pop star's legendary incantatory wails float out of the character Selma's mouth, producing an acoustic rhapsody for which her fans, at least, have been waiting. In this sense, the paradox of Björk herself inhabits these scenes—and the voice of the star is heard separate from, yet also within, that of the character.

The "difference" then, heard in this particular voice, creates a gap between performer and character as both are represented by the imaginary acoustic figure on screen. There is a strong work on the part of this narrative, moreover, to close this gap, to join these voices, to attach Björk's voice to Selma's body, to identify it as Selma's, rather than as belonging to the extra-diegetic pop star. This progressive apparent unification of the two vocal bodies takes place as a movement from asynchronicity to synchronicity. The early musical sequences, that is, where Selma sings in the factory and again on the train tracks, follow an MTV practice of post-synchronization of her singing. The voice is almost a voice-off, "dubbed" over the images to appear in synch, laid over the cuts for an illusory impression of continuity and smoothness. Such a voice, again, brings us nearer to Björk and to her persona as star and performer, separating us, subtly, from Selma's character at the very moment in which her internality finally sounds. This performance is not stressed as a rendition sung by Selma (as it would be more clearly if sung in sync by the "character" on the set, surrounded by the acoustics of diegetic space). Moreover, as we know, other characters in the diegetic space cannot hear her. In fact, like most forms of voice-off, this voice is directed largely at the viewer, the privileged recipient of the song. The very voice that carries the subjectivity of Selma to us, thus, simultaneously invokes our sense of her split, of her disconnection from the "real" of the film text, and reminds us of who she "really" is—Björk, singing what Selma feels.

Once Selma has been imprisoned, this "distance" between the voice of Selma and that of Björk narrows. In her cell, Selma sings a rendition of "Raindrops on Roses," mournfully crooning next to the ventilator shaft, where hymnal strains from the chapel have brought the requisite inspirational rhythms to her ear. This scene, unlike the preceding songs, is not post-dubbed but rather is pieced together from Björk's improvisational synch performance. As such, edits between shots are more noticeable, and vocal phrasing has a halting, wavering, tortured tonality. Only the faintest musical accompaniment breathes under Björk's voice here, as opposed to the sweeping, cathartic strains that swell in other scenes. The effect of this new "synch" status to the voice (reprised in the final "next to the last" execution song) is to solidify the apparent unification of star with character, of Björk to Selma. The "gap" between them closes, as does the gap between voice and body, as the voice is formally "yoked" to the image. In this she is a good example of a voice that has been "pinned" to a body, after initially enjoying asynchronous freedom. And while a degree of "claustral constraint" is indeed implied (even fairly overtly by the plot of the film itself), this subtle metamorphosis simultaneously conveys an enhanced expression of Selma's internality. On one hand, Selma's physical imprisonment is stressed—she suffers a loss of imaginary mobility enhanced by the limitation, now, of sound to screen space. But with this physical constraint a greater metaphysical, or spiritual, freedom seems accessed by the character. In these scenes, finally, Selma "really" sings— the voice she possesses, and which possesses her, is no longer a fantasy, but her own. Strapped to the board in the hanging room, Selma now also has an "audience" (albeit a grim one) in the witnesses who have come to watch her die, but who first will hear her sing. Finally, her voice affects others—they stare at her in wonder at the sound she produces, and the kindly prison guard turns her head in a sympathy of emotion on hearing Selma's tones. Thus, in this final "pinning" of Björk's voice to Selma's body, Selma finds her greatest subjective power—moving others as she has been moved, expressing an internality that has been locked inside her for the bulk of the film, traversing her otherness to find solace in the passion her voice creates. That Selma's redemption comes at the price of her life, and indeed, of her voice (she is silenced by patriarchy—a fact that is underscored by the stripping of the sound track once she is hanged) does not alter the power of her subjective expression. Like Lisa in *Letter from an Unknown Woman*, her scripted fate is determined by social reality. Yet her voice speaks here of a transcendent ascension within which her suffering becomes publicly recognized, becomes a form of art. Indeed, this silence is the "other side" of the voice, rendering it in its very absence as a profound reminder of the paradoxes that surface across the textual field of this film. The heterogeneous consciousness between Björk/Selma and the viewer is sustained, a feminine subjectivity expressed, and a feminist discourse articulated, alongside the more obvious patriarchal forms and meanings also structured into this film, as we have seen in the other films discussed in this book.

Reading *Dancer in the Dark* metaphorically, we can define difference, in the cinema at least, as an ecstatic divide created, traversed, and culminated in the female voice. This film, which cannot be tied to a feminist author, and which bears a contradictory ideology, nonetheless allows for an evocation of a transcendent subjectivity associated to the female protagonist. The filmmaker, Lars von Trier, indeed may not have even intended such subjectivity to emerge. While von Trier's film is clearly absorbed with the question of female voice, this is not to say that it is a self-consciously feminist film. I will not extrapolate at length on the film's patriarchal "side" (a harsh condemnation of Selma's naïveté and passivity), which is not difficult to perceive. In this way, *Dancer* provides a contemporary corollary to the other texts discussed in this book: strong contradictions are at work within it, and patriarchal underpinnings move in active paradox to an evocation of feminine subjectivity. Still further, the expression of such a transcendent subjectivity is due precisely to these powerful paradoxes created and sustained by the foregrounding of the female voice within the film. The female voice has a pronounced relationship to asynchronous, heterogeneous signification and it establishes tension to the objectification posed by the image. It brings forward representations of internality, consciousness, and vortexicality in opposition to contrary discursive modes. This book offers a method for approaching such difference, a method that I hope will serve to open up new debate in feminist studies of film generally, and, more specifically, about the potential for films to represent or communicate difference in positive, rather than negative, terms.

Within these pages, a number of criticisms have been brought forward in regard to canonical texts in the field of cinema studies. My intent, in reexamining these vastly influential works, is in no way to dismiss their undeniable contribution to both film studies and feminist film theory, but to suggest that, unfortunately, the very seeming invincibility of some of these writings may have led us to prematurely consider the "case closed" on some particularly thorny issues. A number of problems need now to be explored in new directions, to be reconceptualized, the relationships between them rethought, and the ideological assumptions that underlie them reconsidered. In particular, my charge, while writing this volume, was to consider whether feminine subjectivity can be expressed in the classical Hollywood cinema despite the objectifying force of the image. A strong legacy within the field implies that such representation is muffled at best: a deep pessimism rules the bulk of work that has been conducted in this arena. In this respect, I suggest, feminists writing about film may have painted themselves into a theoretical corner. An intimidating edifice of assumptions has been constructed regarding the nature of subjectivity itself, the primacy of the image over sound in representational weight in cinema, the importance of causality and linearity over stasis and circularity within narrative, the "external" place from which enunciation and discursive authority emerge, the inviolate dominance of patriarchal ideology, etc. Studies of voice, and particularly female voice (to which many minds were turned in the late 1980s and early 1990s, along with sound generally, as a potential arena within which a feminist critique of the image might emerge), have functioned to bolster this edifice, rather than to question it or overturn it. The result, in fact, has been a retreat from feminist theory in film studies in general—for where is the pleasure in reminding oneself of the futility of one's work, in repeating a depressing analysis, within a new context, perhaps, of a process of repression and objectification that has been "proven" a million times over, and which forces the female writer into an absurd position in which she must acknowledge she is not a subject?

My goal, in writing this book, then, was in part to counter this stultifying system of assumptions with a more open structure, one that might allow for alternative interpretations of a number of these vital, and fundamental theoretical questions. To the question of subjectivity, I have offered an alternate reading of psychoanalytic texts that account for the workings of voice and consciousness in allowing for the sustaining, rather than the foreclosing, of feminine (or other) difference. Critiquing the hierarchy implicit between image and sound tracks in determining cinematic representation, this book extends important work on sound done by Rick Altman and others into the specific terrain of the voice-off and its effects. Questioning narratological work that identifies causality and linearity as progressive textual features promoting access to character subjectivity, I have looked to the constructive force of vertical narrative movement, temporal spirals, digressions, and inward circling repetition as symptoms of a vortexical, paradoxical advance, wherein contradictions construct and evoke a simultaneous perception of the complex spatialities and temporalities of narrative. Finally, this book suggests that contradictory, plural discourses can be expressed simultaneously within representational forms produced in patriarchy.

This book also seeks to reopen the door onto the study of sound, and of the voice in particular, by feminists and others concerned with understanding the representation of women in film. Within this manuscript, I locate the female voice-off as a particularly powerful formal feature that provokes an awareness of heterogeneous consciousness, plural point of view, and discursive paradox within a number of classical texts that might seem, due to their mode of production, authorship, and conventional form, unlikely to promote or sustain difference. However, the voice is only one aspect of the sound track that, as others have pointed out before me, is excessively complex, has been sorely misrepresented in much film theory, deserves the same kind of ardent detachment that has spawned so many important reflections on the functioning of the image of film, and is ripe for further theoretical and critical exploration along many avenues.

The methodology adopted in this book, moreover, by providing close textual analysis of the films discussed, is likewise motivated by a sense that the merits of this approach to analysis have been prematurely rejected, with the advent of cultural studies and its valuable contribution to film theory. The method illustrated within these pages is intended to emphasize the importance of a sustained examination of the fabric of any cinematic text. In this temporal medium the progressive structuration of meaning(s) across the text need to be carefully observed in all their relations.

This book, in short, tries to "unsettle" the definitions that have become "self-evident" within the field, while at the same time, as Trinh T. Minh-Ha puts it, "pointing insistently to difference."[1] As a woman both writing about film and making films, the desire to find a space within which difference could empower rather than paralyze me catalyzed the theories that I have offered here. Difference can be understood as a forcible voicing of contradiction, as heterogeneity sustained as consciousness, as perspectival plurality, as an affirmation of discursive antilogy. Viewed as a dynamic, difference can be said to be both represented and sustained within even classical film texts, which most feminist film theory has written off, pointing to mechanisms of fetishization, objectification, repression, and misogyny that foreclose feminine otherness. This fundamental dialectic of image to sound needs to be reassessed by film theory. The female voice-off in cinema, in particular, articulates and exacerbates our awareness of the constructive force of difference. It opens perception onto a space of positive paradox, within which contrary meanings are recognized simultaneously, and in relation to which subjectivity itself can be understood outside traditional models which center an ideal of male transcendent vision. As such, the voice-off offers us a way of reconceiving difference itself and allows us, indeed, to reassess the place of the feminine in film.

notes

Prologue

1. Bordwell et al. have argued that, relatively speaking, the "crisis" sound posed was minimal—as little as a two-year period of representational upheaval. *Classical Hollywood,* 301–8. Certainly by 1935 the formal importance of sound in film would seem securely entrenched—for by this date "the supervising dubbing mixer attained about equal rank with the editor of the picture" in the postproduction hierarchy. Stewart, "Evolution of Cinematic Sound," 49.

2. Amy Lawrence refers here to films from the early sound era—the class of films frequently referred to as "hybrids." *Echo and Narcissus,* 71.

3. Altman, "Four and a Half," 37.

4. Renov's *Hollywood's Wartime Woman* and Doane's *The Desire to Desire* are two excellent explorations of the historical conjunction of wartime propaganda and women's films. Whereas Doane is interested in the rise of consumer culture and its impact in brainwashing women into identification with popular-culture imagery, Renov links the Hollywood machine to that of the War Office, in examining the repercussions of the war on both real and represented women.

5. Houseman, *Unfinished Business,* 286; Berstein, *Walter Wanger,* 210–14, 443.

6. Obviously, many films do not fit this generalization. Some films, shot on sound-stages with artificial sets and the like, might be said to bear highly contrived image tracks—eschewing the accidental details that the real offers and that so many filmmakers embrace as one source of the sublime in film. Likewise, some filmmakers abhor the artificially composed sound track. The point here, however, is simply to remind that creating a sound track requires *at least* as much deliberation as putting together the image.

7. Doane, "Voice in Cinema," 40–43; Silverman, *Acoustic Mirror,* 46–54, 58–65; Silverman, "Dis-Embodying."

8. Silverman, *Acoustic Mirror,* 186.

9. Deleuze and Guattari, *Thousand Plateaus,* 93. Emphasis in the original.

10. They refer to such constants as "pseudoconstants." Ibid., 91.

11. Ibid., 91. Emphasis added.

12. Ibid., 90. Emphasis added.

13. To clarify here—my use of the terms "feminine," "the female subject," and "women" within this text is based on the following assumptions: the feminine relates to the psychoanalytically constructed subject (usually women); the female, the biological subject; and women, historical subjects. There is still the problem of defining what one means by "female voice"—part of the object here, indeed, is simply to clarify and propose a tangible, useful way of conceiving this term relative to film. On a superficial level, and in order to facilitate a means for entering into a discussion of such complex issues at all, the notion of the female voice will be thought of as generally the voice one assumes is produced by a female, but also one that relates to the feminine subject (as in how the feminine speaks through the female) as well as to women (for speech is always political).

14. Mulvey, "Visual Pleasure," 6–18.

15. Turk, "Deriding the Voice," 105.

16. Altman's "Sound Space" (46–64) traces the representational legacy of radio, phonography, theater, and public address as representational systems upon which evolving sound cinema "leaned" while developing its own "new form of representation." Lawrence is particularly interested in the ideological imprint of the history of phonography, in which she sees a bias *against* the female voice that marks it as a troubling signifier in the nascent sound film. Lawrence, *Echo and Narcissus,* 11–34. Lastra looks to silent cinema itself as the discursive system that provides the *codes* by which sound represents itself in film. Lastra, "Reading, Writing," 79–84.

17. Altman, "Four and a Half," 35–37.

18. See Metz, *Imaginary Signifier.*

19. Metz, "Aural Objects," 27–29.

20. Rick Altman's work (especially "Material Heterogeneity," 15–31) offers rich inspiration for thinking about the complex dimensionality and materiality of sound. The voice-off embodies a similar "material heterogeneity," while bearing other unique characteristics not necessarily applicable to all sound.

21. Copjec, *Read My Desire*, 17–19.

22. Silverman, *Acoustic Mirror*, 47–48.

23. A number of films from this period that bear little or no voice-off offer some interesting parallels to these films. They highlight women's speech or feminine discourse through other pronounced means, such as the obsessive production of and (re)reading of letters in *All This and Heaven Too*. Amy Lawrence (in *Echo and Narcissus*, 109–46) has analyzed this same tension with regard to a condition of muteness contrasted with hyperverbosity (*The Spiral Staircase*) and obsessive telephoning (*Sorry, Wrong Number*).

24. The work of both Kozloff and Smoodin, heavily influenced by the narratological theory of Gérard Genette, bears vestiges of this tendency. See Kozloff, *Invisible Storytellers,* and Smoodin, *Voice-over: A Study.*

25. Altman, "Four and a Half," 39. Emphasis added.

26. Silverman, *Acoustic Mirror,* 42–71.

Chapter 1: A Metapsychology of the Voice-off

1. Lacan, *Four Fundamental,* 102.

2. Ibid., 84. Emphasis added.

3. Ibid., 84–85.

4. Ibid., 75. Emphasis added.

5. Ibid., 195. Emphasis in the original.

6. Barthes, *Pleasure of the Text,* 66.

7. Metz, "Aural Objects," 24–27.

8. The word "uncanny" is often deployed in descriptions of voice (and voice-off) in cinema, and indeed is apt. "Unheimlich," according Freud, designates opposite meanings simultaneously. The "strange" and the "familiar" co-signify in this word as though they were one: the "uncanny" is paradoxical. Freud, "The 'Uncanny,'" 122–61.

9. Rosolato, *Le Relation d'Inconnu,* 42, 51. My translation.

10. Ibid., 51. My translation; emphasis added.

11. White, "Writing in the Middle," 185. White discusses the middle voice in this essay specifically with an eye to its literary applications. White also notes that, for Barthes, "writing in the middle voice is a perfect example of a . . . 'performative' . . . 'speech act'": voice-off seems another obvious instance of a "performed speech act." Ibid., 187. Martin Jay, in the essay "Experience Without," 146, exploring the "middle voice" as understood by Walter Benjamin, similarly notes Benjamin's tracing of this voice to traditions of oral storytelling.

12. Freud, "Instincts," 125. Emphasis in the original.

13. Jay, "Experience Without," 147.

14. See Baudry, "Ideological Effects"; Metz, *Imaginary Signifier;* Mulvey, "Visual Pleasure" and "Afterthoughts"; De Lauretis, *Alice Doesn't;* and Doane, "Film and the Masquerade."

15. Baudry, "Ideological Effects," 289. Emphasis added.

16. Ibid., 292.

17. Baudry points out the importance of visual precocity in the child after birth. But the child has already been hearing for quite some time. Thus, "auditory precocity" must be at least as powerful, if not more so, than the visual capabilities of the child even as it is born. Ibid., 294.

18. Ibid., 295.

19. Branigan has pointed out the slipperiness of this term, which has transmogrified in film theory from a role of an "object" that records reality to a metaphor for primary identification, and finally, to "a reading hypothesis about space." "What Is a Camera," 97. Interestingly, no such all-encompassing mechanical metaphor exists for the producing apparatus of sound. We never talk, for example, about the "mike" as if it were the sound track or, alternately, the listener's "ear."

20. Williams leans on Baudry's *other* famous essay, in which he draws an analogy between cinema and Plato's allegory of the cave. In this essay, Baudry does touch on sound to assert both that it is "more real" than the image ("reproduced and not copied") and, in a point Williams leaves dangling, that it *introduces ambiguity.* This ambiguity would seem to be at cross-purposes with much of Williams's critique of Baudry. It is, however, very much in line with my own reading of the voice as raising contradictions to the image, rendering its meaning unstable in important ways. Baudry, "Apparatus," 110; Williams, "Is Sound Recording," 51–66.

21. For a fascinating overview of the evolution of the debate on whether sound is "perfectly reproduced," suffers no ontological distortion, or has only a "partial," "distorted . . . correspondence to the original event," see Lastra's "Reading, Writing," 65–66.

22. See, for example, McClary's *Feminine Endings,* which explores the structuring representation of sexual difference in music. The groundbreaking work of Altman and Lastra brings the "point of audition" of the subject into relief. See Altman, "Sound Space," and Lastra, "Reading, Writing."

23. Williams acknowledges moreover in his essay that "for the purposes of simplicity, I am assuming a recording made with only one microphone." Williams's argument depends, unfortunately, on a premise that severely misrepresents the standard practices of sound recording technology in film, limiting its usefulness. Williams, "Is Sound Recording," 53.

24. Ibid., 53.

25. Altman has pointed out the importance of considering the role of *reverberation* in appreciating sound dimension. See Altman, "Material Heterogeneity," 24, 27–28.

26. Though many technicians in the early 1930s apparently resisted this multiplicity, which they felt created a "monster spectator" with "five or six very long ears, said ears extending in various directions," it evolved into common practice by the late 1930s. Today, mixing between different mikes frequently occurs during the original recording of sound as well. See Altman, "Sound Space," 49.

27. He goes on to remind that because of these particular characteristics, "*no* microphone produces an entirely faithful sound record." Altman, "Material Heterogeneity," 26.

28. Experimental films, of course, blur these distinctions—often with the express purpose of disrupting the codes of transcendent spectatorship critiqued in these pages. There are also moments in many classical films in which we do perceive more than one image angle at a time—notably, superimpositions and dissolves. In fact, these decentering visual pluralities mark an intriguing correlation in the image to the contradictions posed by sound. They operate in ways similar to the female voice-off in creating a consciousness of difference for/in the spectator.

29. Altman, "Sound Space," and Lastra, "Reading, Writing." Both these articles are fascinating and complicated, and I cannot completely do them justice here. Lastra's article leans heavily on Tom Levin's "The Acoustic Dimension." Levin extends Williams's demonstration that sound is a representation rather than a reproduction. He argues (among other things) that sound is always transformed by the technology that reproduces it. We can never hear, that is, the sound as it was in the original space. It only seems the same to us because of "a socially constructed auditory practice that emphasizes the similarity of such sounds in order that they can be understood . . . by the hearer." Levin, "Acoustic Dimension," 62.

30. Altman, "Material Heterogeneity," 19.

31. As Metz defines it, "identifying with one's look is . . . *primary cinematic identification,*" implying (by default) that "identification with one's hearing" is not primary (and possibly not cinematic). Even secondary identification (identifying with characters) in his schema is linked to vision—through point-of-view shots, for example. Metz, *Imaginary Signifier,* 56. Emphasis in the original.

32. Ibid., 60.

33. Lacan, *Four Fundamental,* 118.

34. Rosolato, "Les hallucinations acoustico-verbales," 280. My translation.

35. Ibid., 280. My translation.

36. Ibid., 277–78. My translation.

37. Both Lacan and Rosolato stress this side to the acoustic register, remind-

ing that (in the field of the unconscious) "the ears are the only orifice that cannot be closed." Lacan, *Four Fundamental,* 195.

38. Metz, *Imaginary Signifier,* 51.

39. Rosolato, "Les hallucinations acoustico-verbales," 276. My translation.

40. Lastra, "Reading, Writing," 83. Lastra here is quoting Tom Levin in making this point. See Levin, "Acoustic Dimension."

41. Lastra, "Reading, Writing," 84. Emphasis added.

42. Ibid., 85.

43. Ibid., 86. Lastra here quotes Stanley Cavell from Cavell, *The World Viewed.*

44. Ibid., 84.

45. Ibid., 85.

46. Metz, *Imaginary Signifier,* 73.

47. Ibid., 73–74. This description is striking, in that it speculates about a very specific semantic and/or discursive function of (a very specific use of) voice-off, rather than offering a metapsychological metaphor on the nature of the auditor's relationship to sound or voice, à la the bulk of *The Imaginary Signifier.*

48. Ibid., 73.

49. Doane, "Voice in the Cinema," 34.

50. Ibid., 34. The evolution Doane sees here toward increasing acceptance of the asynchronous signifier is at odds with Amy Lawrence's view that early hybrid cinema allowed for breaks in classical style that progressively became subsumed as conventions solidified. Lawrence, *Echo and Narcissus,* 32, 71.

51. Doane, "Voice in the Cinema," 35.

52. Ibid., 40.

53. These benshi-like commentators, in turn, represent a continuation of the ballad-singer who toured rural festivals and "declaimed in a singsong manner" a story implied by a series of paintings. Another link on this evolutionary chain is the lantern-slide lecturer whose narrative coincided with the projection of often hundreds of photographs. Berg, "Human Voice," 167–68. Norman King mentions also that the live voice-over "lecturer" tradition was alive and well in French Provence "as recently as 1981." King, "Sound of Silents," 3.

54. Berg, "Human Voice," 166–67, 173–74. Berg quotes from Ernest Lindgren, *The Art of the Film,* 137.

55. Tom Levin underscores this dialectic when he claims that "[t]he history of the development of cinema sound can . . . be read as an oscillation between its difference understood as supplement and its difference understood as threat." Levin, "Acoustic Dimension," 63.

56. Levin, "Acoustic Dimension," 60. Levin here is citing Manvell and Hunty, *Technique of Film Music,* 20–22.

57. Belton, "Technology and Aesthetics," 66. Levin's work also points to the

pleasurable affect of the sound/image dialectic. He cites Adorno and Eisler in postulating that the acoustic register's "spatial dimension" contributes to the *aura* ("A-effect") that simultaneously brings out the *difference* between sound and image. Fascinatingly, Adorno and Eisler were most interested in sound in that they felt it "foregrounds the *mediated* character of the visual register"— they understood the "acoustic supplement [as potentially] threaten[ing] to discredit and even displace the visual domain it was meant to support and strengthen!" Levin, "Acoustic Dimension," 63; emphasis in the original. See Adorno and Eisler, *Komposition für den Film*.

58. Doane, "Ideology and Practice," 55–56.

59. Ibid., and Doane, "The Voice in the Cinema."

60. Doane, "The Voice in the Cinema," 40.

61. The advisability of locking discourse to representational form in the way Doane does here, in fact, seems questionable. She herself acknowledges that these "two radically different modes of knowing (emotion and intellection)" cannot always be attributed to the sound track and image track, respectively. I would propose that such "different modes of knowing" produce meaning between them that "belongs" to neither. Doane, "Ideology and Practice," 56.

62. Doane, "Voice in the Cinema," 41. Doane's translation; emphasis in the original. Here Doane is citing Bonitzer, "Les silences de la voix," 25.

63. Doane, "Voice in the Cinema," 41. Doane's translation.

64. Ibid., 40. Emphasis in the original.

65. Ibid., 44.

66. Rosolato, *Relation d'Inconnu*, 37. Emphasis in the original.

67. Ibid., 37. Emphasis in the original.

68. Doane, "Voice in the Cinema," 48–49.

69. Ibid., 49.

70. Rosolato, *Relation d'Inconnu*, 34. My translation; emphasis added.

71. Doane, "Voice in the Cinema," 50.

72. Haraway has pointed out that in taxidermy, the adult male version of the species and its characteristics stand in for the species itself. The female is simply assumed to be a variant of the male "perfect expression" of the species. Haraway, *Primate Visions*, 41.

73. Silverman's revaluation of the visible signifier of feminine difference as not *in itself* lacking (rather representing a repository where masculine lack can be worked through) suggests that the sex of the viewer/spectator may indeed bias or determine the *reading* of the *image* (and, in this scenario, not "being" the lack, the female spectator may indeed perceive her specular counterpart differently than a male spectator).

74. See Silverman, *Acoustic Mirror*, 119–26. Silverman "replaces" the pre-Oedipal "chora" postulated by Kristeva as the time of desire between the little girl and the mother with this Oedipal moment she links to the entry into lan-

guage. In fact, Silverman suggests, there are *two* Oedipal crises/desires—one negative and one positive—between which the female is destined to oscillate. Silverman suggests that these two desires "cancel each other out," calling them "irreconcilable." She stresses that "desire for the mother can never be anything but a contradiction" (Ibid., 123). Since I see contradiction as a site of flex, of positive paradox, I am inclined to view this description of female desire as refreshingly reversible and fluid, allowing for difference even in the self, rather than self-annulling.

75. Ibid., 123.

76. Ibid., 124.

77. Ibid., 41.

78. Ibid., 41.

79. Ibid., 32.

80. Ibid., 49–50, 72. Silverman quotes Chion, *La Voix,* 57. It is true that Chion appears to be far less *conscious* of the implications rendered by his poetic ruminations and drastic metaphors than is Silverman. Silverman, however, points out the negative thrust of his vocabulary only to posit it as, on some level, appropriate to the kinds of films he is discussing—an accurate rendering of the state of things in "Hollywood." However, in this respect Chion is much more "democratic" than Silverman is—fairly impervious to historicity or genre in his analyses, he flits from classical cinema to Duras to Mizoguchi and back again in painting his absolutist portrait of "the voice." Thus whereas Chion rather randomly mobilizes both this image of "umbilical night" and its opposite "fantasy" (the soothing maternal voice that wraps the subject in a "sonorous envelope" drawn by Rosolato) relative to both classical and "alternative" cinema, Silverman erects a wall between Hollywood and feminist filmmaking, implying that in one, female voice-off works one way; in another, it works quite differently. In this sense, she seems overly dismissive of one cinema and idealistic about the other. Thus, despite Chion's less than rigorous historiographic approach, he seems more in touch with the workings of individual films. See Chion, *La Voix.*

81. Silverman, *Acoustic Mirror,* 50.

82. Ibid., 67. Silverman's suggestion that "Hollywood draws . . . upon the paradigm of female sexuality championed by . . . [Ernest] Jones [which equates] woman's voice with her vagina" leads to her conclusion that via these sites "subjectivity is introduced into her." Ibid., 67. Silverman never explains what kind of subjectivity this might be.

83. Ibid., 186.

84. Ibid., 50, 53–54.

85. Ibid., 25, 49.

86. Ibid., 54.

87. Ibid., 48–49.

88. Ibid., 39.

89. This is something I am sure Silverman does not mean to suggest. Indeed, she concurs entirely with Bellour's tracing of the relayed gaze via Sean Connery's character to Hitchcock and back to the spectator in *Marnie* as a typical, if flamboyant, process of phallic identification. Ibid., 203–4. See Bellour's "Hitchcock, the Enunciator."

90. Silverman, *Acoustic Mirror,* 24. Silverman stakes her claim that Hollywood "plays more than a reproductive role in the construction of sexual difference" on what she calls the increasing "specularization of woman" coincident with its appearance in the history of Western forms of representation. She notes a concomitant "despecularization" of the male. How this theory fits with obvious fetishizations of the male body in films, she does not elaborate.

91. As remarked earlier, the uncanny can be read as an experience of paradox. If the male subject recognizes himself in female sexuality, we may, along with Silverman, claim that this is a recognition of "woman's otherness ... [that] impinges dangerously upon male subjectivity." We may, however, also see this as a sign of the ambiguous basis of sexual difference, and as an experience in which difference is sustained as itself. Freud's insistence that "unheimlich" *simultaneously* renders the familiar and the strange suggests a (subliminal) recognition on the part of the subject that difference is what he or she *is.* Ibid., 17.

92. Ibid., 39.

93. Silverman notes, too, that *Peeping Tom* is aberrant within the classical system, unpleasurable in many ways. Her reading of the film, which looks only to ways in which the film structures masculine subjectivity, is only half the story. She hints that the female spectator is someone in conflict, struggling to understand herself via this ricochet of violent male desire, positing the character of Helen as a model for this condition (as well as, intriguingly, a mirror of Silverman's own position as theorist). Ibid., 41.

94. Even as she implies this discursive divide, Silverman does not want to entirely forsake the possibility that the female voice-off offers *special* resistance to the image—that through it particularly the woman can be heard or addressed. Though she criticizes Irigaray's "essentialism," she celebrates ways in which the voice as such contributes to the collapse of limits and boundaries in feminist films, echoing Irigaray's vocabulary of blurred inner and outer spaces, fluidity, permeability, multiplicity within the self. Ibid., 183.

95. Ibid., 33.

96. Silverman, "Disembodying," 134.

97. Ibid., 136.

98. Silverman, *Acoustic Mirror,* 166–67.

99. Silverman's notion of "disembodiment," it should be noted, relies heavily on Doane's article, "Voice in the Cinema." Doane's definition of the dis-

embodied voice is of a voice-over, as in those voices never "placed" relative to a body, as is often used in conventional documentaries. Such a voice, "radically other," outside space and time, and "beyond criticism . . . censors the questions 'Who is speaking?' 'Where?' 'In what time?' and 'For whom?'" Doane points out that the model on which she bases these observations of the properties of the disembodied voice is more or less *male*. Doane, "Voice in the Cinema," 42.

100. Silverman, "Disembodying," 137.

101. At the limit, she seems to share Peter Gidal's suspicion of the image, and to hold that the image itself always renders Woman a fetishized other. See Gidal, "Against Sexual Representation."

102. Were it so obviously taking place, the textual placement of the female spectator in a "narcissistic" position seems arguably a positive mechanism, given that her placement at all has by no means been established by Silverman as even having this definable characteristic in Hollywood cinema, since all texts ultimately "recover" the female body. The use of the word narcissistic here is clearly moral, not psychoanalytic. (Silverman's take on narcissism in *The Acoustic Mirror,* it should be noted, is much less puritanical than it is in this earlier essay.)

103. Silverman, "Disembodying," 136. Emphasis in the original. Silverman also notes here that Lisa's narration is not only "at every point anchored to a specific female body, but the temporal interval which separates it from that body constantly diminishes as the film unfolds" (Ibid., 136). She does not explain how she understands this notion of diminishing temporal interval; if my guess is correct, she means to imply that Lisa's voice comes closer to being "over" her own image as it produces the letter (her torso slumping over the candles at the end, for instance) rather than exclusively over the image of Stefan at his desk at the end of the film. Again, the stress laid on the problem of Lisa's body, which is obviously an important one to address in this film, centers on a highlighting of the "specific" female body as the one for feminists to work past, in some sense, as if a "non-specific" female body, as described in the avant-garde films that she discusses, somehow skirts the objectionable processes of fetishization and occultation. Indeed, though the specific/non-specific (or multiple) dichotomy she sets up is interesting, the way she describes the voice relative to image in these avant-garde films tends to displace the problem of the voice as such onto the visual, to reduce it to its narrative function, its status as language, and to assume that in distance from synchronization resides an "essential" resistance to the patriarchal use of the female body.

104. He may be said, in a sense, to overhear *telepathically,* through a sympathy the voice-off establishes between the two characters. In *I Walked with a Zombie,* similarly, Frances Dee's voice-off is "overheard" by Tom Conway in just this way. Conway interrupts her voice-off reverie of delight as she stands

looking at the sea to insist that the ocean (and the world) are not as beautiful as she thinks. His ability to "hear" her thoughts presages their empathetic liaison later in the film.

105. Many critics have pointed out Stefan's dubious character. See Modleski's "Time and Desire."

106. Heath, "Question Oshima," 146–48. Emphasis in the original.

107. Ibid., 150. Emphasis in the original.

108. Studlar, "Masochistic Performance," 42.

109. Although Studlar explicitly criticizes theoretical work that "'psychoanalyz(es)' characters," the bulk of this essay is, in fact, dedicated to proving how well Lisa fits this particular psychoanalytic model. Studlar aims in this to upset the doxa that holds masochism as a purely passive and painful position, demonstrating how it may be understood as representing active and pleasurable subjectivity. Ibid., 36–37.

110. Fischer, "Shot/Countershot," 109. Fischer sees Lisa as "an artist of love" whose position of suffering is ultimately denied by the film. Ibid., 95, 101.

111. Modleski, "Time and Desire," 326–32.

112. Silverman, *Acoustic Mirror,* 57–58.

113. Kaufmann, *Discourses of Desire,* 17–20.

114. White, *Cinema of Max Ophüls,* 142–43, 147.

115. Ibid., 138. Emphasis in the original.

116. Ibid., 149.

117. Branigan, *Narrative Comprehension,* 177–79.

118. Ibid., 184.

119. Ibid., 187–89. Emphasis in the original.

120. White, *Cinema of Max Ophüls,* 140. As Amy Lawrence suggests relative to a similarly vortexical flashback structure in *Sorry, Wrong Number,* "dissolves . . . imp[ly] the *connection between spaces* rather than the distance that separates . . ." Lawrence, *Echo and Narcissus,* 139. Emphasis added.

121. Even the "offscreen" voices-off of Stefan and little Stefan work in this direction—as when they both repeat the ominous words, "Two weeks . . . !" These voices cut a swath through the narrative's progression, echoing each other.

122. Branigan mentions that the courtyard scene "contains a future tense." Branigan, *Narrative Comprehension,* 189. The fact that the view of Stefan's hands, a literal "mise-en-scene" of Lisa's desire, takes place while she is daydreaming, points to the representation of the shot as her fantasy. Significantly, Lisa's fantasy is creative of the film itself and seems only marginally masochistic (if wishing to sit at someone's feet in a wash of music is the wish of a masochist). At the very least, we see here a staging of her desire that "comes true" (however briefly) and of "the making visible, present, of what isn't there, of what can never *directly* be seen" (Cowie, "Fantasia," 75; emphasis in the

original). Is the representation of Lisa's fantasied glimpse of where she will be (without seeing it when she is there) a way of figuring female desire?

123. Branigan, *Narrative Comprehension,* 190. Emphasis added.

124. Ibid., 191.

125. Jacqueline Rose discusses the problem of the visible and points out Lacan's interest in exposing the farce of the value "accrued" to the visible. She seems at a loss, however, to explain how or if Lacan suggests a means for the female to be conceptualized beyond the "masquerade" she figures, and suggests that Lacan's theory of value, like Levi-Strauss's, "presupposes the subordination which it is intended to explain." *Feminine Sexuality,* 42–45.

126. Perhaps one of the most important points of Vasse's work regards the relation between the voice and writing—both, in his view, "always betray something of the unconscious." Vasse, *L'ombilic,* 8. My translation.

127. Chion, *The Voice,* 112–14.

128. Other psychoanalytic texts, obviously, can also be scrutinized in this regard—not only original works by Lacan and Freud that Vasse and Rosolato interpolate, but theories offered by feminists like Irigaray and Kristeva. Interestingly, Slavoj Žižek has recently reinterpreted Chion's notion of the *acousmatique* itself, and "used" it to figure the "object voice." See Restivo, "Recent Approaches" 137–39.

129. Doane, "Voice in the Cinema," 35, 40.

130. Rosolato, "Relation d'Inconnu," 51. My translation.

131. Dolar, "The Object Voice," 17, 28.

132. Vasse, *L'ombilic,* 12. My translation.

133. Ibid., 14, 16, 17. My translation; emphasis in the original.

134. Ibid., 20. My translation; emphasis in the original.

135. Ibid., 183–85. This opposition of "savoir" and "lieu" is a crucial element of Vasse's theory of the voice. He later declares that "the unconscious is the instance of place (lieu) and the conscious is that of knowledge (savoir)." The unconscious has "something to do with the body and the question of its origin in the place . . . the conscious . . . elaborates a system of abstract representations, separated, outside the place, articulated in *time* . . . and *is the consequence, outside the place, of what goes on there.*" The voice, "between" these two, founds them and is constituted of them. It speaks of an impossible heterogeneity, what can be "said" and what "is" speaking (ça parle). Ibid., 194, 196. Emphasis in the original; my translation.

136. Doane, "Voice in the Cinema," 47–50.

137. Vasse, *L'ombilic,* 12. My translation.

138. Italics indicate emphasis in the original; underlining indicates added emphasis. Lacan has affirmed, moreover, that in verbal hallucinations, "the subject is immanent"—*there,* in the voice. Lacan, *Four Fundamental,* 258.

139. Lawrence's reading of Rosolato corroborates this conclusion. She

affirms, "The 'feminine' quality of the maternal voice . . . is one of the aspects projected onto it at a later stage, *after* the recognition of difference." Lawrence, *Echo and Narcissus,* 27. Emphasis in the original.

140. Music, he also reminds, in "its archaic forms [has] . . . a rapport with . . . religious themes of sacrifice." These connections may explain the powerful alignment of female voice-off and music in melodrama. Rosolato, *Essais sur le symbolique,* 296. My translation.

141. Turk further claims that "music, as contrasted with language, may remain a 'good' acoustic object." He goes on to argue that the films of Jeanette MacDonald and Nelson Eddy, where "song assume[s] primacy over dialogue . . . intimate notions of subjectivity that confound mainstream assumptions concerning sexual difference. [Their acoustic and textual operations] promote extraordinary eruptions of freely circulating, virtually *decorporealized* libido." Turk, "Deriding the Voice," 104, 109, 111. Emphasis added.

142. What Silverman terms Stefan's "willingness to read" should rather be described as a state of acoustic receptiveness, a suspension of limits that allow her voice to permeate, to fascinate, to be heard "in" the words he reads. Silverman, "Disembodied," 136.

143. The recognizability of the "star-voice" clearly comes into play here. Whereas contemporary audiences may or may not have recognized Fontaine "in" her voice here, within the *story,* she has not been revealed visually and remains anonymous. Certainly today's audience would recognize most of the famous voices in these films before seeing the actresses' faces. Here Hollywood capitalizes in an obvious way on star "visibility" even as that star is not visible. If the star's *body* is thereby perceived, that body still emerges in vocal form and is subject to the same plurality in/of space described earlier. This multiplicity may be even aggravated—as the character is also "someone else," the voice is also "someone else's"—a "star's."

144. The voice-off's implied awareness of what is going on in the image leads me to disagree with White that Lisa "is not privileged to witness the images her narrative induces." On the contrary, Lisa's voice-off seems to lovingly resurrect these images, her story, for Stefan, and to "watch" them with him in their sharing of an imaginary past. White, *Cinema of Max Ophüls,* 138.

145. Deren et al., "Poetry and the Film," 173–75, 179, 183–85.

146. Fischer sees the "intricacy" of *Letter*'s structure as symbolic of "psychic entrapment." She adds that the stasis in the film is "counterpoint[ed]" . . . by Ophüls's "formal reliance on camera movement." Thus, even on the image track, a work of contradiction is fundamental here. Fischer, *Shot/Countershot,* 107. Emphasis in original.

147. Modleski, "Time and Desire," 332, quoted in Joan Copjec, *Flavit et Dissipati Sunt, October,* 18 (Fall 1981): 21. Modleski quotes Freud as quoted in Copjec, *Flavit et Dissipati Sunt.*

148. Ibid., 332.

149. "Like desire, the love letter waits for an answer; it implicitly enjoins the other to reply, for without a reply the other's image changes, becomes *other*." Barthes, *Lover's Discourse,* 158. Emphasis in the original. In fact, Lisa gets her "reply": Stefan's mirroring of her self-sacrifice.

150. Rosolato, *Essais sur le symbolique,* 303. My translation.

151. Lacan, *Four Fundamental,* 195; Barthes, *Lover's Discourse,* 1.

152. Barthes, *Lover's Discourse,* 158. Emphasis in the original.

153. Ibid., 158. Emphasis in the original.

154. White, "Writing in the Middle," 181–87.

155. Ibid., 186.

156. Ibid., 187.

157. Ibid., 185.

158. Jay, "Experience Without," 151. Jay is technically referring here to "free indirect style," which he defines as a kind of middle voice. Ibid., 150.

159. Freud, "Instincts," 123. Cited in White, "Writing in the Middle," 183.

160. Freud, "Instincts," 125; White, "Writing in the Middle," 184 (emphasis in the original).

161. White, "Writing in the Middle," 184. Emphasis in the original.

162. See Studlar's "Masochistic Performance."

163. White, "Writing in the Middle Voice," 185.

164. Jay, "Experience Without," 155.

165. Kainz, *Paradox, Dialectic,* 27.

166. Jay, "Experience Without," 155; Branigan, *Narrative Comprehension,* 191.

167. Kainz, *Paradox, Dialectic,* 32.

168. Kainz, *Paradox, Dialectic,* 27. Emphasis added.

169. Lacan, *Four Fundamental,* 22–28, 31, 44. McGowan offers a comprehensive critique of the misreadings film theory has made of Lacan's theory, of which this "mastering gaze" is one such reduction. McGowan reminds that the gaze is also "the site of a traumatic encounter with the Real, with the utter failure of the spectator's seemingly safe distance and assumed mastery." McGowan, "Looking for the Gaze," 29.

170. Jay, "Experience Without," 151.

171. Modleski, "Time and Desire," 333.

172. Heath, "Question Oshima," 148.

173. Fischer has also noted the simultaneity of this moment and that "the film depicts Lisa enraptured with desire for Stefan [although] she conceives of herself as being desired by *him*." She sees Lisa's voice-off here as a *denial* of feminine desire, rather than an actively signifying contradiction. Fischer, *Shot/Countershot,* 100. Emphasis in the original.

174. Vasse, *Le poids du réel,* 47. My translation. The ritualistic symbolism of

the duel may then very well reflect not so much the imperative of punishing Stefan, but the relation of sacrifice to love and transcendence in representation. Rosolato also explores the relationship of art to suffering and sacrificial ritual. "Essais sur le symbolique," 184–98.

Chapter 2: Point of View and Paradox

1. Silverman, *Acoustic Mirror*, 39. Certainly, in the classical Hollywood cinema, few men scream. Even in alternative or "art" cinema, manifestations of this voice are rare, with the famous cries of Michael Lansdale in Marguerite Duras's *India Song* being one notable, provocative exception.

2. Metz, *Imaginary Signifier*, 190; Kuntzel, "Film Work," 59–61.

3. Poizat, *L'Opéra*, 133, 130. My translation. Poizat cites Lacan from Juranville, *Lacan et la philosophie*, 231.

4. Doane, for example, has expressed this view of the film. She also notes that the voice-over given the male character is "very misleading" (opening the door to further analysis). Doane, *Desire to Desire*, 150–51.

5. Nick Browne detaches of the notion of point of view from literal camera placement and prioritizes the rhetoric of narrativization. He sets out the possibility for a description of point of view that does not necessarily "belong" to a character per se, but rather reflects the spectator's grasp of perspective in an abstract sense. His model suggests, then, a means for theorizing the (simultaneously) "multiple" point of view I allude to above. Browne, "Spectator-in-the-Text," 26–38.

6. See Branigan's *Narrative Comprehension* for a rigorous model of the multiple complexities of narration, meaning, and cognition. Branigan's discussion of sound within this book, unfortunately, is much less developed than his discussion of the schematics related to and the cognition of the image.

7. This is Altman's term, a useful one to be sure, explored in more depth later in this chapter. See Altman, "Sound Space," 60–61.

8. See Burch, *Theory of Sound Practice*, 17–32.

9. Browne, "Film Form/Voice-Over," 239. Emphasis added.

10. Branigan, *Narrative Comprehension*, 170.

11. Smoodin, *Voice-over: A Study*, vi–vii. Emphasis added.

12. Telotte echoes Smoodin's vocabulary: ". . . even if a voice *disappears* after introducing or moving us into the flashback, it maintains proprietary *control* over the narrative." Telotte, *Voices in the Dark*, 41. Emphasis added.

13. Kozloff, *Invisible Storytellers*, 11–12. Kozloff cites Metz from *Film Language*, 54. In her other book, Kozloff sees a similar "feminizing" discredit applied to the level of dialogue itself. *Overhearing Film Dialog*, 13.

14. Kozloff, *Invisible Storytellers*, 11. The debate continues on whether sound is "equal" to image. Branigan suggests that "[o]f the many false statements

about sound offered by theorists, perhaps the most misleading is to say that sound and image have an equal status in film." *Narrative Comprehension,* 267. Overall, blanket demotions of either image or sound relative to the Other seem a dead end for film studies. There are films (like those of Brakhage) that work toward "pure" visuality, and others obsessed with "pure" sound (Straub/Huillet and some of Duras's films). Many silent experimental directors, of course, expressly tried to "evoke" sound through image in films like *Symphonie Diagonale* and *Rhythmus II.*

15. Lawrence has made a similar connection in her analysis of several films from the 1940s, within which she sees a "textual association of man with the image and woman with sound [that] accentuates the way cultural values associated with gender are assigned to cinema's image/sound hierarchy." Lawrence, *Echo and Narcissus,* 112.

16. Arnheim, who views sound as a demon-seed come to pollute, disable, and destroy the plastic integrity of the "silent" film, notes that speech "interferes with the expression of the image," and impoverishes this "pure" art form, turning it into "an unstable hybrid." Arnheim, "New Laocoön," 114–15.

17. Kozloff, *Invisible Storytellers,* 41, 128.

18. Ibid., 128.

19. Gledhill, "*Klute:* Part 1," 16.

20. Telotte, *Voices in the Dark,* 15.

21. See Renov, *Hollywood's Wartime Women,* and French, *On the Verge.*

22. Telotte, *Voices in the Dark,* 16.

23. Ibid., 15.

24. Branigan, *Narrative Comprehension,* 113.

25. Ibid., 98.

26. Telotte, *Voices in the Dark,* 15–16.

27. Kainz, *Paradox, Dialect,* 27.

28. Kawin, *Mindscreen,* 10.

29. This "prologue" was a sore point of contention between director Lang and the studio bigwigs at Universal-International, who felt it was both "too long" and "foolish, semi-Freudian, unrevealing nonsense." Their initial recut of the entire opening of the film to drop the prologue, the death of Celia's brother, and her trip to Mexico/honeymoon with Mark brought Lang's relationship with producer Walter Wanger to a crisis point. Bernstein, *Walter Wanger,* 213.

30. Bruce Kawin coined this term in contradistinction to the physical eye in elaborating his view of "mindscreen"—"the field of the mind's eye." He goes on to insist that the "question of voice becomes . . . the question of mind, and both are inseparable from the question of meaning." Kawin, *Mindscreen,* 7, 10, 22.

31. Lawrence, *Echo and Narcissus,* 97.

32. As Bergstrom has noted, in this sequence the film "seem[s] to indicate the keys to its interpretation." Bergstrom, *Logic of Fascination,* III-2.

33. Freud, *Interpretation of Dreams,* 564.

34. Kawin's linguistic-inspired distinctions between "first person," "second person," and "third person," though interesting, are only awkwardly transposed onto film. Kawin, "Outline of Film Voices," 40–45. In fact, Nick Browne claims that with regard to "the structural role of the voice-over," film both "continues its affinities with and proclaims its discontinuity from literature." Brown, "Film Form/Voice-Over," 233. The shifting described in this scene is very subtle, and should be understood expressly in terms of an evolving relationship between image and sound, and how, in their progression, they construct narrative space and hail the spectator.

35. Freud, *Interpretation of Dreams,* 530–31.

36. Doane, *Desire to Desire,* 108–9. Emphasis in the original.

37. Ibid., 109, 19.

38. Bellour describes this elemental relation of repetition and alternation as the "silent weave" of the (above all, classical Hollywood film) text. In this "serial structuring," he sees "the fundamental condition of textual expansion." Bellour, "Cine-Repetitions," 66, 68, 69.

39. Thinking along Deleuze-Guattarian lines, such forms, linked as they are to the female voice (and the contradictions of female experience) may be the abstract machine *devenir-femme* (becoming-woman). Of the rhizomatic text, Deleuze and Guattari note that "no entrance is more privileged [than another] even if it seems an impasse." Deleuze and Guattari, *Kafka,* xxvi, 3.

40. Heath links the distraction of the eye (in a scene in *Suspicion*) to the digressive suturing of narrative. Heath, "Narrative Space," 19–24.

41. Barthes, *S/Z,* 75. Underlining indicates emphasis added; italics indicate emphasis in the original.

42. Burch and Dana, "Propositions," 50.

43. Ibid., 50. Bergstrom has critiqued Burch and Dana's generalization in respect to the reformulation of codes she observes at work in Lang's film, noting the many reversals, doublings, and repetitions that complicate the film's structure, mise-en-scene, and significations. Bergstrom, "Logic of Fascination," III, 1–28.

44. Burch and Dana expressly point to the elaborate camera movement that links the two Hacienda scenes: in the first scene it "stands out" as excessive, in the second it makes "everything fall into place, . . ." "tie[s] the final knot" back to linearity. But this camera movement also re-inscribes the "excess" of the prologue's tracking movement, as well as those in the wedding scenes—and serves thus to collapse time, suggesting that all four movements could be taking place simultaneously, "in" Celia's mind as she swings on the ham-

mock, wondering (and wandering) in her mind about the "stranger" in her arms. Burch and Dana, "Propositions," 51.

45. White, *Cinema of Max Ophüls,* 351, note 103.

46. Lacan, *Four Fundamental,* 83–84, 182.

47. This scene bears striking similarities to Lisa's "staging" of the long-desired encounter with Stefan in *Letter from an Unknown Woman.* Lisa, too, wants to meet Stefan "on her own ground"—and she traps him, so to speak, in the scenario she knows he cannot resist. But in the case of Lisa (as opposed to the *other* women he thinks *he* traps), she is fully in control of this seduction, setting herself out to be seduced. In this sense, Lisa's ultimate entrée into Stefan's apartments does not seem the ruthlessly depressing scenario it has been painted by many critics. Where once she was a powerless, wretched voyeur on the stairs, unable to enact her desire, she now is participating in life and its risks. That we see her from the stairs underscores the fact that she knows the risks, and *we know she knows how she looks from there.*

48. Bergstrom has noted the confluence of "doubling" between Celia and Mark throughout this film, a thematic she links obliquely to Lang's Expressionist roots. Bergstrom, "Logic of Fascination," III, 21–23.

49. The symbolic workings of their speeches here are rich in suggesting a shared romantic fatalism, a fairy-tale view of love that waits for the One ("Sleeping Beauty" and her prince) as well as a (perhaps equally romantic—and Freudian) sadomasochistic configuration of sexual passion (Celia's and Mark's "real feelings" awakened by the sight of blood).

50. These remarks are partially inspired by the work of Poizat on the functioning of silence in opera. Poizat, leaning heavily on Lacan, defines a "voix-pure" as a voice that is "heard" apart from speech, a voice heard for itself. In this respect, we can associate the "voix-pure" with silence (as well, tangentially, with music). Poizat states, "[a] paradox appears perhaps to be in effect lifted when we envision the question of silence not in its opposition to sound, but in its opposition to speech." He goes on to associate silence closely with "the cry" (another form of "voix pure" in that it renders the sense-giving aspect of the voice unintelligible, incidental). Poizat, *L'Opéra,* 130. My translation. In the continuum he draws (silence and the cry on one side, speech and meaning on the other—with song mediating between), I would place female voice-off close to *song*—for its musicality, its poetry, its dynamic relation to silence and its corporeality. As Barthes notes, "we rarely listen to a voice *en soi,* in itself, we listen to what it says." In some sense, then, perhaps Celia is really listening to Mark's "voix pure." Barthes, *Grain of the Voice,* 183.

51. Poizat, *L'Opéra,* 124. As Poizat interprets Lacan, the "objet-voix is not an . . . object . . . [but] . . . a process inherent to each individual, a process by which the voice constitutes itself as object, as drive, and as an object which is marked as lost . . ." Poizat, *L'Opéra,* 142. My translation.

52. Branigan's position, that ". . . in a [deep] . . . sense, a character's glance is an important measure of the *acquisition of knowledge* by character and spectator," seems admirably demonstrated in this scene. Branigan, *Narrative Comprehension,* 53. Emphasis in the original.

53. Waldman has argued that the gothic structure of the mansion in *Secret* is a metaphor for the domestic isolation of the woman in the home. "Architectural Metaphor," 55–69.

54. Doane's brief comments on this scene merit note. Describing the voice-off here as "convey[ing] her [Celia's] thoughts . . . [to] herself," she describes the shot (somewhat inaccurately, as she states that the image of the door *follows* Celia's words, when the words actually *coincide* with the image) as "ruptur[ing] the spatial continuity of the scene . . . appear[ing] from nowhere. . . . [T]he markers of subjectivity or interiority (a dissolve, extreme close-up concentrating on the eyes, loss of focus) are absent. . . . Because [the door] is not present in the space occupied by Celia, it could not be the object of a point-of-view structure." Doane, *Desire to Desire,* 138. It is curious that Doane does not consider the voice-off a "marker of subjectivity" (especially, as she notes its representation of Celia's internal thoughts a moment earlier). Doane's reading of point of view here relies entirely on the image, discounting sound and voice. Moreover, her comments imply a strict association of point of view with immediate diegetic space.

55. Doane has suggested that "the central concern of [Celia's] investigation is the discovery of what her husband . . . keeps behind the locked door labeled 7." Only a secondary concern is "analyzing her relation with Mark." Surely, if this were true, the film's *raison d'être* would be fulfilled with the opening of the door, and the narrative would have nothing left to resolve (for a still lengthy chunk of time). Doane, *Desire to Desire,* 150.

56. Doane views the moment of unlocking the door, and "[confronting] . . . an aspect of herself," as "a process of doubling or repetition [that] lock[s] the woman within a narcissistic construct." Doane, *Desire to Desire,* 137. The notion that self knowledge equals narcissism is a perplexing one, as is the implication that narcissism is by definition a negative attribute for the female character in "locking" her (to herself?).

57. Ibid., 151. Doane's statement here is debatable, as Celia's voice-off does pick back up later in the film, following Mark's "interruption," albeit in a transformed modality, as I shall discuss.

58. Ibid., 151.

59. Poizat, *L'Opéra,* 202. My translation.

60. Ibid., 172. My translation. Turk has noted other connections between the soprano and the scream. He suggests that because song can be construed as a heightening of the scream's erotic dimension (desire), the high-pitched female voice has a particularly charged paradoxical affect. He claims, "the

soprano is the manifest sign of . . . power . . . in a libidinal transaction that . . . embraces the feminine . . . [and] takes male subjectivity *to be dependent upon it and incomplete without it . . .*" Turk, "Deriding the Voice," 112–13. Emphasis added.

61. Doane, *Desire to Desire,* 151. She goes on to suggest that the void "gives witness to . . . the death of female subjectivity." My sense is that this image rather represents a risky plunge into a subjectivity *between* female and male.

62. Branigan, *Narrative Comprehension,* 142–60.

63. Browne, "Spectator-in-the-Text," 36. See also Lacan, *Four Fundamental,* 75.

64. The abstract images of the "trial," in fact, are those singled out for censorship for the television version of this film, which is more widely available on video than the original cut.

65. Bernstein, *Walter Wanger,* 214–15. Lang "accused Bennett of violating 'her duties and obligations as a stockholder' in dubbing the new narration." This was the final nail in the coffin of the uneasy alliance between the Wangers and Lang. Bernstein, *Walter Wanger,* 214.

66. Ibid., 215; Rolfe, "The Perfectionist," 3. According to Bernstein, "Wanger had . . . purchased the *Redbook* story at Lang's request"—also, he had an uncommonly (for him) harmonious relationship with the scriptwriter, Silvia Richards (they were "more than a writing combination"). Setting himself up in competition with Hitchcock, moreover, "Lang claimed that with *Secret Beyond the Door* he was interested in the *mood of a fictional space,*" comparing the project to *Rebecca.* Bernstein, *Walter Wanger,* 209, 215. Emphasis added. This convergence of formal challenge, personal investment, and reflected directorial status may well explain the barely repressed rage in his later rejections of the film. According to Hilda Rolfe, his secretary at the time, "he could hardly bring himself to discuss" it. Rolfe, "The Perfectionist," 3.

67. Kainz, *Paradox, Dialectic,* 27. Emphasis added.

68. Ibid., 27.

69. Doane has pointed to *Secret Beyond the Door* as belonging to a cycle of "'paranoid woman's films' . . . [in which] the institution of marriage is haunted by murder." Doane goes on to describe Celia's voice-off as "surprised" at realizing she is marrying a stranger. Celia's intonation, in fact, is rather one of fatalism—cognizant of danger, but also excited. The point is not that she is worried about "an overly hasty marriage," as Doane suggests, but that her desire is, specifically, to unite with this man she does not know, so that in learning who he is (since he is her desire) she may know herself. Doane, *Desire to Desire,* 123–24.

70. Kozloff, *Invisible Storytellers,* 5. Kozloff mentions the opening of Renais's *Hiroshima Mon Amour* in this connection, a sequence that also introduces and expresses a thematic of conscious subjective identification between a man

and a woman such as haunts the course of this film's narrative. The ending of Mankiewicz's *The Honeypot* also bears a zany inflection of this technique.

71. The union between them is also represented in their dialog (Celia's acknowledgment that she knows he loves her—that is, she can read his mind or hear his thoughts).

72. Branigan has noted how misleading the term "point of view" is in general in that it "suggests that there is a single principle (a 'point') that accounts for the unity of a perceptual judgment (a 'view'), rather than a series of relationships spanning a range of mental activities." Branigan, *Narrative Comprehension,* 255.

73. Kozloff suggests this may be an effect of any voice-over narrator, even those with a much shorter lifespan than Celia's. My sense is that such voices may initiate or elaborate a point of view, as I've described here, without even really functioning as a *narrating* presence in the film over all. Kozloff, *Invisible Storytellers,* 4.

74. Heath, *Questions of Cinema,* 136.

75. *I Walked with a Zombie,* another oft-cited film with multiple voices-off, differs in interesting ways from both *Secret* and *Eve,* in that the main female voice-off "shares" the voice-off not with another character but with a completely non-localizable "voice-of-God" that emerges only in the last moments of the film, speaking with a Haitian accent, quoting a dark bit of Scripture. The nurse's voice-off may ultimately still be read as "sharing" this final voice-off—for her character has evolved to ever higher levels of identification with the "space" from which this voice-of-God is delivered—that of the "natives," and that of "religion/superstition."

76. Kozloff, *Invisible Storytellers,* 64–68.

77. Ibid., 68–69. Kozloff also suggests that Addison's power is compromised at the end, when "the image maker" has the last word and shows us the other side of Eve's triumph. Kozloff, *Invisible Storytellers,* 70–71.

78. Ibid., 68.

79. Since the studio (Twentieth Century Fox) went over Mankiewicz's head to cut out the voices of women, however, there certainly could be a strong argument for an ideological agenda taking place subliminally here, in the doctoring of the film to reassert the male voice-off's primacy. Ibid., 68.

80. Ibid., 66–67. The question of what Barthes calls the "grain" of the voice, its definition, has found myriad interpretations in film studies. Pamela Robertson, for example, considers the "ironic" tone of male voice-over in noir films a manifestation of grain. I see the irony (or sincerity) as a function of performance and script (or even point of view), rather than as an attribute of the voice per se. The grain referred to here is in the thickening of Addison's voice when he first pronounces the name "Eve," the texture of desire infecting his voice, so to speak, physically. Robertson, "Structural Irony," 45.

81. Although Eve never possesses a voice-off in the film, she nonetheless bears a marked preference for offscreen space. She frequently speaks from offscreen, as she does here, hovers offscreen, invisible to others who do not know she is watching (as when she interrupts Margo and Bill's good-by kiss at the airport), always seems just outside the frame, knowing more about others than is known about her (in this sense, perhaps, like Addison, she is outside the story).

82. Girard, *Deceit, Desire,* 1–52, 83–95.

83. Doubtless the female subject here seems defined in terms of narcissism, but so is the male subject (Addison desires himself through Eve, that is, to be that powerful critic she worships). Girard's whole theory really rests on the premise that all desire is narcissism mediated through others who appear to have accessed a narcissistic wholeness without difficulty. Despite its pessimism, his model is of interest for feminism, as it defines desire as metaphysical, sidestepping the thorny dichotomies of sexual difference.

84. Pamela Robertson calls female voice-overs "earnest"—"unlike typical male narrations [they are] almost never ironic." Robertson, "Structural Irony," 44–45.

85. Barthes continues: "In fact, it suffices that the cinema capture the sound of speech *close up* . . . to succeed in shifting the signified a great distance and in throwing, so to speak, the anonymous body of the actor into my ear . . ." Barthes, *Pleasure of the Text,* 66–67. Emphasis in the original.

Chapter 3: Discourse, Enunciation, and Contradiction

1. Mary Ann Doane has defined discourse as "a statement which exhibits or foregrounds its 'I.'" Doane, *Desire to Desire,* 10.

2. Jacobs, "*Now Voyager:* Some Problems," 90. Jacobs describes enunciation further by quoting Jean Dubois: "Enunciation is defined as the attitude of the speaking subject in the face of his [*son*] *énoncé*." "Enoncé et énonciation," *Les Languages,* no. 13, 104; Jacobs's translation, Dubois' emphasis.

3. Gledhill, "*Klute:* Part 1," 13.

4. Telotte, *Voices in the Dark,* 51.

5. Metz, *Imaginary Signifier,* 91.

6. Silverman, *Acoustic Mirror,* 200.

7. See Freud's "A Case of Paranoia Running Counter to the Psycho-analytic Theory of the Disease," xiv, 261–73 (1915 standard edition), cited by Rosolato, *Essais sur le symbolique,* 200–201.

8. Metz, *Imaginary Signifier,* 94–95. Metz's allusion here, in its evocation of ravishment, is a curious way of imagining subjectivity.

9. Ibid., 96.

10. Silverman compares Metz's image-fixation to a Bazinian nostalgia for the real. It also parallels Rudolf Arnheim's plaintive call for a "pure" segregation between the perceptive faculties, in the name of art. Arnheim, however, acknowledged that sound affected meaning, if only through "adulteration." Silverman, *Acoustic Mirror,* 201, and Arnheim, *Film as Art,* 211.

11. Silverman, *Acoustic Mirror,* 200.

12. Metz, *Imaginary Signifier,* 96.

13. Doane, "Voice in the Cinema," 39.

14. Foucault, "Orders of Discourse," 8–9. Emphasis added.

15. Ibid., 8.

16. *The Acoustic Mirror,* 208–9. Or, as she intimates here, through the gendered interference of the author's voice. Silverman claims that both intentional and "unconscious" feminine attributes can be projected onto a film by a female director's desire. Ibid., 178–86, 225–34. A similar argument characterizes Flitterman-Lewis's study of female authors, *To Desire Differently.*

17. Mulvey's famous essay "Visual Pleasure" is the key text for the linking of the feminine to stasis and specularity in film. "Regressive" is the term Silverman uses to describe the flashback "journey" of Crawford's character in *Possessed:* it is a term she leans on frequently in her *The Acoustic Mirror,* to describe a pejorative effect. Silverman, *Acoustic Mirror,* 59.

18. Doane, *Desire to Desire,* 148. The sequence Doane describes in this way is from *The Spiral Staircase.*

19. Doane, "Voice in the Cinema," 40–42. Emphasis added.

20. See Baudry, "Ideological Effects." Of course, the "distance" Brecht calls for requires self-consciousness—the opposite, in fact, of the cloaked position of transcendence described by Baudry and Metz.

21. This ontological and socio-political relationship, specifically as implied by "voice" in the documentary film, has been brilliantly excavated by Bill Nichols. See "Voice of Documentary."

22. She agrees with Doane, Chion, and Bonitzer on this point. Silverman, *Acoustic Mirror,* 49. Emphasis in the original.

23. Ibid., 51. In discussing the male "voice-over" (a category she borrows from Doane), Silverman not only notes its rarity but also states that when it does appear, "it is usually associated with a diegetic figure." Ibid. She seems to be saying in fact that it is not a "disembodied voice-over" at all, but (in her terminology) an *embodied* voice-over. Moreover, one of the "disembodied" voice-over examples she gives, the voice that opens *Johnny Belinda* (1948) is the voice of a diegeticized male character, the rapist. If one were to go fishing for examples of male voice-off "embodiment" that lead to narrative containment, this voice provides ample fodder—his voice-off mis-leads us at the outset, suggesting he has some distance on the story about to unfold, then

disappears "into" an unlikable character who exemplifies the abuse of power, until, finally, he is "silenced" altogether by the mute female lead, who shoots him. Silverman reads this film in terms that portray the woman's objectification and impotence. However, this film may also be viewed as a good example of discursive contradiction, wherein the voice of male oppression is read as such. For Silverman's discussion of the film, see *Acoustic Mirror,* 67–70.

24. Ibid., 53.

25. Ibid., 53.

26. Ibid., 53.

27. Ibid., 53.

28. Ibid., 53. Silverman never demonstrates the aggressive "auditory mastery" of the spectator relative to internal monologue through specific textual analysis—in fact, the point is far from obvious.

29. Doane is, of course, critical of the ideological burden of this "directness" (expressive of patriarchal authority). Interestingly, she notes later that, in trying to countervail this burden, many documentary filmmakers have eschewed the voice-over. Doane suggests that the "silencing" of the voice of authority, however, "promotes . . . an illusion that reality speaks and is not spoken, that the film is not a constructed discourse." One can only feel somewhat sympathetic towards documentarists, who apparently just cannot win, one way or the other. Doane, "Voice in the Cinema," 42, 46. Emphasis in the original.

30. Ibid., 43.

31. Silverman, *Acoustic Mirror,* 53.

32. Ibid., 56.

33. This central scene also provides a contradictory "key" that renders the ending of the film unstable. For, though we have "seen" that Nancy was subjected to a brutal experience as a child, we also see that the trauma arises at *not being believed.* In important ways, Nancy is a victim of male paranoia in this film, a persecution that she finally internalizes and claims as a "true" self-image.

34. Ibid., 54. Silverman associates the male voice-off with "regressive journeys" to the interior of the diegesis a few paragraphs earlier—her segregationist conclusion here thus seems excessively absolute, even by her own argumentation.

35. Ibid., 54–63.

36. McClean, "It's Only That I Do," 6–12.

37. Bordwell, Foreword to Branigan's *Point of View,* xii.

38. Silverman, *Acoustic Mirror,* 62.

39. Ibid., 62.

40. She celebrates this fluidity in its emergence in films by women. Only there, "freed from it from its claustral confinement within the female body," does the female voice demonstrate its "enormous conceptual and discursive

range." As her own discussion goes a long way to prove, however, the voice is never really "free" of the body. Ibid., 186.

41. Ibid., 71.

42. Ibid., 212–34.

43. Ibid., 211.

44. Foucault, *History of Sexuality: An Introduction,* 45. Emphasis in the original.

45. Foucault, *Archeology of Knowledge,* 150.

46. Ibid., 150. One should perhaps be wary of all theories that are too self-contained, too well constructed, marked as "givens" for this reason.

47. Ibid., 151.

48. Foucault, "Orders of Discourse," 28.

49. Kainz, *Paradox, Dialectic,* 27; Foucault, "Orders of Discourse," 20.

50. Foucault, "Orders of Discourse," 20.

51. Bergstrom, "Rereading the Work," 25.

52. Ibid., 26–27. Bergstrom refers to Heath's analysis of *Touch of Evil* in particular in responding to Johnston's thesis.

53. Ibid., 26, 28.

54. Ibid., 30.

55. Suter, "Feminine Discourse," 93.

56. Ibid., 93. In suggesting that discourse, to be invulnerable to such "usurpation," needs to be "ec-centric" to the narrative structure, Suter aligns herself implicitly with a logic that, again, sees discursive subjectivity as a position of exterior authority.

57. Ibid., 101. The sequence Suter points to as enunciating the character Cynthia's desire involves Cynthia's "voice-off" (speaking post-coitus from off-screen space) while her body and that of her lover remain offscreen. Suter suggests the offscreen evocation of desire "elide[s] all explicit signifiers of sexuality." Cynthia's voice-off, to the contrary, strongly suggests her subjectivity and desire, invoking our perception of erotic bodies in space, rapt in their own pleasure and inaccessible to our gaze. A more sustained analysis of the workings of voice and sound in the film might bolster the "strength" of the feminine discourse that Suter considers excessively frail in her account. Ibid., 97.

58. Suter suggests "the importance is that the feminine *does* exist" (in the film). Ibid., 97. Emphasis in the original. Mulvey's recognition of the feminine is more qualified, in that she claims it escapes specularity only in the uneasy processes of identificatory transvestitism. Mulvey, "Afterthoughts," 69–79.

59. Bergstrom, "Enunciation and Sexual," 57.

60. Ibid. See also Bergstrom, "Alternation." In the interview, Bellour insists that ". . . in the American cinema as a whole . . . the central place assigned to the woman is a place where she is figured, represented, inscribed in the fiction through the logical necessity of a general representation of the subject of

desire in the film, *who is always, first and last, a masculine subject.*" Bergstrom, "Alternation," 94. Emphasis added.

61. Indeed, *Blackmail* could be said (if one wanted to construct hierarchies between sound and image) to favor sound over image—sound, moreover, that structures subjectivity in terms of the female character rather than the male. Consider, for instance, the famous scene in which the character Alice's inner thoughts are a torment of subjectivistic sound—the increasingly loud and rapid repetitions of the word "knife" uttered by her gossipy neighbor. This is a fascinating moment of voice-off, illustrating its rhetorical and psychic heterogeneity well, for this voice-off can be read not only as the offscreen sound of the neighbor speaking, but also as the main character's inner thoughts as well. Amy Lawrence, in a compelling analysis that stresses the discursive contradiction at work here, describes Alice's painfully experienced struggle to speak as self-consciously underscored by the film. In *Blackmail,* she argues, "patriarchal culture is indicted with the exposure of its intentional suppression of the woman's voice." Lawrence, *Echo and Narcissus,* 116.

62. Bellour, "Obvious and the Code," 7–17.

63. Berstrom, "Alternation," 94.

64. Silverman, who is extremely critical of Bellour's nostalgic auteurism and his obvious identification with Hitchcock et al., via the relaying gaze, ultimately agrees with him on this sweeping view of classical cinema. "[H]e is correct in assuming that the authorial system of most Hollywood films forecloses upon the female voice. If we were to ask . . . where [this discourse] come[s] from . . . the answer would resoundingly be: 'The male subject.'" Silverman, *Acoustic Mirror,* 205.

65. Ibid., 51.

66. Doane, "Voice in the Cinema," 40.

67. Bergstrom, "Alternation," 94.

68. Ibid., 94.

69. Suter, "Feminine Discourse," 89–90.

70. Ibid., 93.

71. Ibid., 89.

72. Foucault, "Orders of Discourse," 8.

73. The invocation of the notion of a "direct" relationship to the viewer established by the voice-off here obviously differs from Silverman's outlined earlier. In my view, such "directness" implies a discursive relationship in which the voice-off is not merely "heard" by a viewer (intrusive or otherwise), but rather is understood to have enounced words/speech *in order to be heard.* In those cases where voice-off represents thought, rather than speech, this schema is also at odds with Doane's, in that within it such moments may in fact mark the most "direct" relationship between viewer and voice-off. The viewer understands these thoughts to be those of a consciousness that speaks, as it

were, telepathically, thus bringing about a deeper complicity than is possible with the "authoritative" voice-over.

74. This "speaking to" stance parallels, on the image track, those moments when a character looks directly in the camera. However, such analogies have their limitations, given that the spectator's metapsychological relationship to the voice differs markedly from that which he or she takes up via the gaze.

75. Male voice-off also works this way, perforce the direct and self-imbricating stance of the narrator. However, the "subjective" overlay that is so common to the female voice-off (in its association not only to an especially complicit direct address and to an effect of shared consciousness between the character and viewer) foregrounds a specifically feminine discourse. She not only "speaks," but "speaks to" the spectator with a candor and vulnerability unthinkable, for example, for the noir voices-off of *Out of the Past, Dark Passage,* and *Murder My Sweet.* The female voice-off, that is, implies *it knows* it speaks to/for women.

76. Gene Tierney's reluctance and failure to marry again in *The Ghost and Mrs. Muir* similarly reflects this feminine desire to possess a home in her own right.

77. Stanwyck's carefully modulated lyricism here, and the subtly orchestrated mix of her voice's syncopated rhythms and tones with the musical score, strongly reminds of Fontaine's voice-off in *Letter from an Unknown Woman* and *Rebecca,* as well as the voices-off in *Secret Beyond the Door, All about Eve,* and *Brief Encounter.* In fact, the female voice-off is almost invariably "musical"—the greatest exception being Crawford's voice-off in *Mildred Pierce.* This exception seems due to the effort to employ this voice-off as a "noir" narrator, an attempt that backfires, given the prototypical vulnerability of her address (as opposed to male voice-off irony). See Robertson, "Structural Irony."

78. Renov points out this slippage in Claire Trevor's voice-off, noting how her voice "at moments provid[es] expository overlay but more often produc[es] a commentary of emotional response." Renov, "*Raw Deal:* The Woman," 20.

79. Ibid., 20.

80. Ibid., 19.

81. Albeit via metaphors of distance, which seem singularly inappropriate in explicating the subjective position enjoined by voice-off, particularly in this film. Ibid., 22.

82. Girard has noted how envy and jealousy are dead giveaways of desire: the jealous wife in "hating" Addie betrays her true feeling of admiration (and vice versa). Girard insists that to understand such a desire as (merely) homosexual is to miss the point. Rather, the desire for the object (Brad) is an illusion, an erotic value conferred because of a passionate attachment to the "fascinating rival." All desire (and *A Letter to Three Wives* certainly seems a tribute to this theory), Girard suggests, is triangular. *Deceit, Desire,* 46–51.

83. Hollinger describes the film's "narrational perspective" as "extremely confused." Hollinger sees Addie's narration as "casting an ironic light on the wives" when they renew their dedication to their marriages. She shows Addie's power to reside in the contempt she holds for the women's concessions to marriage, but fails to account for the patriarchal discourse Addie delivers along with her enunciation of power, independence, and female beauty. Hollinger, "Listening to the Female," 41–43.

84. These are Silverman's words, turned to counter her own argument, "against" classical cinema. She writes here about *The Gold Diggers,* a feminist film, but her description fits Addie's discursive reversibility to a T. Silverman, *Acoustic Mirror,* 180.

85. Ibid., 180.

86. Deborah's insecurity also stems from the difficulty of reinserting herself into a feminine role after life in the military. Her difficulty playing the *femme* was apparently shared by scores of WACS, WAVES, and the like. See Campbell, "Regimented Women."

87. At this moment, Addie's voice operates somewhat like the "auditory master" that Silverman implies the spectator is, relative to interior monologue (but, of course, here the voice is the intruder, not the spectator). (Her voice reminds also of Fritz Lang's experimental "thought-voice" discussed in chapter 2.)

88. They can only communicate via the voice. One could think of the flashbacks that arise in relation to the voice as responding to this idea, as if the women are trying to defend themselves to their husbands telepathically. Their "speech" (enounced by the flashbacks) is underlined by the image of the telephone as a form of possible resistance to Addie's own speech. Speech is thus, again, emphasized by this film as a power relation.

89. Ideologically speaking, of course, this description fits, with uncanny precision, the movie we are watching. One can only wonder exactly how radical Joseph Mankiewicz's politics really were! But, again, the patriarchal speaks along with the feminine here: "It's a joke." (Or is it?) Both and neither are true, finally.

90. Female voices-off function as hallucinations much more frequently than do male voices-off. Often these voices-off are unpleasant memories (like Joan Fontaine's nightmare in *Rebecca,* when her brutal patroness's words, "They say he simply adored her," ring in her head). At other times, the voice is that of the woman herself, such as in *The Two Mrs. Carrolls.* Stanwyck's character shouts at her own voice-off, which rises out of her head to torment her, as she tries to reject the voice-off's suggestion that her husband is going to kill her.

91. This unusual moment coincides with what Heath describes as "subjectivity *in the image*" that differs from the more common relaying of a character's "point of view" via an overlay of first- and third-person modes. This shot comes

across, that is, as *explicitly* first-person—entirely non-objective. Heath, "Narrative Space," 47–48. Emphasis in the original.

92. Doane, *Desire to Desire,* 147–48.

93. This is the first of three "presents" Addie sends the men, fetish-gifts that are calculated to represent her in her absence as the paragon they imagine, according to the specifications of their desire. For Brad, a snob—champagne; for George, a more likable snob—classical music; for Hollingsway, a would-be bourgeois snob—a portrait of Addie in a silver frame. Significantly, however, this first present is *also* for Deborah, Addie's favorite torture subject. Deborah, we will see, is Addie's pet project, in her role as patriarchal missionary.

94. Rita's real "crime," of course, is writing for the radio and making more money than George, who teaches drama. The script's obsession with the poisonous infiltration of popular culture thus neatly meshes with a classic sex-role reversal that is also timely in the post–World War II era. The implication that Rita feminizes George is brought up over and over, just as radio is, in a sense, represented as "feminizing" culture at large (all those soap operas!). Interestingly, Rita is shown as kowtowing to another (wo)man in her job, "Mrs. Manly" (which, apparently, she must become if she keeps working, a kind of sexual hybrid). Thus we are able to applaud when she "stands up for herself" by standing by her man, refusing to "take his place" (become a man), by taking the time to cater to her husband.

95. Addie's husband, it is said, left her. That is why she wants/needs one of theirs. Addie's lack of a husband makes her dangerous—and desirable—not only to the men, however, for all the women's stories imply their longing to be independent (as Addie seems to be).

96. Lawrence has described the public agitation fomented by the emergence of women announcers during the dawn of radio. She claims, "[T]he *speaking* woman puts herself in a position of authority—a definite breach of propriety." This controversy, she adds, ". . . would never in effect be resolved in . . . [the] sound film." *Echo and Narcissus,* 18. Emphasis in the original.

97. When Rita does behave like a stereotypical female, breaking down into tears, she handles George nicely. He stops complaining and supports her. The patriarchal discourse here encourages her to take her power the womanly way, a way that (mis)represents her as weak.

98. Altman, "Moving Lips," 71, 73. Bresson is quoted from Burch, *Theory of Film Practice,* 90.

99. The classic pairing of voice-off to a close-up here suggests both that the voice is an "interior monologue" or a hallucination. In fact, as it is wont, the voice-off drifts from one "status" into another as the scene progresses, becoming more and more "external" to Lora Mae, vised, however, through her subjective perception. Thus, it represents both "types" of voices-off.

100. "Audio spectacle," as this moment might well be described, "guides us

away from 'content' (language, character psychology, exposition) and toward the quality of the sound, irrespective of whether music, voices, or effects are on the sound track." Lawrence, *Echo and Narcissus,* 96.

101. Williams, "Is Sound Recording," 51–66.

102. Excess is in the air here, in the image of the bursting pipe and the sound of an "alien" voice urging her to doubt her indifference to her marriage. It is an excess both patriarchal (she can't "not care" about losing her husband if the story is to continue) and self-reflexive (she recognizes that "man behind the curtain").

103. The power of Addie's lure is brought home by Hollingsway's fixation on the portrait; he cannot seem to stop staring at it. Lora Mae finally disrupts this obsessive gaze by kissing him forcefully, reminding him of her body. After the kiss, Addie's portrait is conspicuously framed *out* of the very wide, final shot of the room when Lora Mae leaves, leaving Hollingsway to now stare befuddled after *her.*

104. One could argue in this sense that Lora Mae understands what Addie "is" better than the other women do. She agrees to "play" Addie, knowing Addie is a construct of male desire. But Addie represents no real threat to Lora Mae, because, like Addie, Lora Mae has no illusions (yet) about being desired for herself.

105. Significantly, the problem of the name is now revised—he is "Mrs. Bishop's husband," *her* possession.

106. In an Oedipal role-reversal here, Deborah accuses Hollingsway of not being "grown up," or "a man," spurring him on to his noble gesture of confession. Five minutes later, he restores himself to the place of the father, referring to her as "just a kid."

107. In this "diva" mode, again, she takes up Addie's voice. Addie, a woman adored and reviled, is a prima donna, "ruthlessly competitive . . . extravagantly vain, and glamorously ornamental." Pope has shown how the voice of the diva in literature by women is used "less as [a] vehicle for seducing men than for empowering women—both [the self] and other women." As diva then, Addie has empowered Deborah finally to speak. Pope, "The Diva Doesn't Die," 139–40.

108. In this sense, she reminds of Pat in *Raw Deal,* as Renov sees her, "speaking for all women." Renov, *"Raw Deal:* The Woman," 20.

109. Hollinger, "Listening to the Female," 43.

110. Hollinger sees Addie as "reduced to [this] ineffectual gesture," implying that the loss of Addie's power is represented thus. Such interference with the image from beyond, on the contrary, clearly exceeds even the usual regime of knowledge and power doled out to (even male) voices-off comparable to hers. Ibid., 43.

111. Ibid., 43. The spirit of Hollinger's analysis here is unquestionably com-

pelling. Her reading of the voice-off in this film, however, relies on a summary "dialog-oriented" reading that neglects the problematic of sound's relationship to the image, or to other sounds. For example, she describes the flashbacks as all triggered by Addie's voice. As we have seen, the configuration of voice-off in these moments is far more complex, strange, and provocative than a simple dialogic description would allow.

112. Ibid., 43, 49.

113. Ibid., 49.

Epilogue

1. Trinh, *Framer Framed,* 186.

bibliography

Adorno, Theodor, and Hanns Eisler. *Komposition fuer den Film.* Frankfurt: Suhrkamp Verlag, 1976.

Altman, Rick. "Four and a Half Film Fallacies." In *Sound Theory Sound Practice,* edited by Rick Altman, 35–45. New York: Routledge, 1992.

———. "The Material Heterogeneity of Recorded Sound." In *Sound Theory Sound Practice,* edited by Rick Altman, 15–31. New York: Routledge, 1992.

———. "MOVING LIPS: Cinema as Ventriloquism." *Yale French Studies* no. 60 (1980): 67–79.

———. "Sound Space." In *Sound Theory Sound Practice,* edited by Rick Altman, 46–64. New York: Routledge, 1992.

———, ed. *Sound Theory Sound Practice.* New York: Routledge, 1992.

Arnheim, Rudolf. *Film as Art.* Berkeley: University of California Press, 1957.

———. "A New Laocoön." In *Film Sound,* edited by Elisabeth Weis and John Belton, 112–15. New York: Columbia University Press, 1985.

Bailbé, Claude. "Le Son: Programmation de l'écoute." *Cahiers du Cinema,* no.

292 (Sept. 1978), 53–59; no. 293 (Oct. 1978), 5–12; no. 297 (Feb. 1979), 44–54; and no. 299 (Apr. 1979), 18–27.

Barthes, Roland. *The Grain of the Voice.* Translated by Linda Coverdale. New York: Hill and Wang, 1985.

———. *A Lover's Discourse: Fragments.* Translated by Richard Howard. New York: Hill and Wang, 1978.

———. *The Pleasure of the Text.* Translated by Richard Miller. New York: Hill and Wang, 1975.

———. *S/Z.* Translated by Richard Miller. New York: Hill and Wang, 1974.

Baudry, Jean-Louis. "The Apparatus." Translated by Jean Andrews and Bertrand Augst. *Camera Obscura,* no. 1, Fall 1976: 104–26.

———. "Ideological Effects of the Basic Apparatus." *Film Quarterly,* Winter 1974–75: 39–47. Reprinted in *Narrative, Apparatus, Ideology.* Edited by Philip Rosen. Translated by Alan Williams. 286–98. New York: Columbia University Press, 1986.

Bazin, André. *What Is Cinema?* Vol. 1. Translated by Hugh Gray. Berkeley: University of California Press, 1967.

Bellour, Raymond. "Cine-Repetitions." Translated by Kari Hanet. *Screen* 20, no. 2 (Summer 1979): 65–72.

———. "Hitchcock, The Enunciator." Translated by Bertrand Augst and Hilary Radner, *Camera Obscura,* no. 2 (Fall 1977): 66–91.

———. "The Obvious and the Code." *Screen* 15, no. 4 (Winter 1974–75): 7–17.

Belton, John. "Technology and Aesthetics of Film Sound." In *Film Sound,* edited by Elisabeth Weis and John Belton, 63–72. New York: Columbia University Press, 1985.

Berg, Charles M. "The Human Voice and Silent Cinema." *Journal of Popular Film* 4, no. 2 (1975): 165–77.

Bergstrom, Janet. "Alternation, Segmentation, Hypnosis: Interview with Raymond Bellour." *Camera Obscura,* nos. 3–4 (Summer 1979): 71–103.

———. "Enunciation and Sexual Difference (Part I)." *Camera Obscura,* nos. 3–4 (Summer 1979): 33–65.

———. "The Logic of Fascination: Fritz Lang and Cinematic Convention." PhD diss., University of California—Los Angeles, 1982.

———. "Rereading the Work of Claire Johnston." *Camera Obscura,* nos. 3–4 (Summer 1979): 21–31.

Bernstein, Matthew. *Walter Wanger, Hollywood Independent.* Berkeley: University of California Press, 1994.

Bonitzer, Pascal. "Les silences de la voix." *Cahiers du Cinéma,* no. 256 (February/March 1975): 22–33.

Bordwell, David, Janet Staiger, and Kristin Thompson. *The Classical Hollywood Cinema: Film Style and Mode of Production to 1960.* New York: Columbia University Press, 1985.

———. "Foreword." In *Point of View in the Cinema: A Theory of Narration and Subjectivity in Classical Film,* by Edward Branigan, x–xiii. Berlin: Mouton Publishers, 1984.

———. *Narration in the Fiction Film.* Madison: University of Wisconsin Press, 1985.

Branigan, Edward. *Narrative Comprehension and Film.* London: Routledge, 1992.

———. *Point of View in the Cinema: A Theory of Narration and Subjectivity in Classical Film.* Berlin: Mouton Publishers, 1984.

———. "What Is a Camera?" In *Cinema Histories Cinema Practices,* edited by Patricia Mellencamp and Philip Rosen, 87–99. Frederick, Md.: University Publications of America, 1984.

Browne, Nick. "Film Form/Voice-Over: Bresson's *The Diary of a Country Priest.*" *Yale French Studies,* no. 60 (1980): 233–40.

———. "The Spectator-in-the-Text: The Rhetoric of *Stagecoach.*" *Film Quarterly* 29, no. 2 (Winter 1975–76): 26–38.

Burch, Noël. *Theory of Film Practice.* Translated by Helen R. Lane. Princeton, N.J.: Princeton University Press, 1973.

Burch, Noël, with Jorge Dana. "Propositions." Translated by Diana Matlas and Christopher King. *Afterimage,* no. 5 (Spring 1974): 41–66.

Butler, Alison. "Feminist Theory and Women's Films at the Turn of the Century." In *Screen* 41, no.1 (Spring 2000): 73–79.

Cameron, Evan William, ed. *Sound and the Cinema: The Coming of Sound to American Film.* Pleasantville, N.Y.: Redgrave Publishing Company, 1980.

Campbell, D'Ann. "The Regimented Women of WWII." In *Women, Militarism and War: Essays in History, Politics, and Social Theory,* edited by Jean Elshtain and Sheila Tobias, 107–22. Savage, Md.: Rowman and Littlefield, 1990.

Cavell, Stanley. *The World Viewed: Reflections on the Ontology of Film.* Cambridge, Mass.: Harvard University Press, 1979.

Chion, Michel. *La Voix au Cinema.* Paris: Editions de l'Etoile, 1982.

———. *Le Son au Cinema.* Paris: Editions de l'Etoile, 1985.

———. *The Voice in Cinema.* Translated by Claudia Gorbman. New York. Columbia University, 1999.

Clement, Catherine. *Opera, or the Undoing of Women.* Translated by Betsy Wing. Minneapolis: University of Minnesota Press, 1988.

Cook, Pam. "Duplicity in *Mildred Pierce.*" In *Women in Film Noir,* edited by E. Ann Kaplan, 68–82. London: BFI, 1978.

Copjec, Joan. *Read My Desire: Lacan against the Historicists.* Cambridge, Mass.: MIT Press, 1994.

Cowie, Elisabeth. "Fantasia." *M/F,* 9 (1984): 71–104.

———. *Representing the Woman: Cinema and Psychoanalysis.* Minneapolis: University of Minnesota Press, 1999.

Crafton, Donald. *The Talkies: American Cinema's Transition to Sound, 1926–1931.* Berkeley: University of California Press, 1997.

De Lauretis, Teresa. *Alice Doesn't: Feminism, Semiotics, Cinema.* Bloomington: Indiana University Press, 1984.

Deleuze, Gilles, and Félix Guattari. *Kafka: Toward a Minor Literature.* Theory and History of Literature, vol. 30. Translated by Dana Polan. Minneapolis: University of Minnesota Press, 1986.

———. *A Thousand Plateaus: Capitalism and Schizophrenia.* Translated by Brian Massumi. Minneapolis: University of Minnesota Press, 1987.

Doane, Mary Ann. *The Desire to Desire: The Woman's Film of the 1940s.* Bloomington: Indiana University Press, 1987.

———. "Film and the Masquerade: Theorizing the Female Spectator." *Screen* 23, nos. 3–4 (September–October 1982): 74–87.

———. "Ideology and the Practice of Sound Editing and Mixing." In *Film Sound,* edited by Elisabeth Weis and John Belton. New York: Columbia University Press, 1985.

———. "The Voice in Cinema: The Articulation of Body and Space." In *Yale French Studies,* no. 60 (1980): 33–50.

Dolar, Mladen. "The Object Voice." In *Gaze and Voice as Love Objects,* edited by Renata Salaci and Slavoj Žižek, 7–31. Durham, N.C.: Duke University Press, 1996.

Dubois, Jean. "Enoncé et énonciation." *Les Languages,* no. 13.

Dunn, Leslie C. "Ophelia's Songs in *Hamlet:* Music, Madness, and the Feminine." In *Embodied Voices: Representing Female Vocality in Western Culture,* edited by Leslie C. Dunn and Nancy A. Jones. Cambridge, Mass.: University of Cambridge Press, 1994.

Dunn, Leslie C., and Nancy A. Jones, eds. *Embodied Voices: Representing Female Vocality in Western Culture.* Cambridge, Mass.: University of Cambridge Press, 1994.

Dyer, Richard. "Resistance through Charisma: Rita Hayworth and *Gilda.*" In *Women in Film Noir,* edited by E. Ann Kaplan, 91–99. London: BFI, 1978.

Eisenstein, Sergei. *Film Form: Essays in Film Theory.* Translated by Jay Leyda. New York: Harcourt, Brace and Co., 1949.

Fielding, Raymond. "The Technological Antecedents of the Coming of Sound: An Introduction." In *Sound and the Cinema: The Coming of Sound to American Film,* edited by Evan William Cameron, 2–23. Pleasantville, N.Y.: Redgrave Publishing Company, 1980.

Fischer, Lucy. *Shot/Countershot: Film Tradition and Women's Cinema.* Princeton, N.J.: Princeton University Press, 1989.

Flitterman-Lewis, Sandy. *To Desire Differently: Feminism and the French Cinema.* Urbana: University of Illinois Press, 1990.

Foucault, Michel. *The Archeology of Knowledge.* Translated by A. M. Sheridan Smith. New York: Harper and Row, 1972.

———. *The History of Sexuality: An Introduction.* Vol. 1. Translated by Robert Hurley. New York: Vintage, 1990.

———. "Orders of Discourse." *Social Science Information* 10, no. 2 (1971): 7–30.

———. *The Use of Pleasure: The History of Sexuality.* Vol. 2. Translated by Robert Hurley. New York: Vintage, 1990.

French, Brandon. *On the Verge of Revolt: Women in American Films of the Fifties.* New York: Frederick Ungar Publishing, 1978.

Freud, Sigmund. "Instincts and Their Vicissitudes." In *On Metapsychology: The Theory of Psychoanalysis.* Vol. 11 of the Pelican Freud Library. Translated by James Strachey. Edited by Angela Richards. Harmondsworth, Eng.: Penguin Books, 1984. First published in 1915.

———. *The Interpretation of Dreams.* Translated by James Strachey. New York: Avon Books, 1965. First published in 1900.

———. "The 'Uncanny.'" *On Creativity and the Unconscious: Papers on the Psychology of Art, Literature, Love, Religion.* New York: Harper and Row, 1958. First published in 1919.

Gidal, Peter. "Against Sexual Representation in Film." *Screen* 25, no. 6 (November/December 1984): 24–29.

Girard, René. *Deceit, Desire and the Novel: Self and Other in Literary Structure.* Translated by Yvonne Freccero. Baltimore, Md.: Johns Hopkins University Press, 1965.

Gledhill, Christine. "Klute: Part 1: A Contemporary Film Noir and Feminist Criticism." In *Women in Film Noir,* edited by E. Ann Kaplan, 6–22. London: BFI, 1978.

Haraway, Donna. *Primate Visions: Gender, Race and Nature in the World of Modern Science.* New York: Routledge, 1989.

Harrison, Taylor. "Trying Hard to Hear You: Jean Arthur and the Problematics of Presence." *The Velvet Light Trap,* no. 39 (Spring 1997): 42–51.

Heath, Stephen. "Film and System: Terms of Analysis, Part I." *Screen* 16, no. 1 (Fall and Spring 1975): 7–77.

———. "Narrative Space." In Heath, *Questions of Cinema,* 19–75. Bloomington: Indiana University Press, 1981.

———. "The Question Oshima." In Heath, *Questions of Cinema,* 145–64. Bloomington: Indiana University Press, 1981.

Hollinger, Karen. "Listening to the Female Voice in the Woman's Film." *Film Criticism* 16 (Spring 1992), 34–52.

Houseman, John. *Unfinished Business: A Memoir.* London: Chatto & Windus, 1986.

Irigaray, Luce. *Speculum of the Other Woman.* Translated by Gillian Gill. Ithaca, N.Y.: Cornell University Press, 1985.

Jacobs, Lea. "*Now Voyager:* Some Problems of Enunciation and Sexual Difference." *Camera Obscura,* no. 7 (Spring 1981), 89–109.

Jay, Martin. "Experience without a Subject: Walter Benjamin and the Novel." *New Formations,* no. 20 (Summer 1993): 145–55.

Juranville, Alain. *Lacan et la philosophie.* Paris: P. U. F., 1984.

Kainz, Howard P. *Paradox, Dialectic, and System: A Contemporary Reconstruction of the Hegelian Problematic.* University Park: Pennsylvania State University Press, 1988.

Kaufmann, Linda. *Discourses of Desire: Gender, Genre, and Epistolary Fictions.* Ithaca, N.Y.: Cornell University Press, 1986.

Kawin, Bruce. *Mindscreen: Bergman, Godard, and First-Person Film.* Princeton, N.J.: Princeton University Press, 1978.

———. "An Outline of Film Voices." *Film Quarterly* 38, no. 2 (Winter 1984–85): 38–46.

King, Norman. "The Sound of Silents." *Screen* 25, no. 3 (May–June 1984): 2–15.

Kozloff, Sarah. *Invisible Storytellers: Voice-over Narration in American Fiction Film.* Berkeley: University of California Press, 1988.

———. *Overhearing Film Dialogue.* Berkeley: University of California Press, 2000.

Kuntzel, Thierry. "The Film Work." *Enclitic* 2, no. 1 (Spring 1978): 39–82.

Lacan, Jacques. *The Four Fundamental Concepts of Psycho-Analysis.* Translated by Alan Sheridan. New York: W. W. Norton, 1978. First published in 1973.

Laplace, Maria. "Producing and Consuming the Woman's Film: Discursive Struggle in *Now Voyager.*" In *Home Is Where the Heart Is: Studies in Melodrama and the Woman's Film,* edited by Christine Gledhill, 138–66. London: BFI Publishing, 1987.

Lastra, James. "Reading, Writing, and Representing Sound." *Sound Theory Sound Practice,* edited by Rick Altman, 65–86. New York: Routledge, 1992.

———. *Sound Technology and the American Cinema: Perception, Representation, Modernity.* New York: Columbia University Press, 2000.

Lawrence, Amy. *Echo and Narcissus: Women's Voices in Classical Hollywood Cinema.* Berkeley: University of California Press, 1991.

———. "Staring the Camera Down: Direct Address and Women's Voices." In *Embodied Voices: Representing Female Vocality in Western Culture,* edited by Leslie C. Dunn and Nancy A. Jones. Cambridge, Eng.: University of Cambridge Press, 1994.

———. "Women's Voices in Third World Cinema." In *Sound Theory Sound Practice,* edited by Rick Altman, 178–90. New York: Routledge, 1992.

Levin, Tom. "The Acoustic Dimension: Notes on Cinema Sound." *Screen* 25, no. 3 (May–June 1984): 55–68.

Lindgren, Ernest. *The Art of Film.* New York: Macmillan, 1963.

LoBrutto, Vincent. *Sound-on-Film: Interviews with Creators of Film Sound.* Westport, Conn.: Praeger, 1994.

Lundeen, Kathleen. "Pumping up the Word with Cinematic Supplements." *Film Criticism* 24, no. 1 (Fall 1999): 60–72.

Manvell, Roger, and John Huntley. *The Technique of Film Music.* New York: Hastings House, 1957.

McClary, Susan. *Feminine Endings: Music, Gender, and Sexuality.* Minneapolis: University of Minnesota, 1991.

McGettigan, Joan. "Interpreting a Man's World: Female Voices in *Badlands* and *Days of Heaven.*" *Journal of Film and Video.* 52, no. 4 (Winter 2001): 33–43.

McGowan, Todd. "Looking for the Gaze: Lacanian Film Theory and Its Vicissitudes." *Cinema Journal* 42, no. 3 (2003): 27–47.

McLean, Adrienne L. "'It's Only That I Do What I Love and Love What I Do': Film Noir and the Musical Woman." *Cinema Journal* 33, no. 1 (Fall 1993): 3–16.

Metz, Christian. "Aural Objects." Translated by Georgia Gurrieri. *Yale French Studies* no. 60 (1980): 24–32.

———. *Film Language: A Semiotics of the Cinema.* Translated by Michael Taylor. New York: Oxford University Press, 1974.

———. *The Imaginary Signifier: Psychoanalysis and the Cinema.* Translated by Celia Britton, Annwyl Williams, Ben Brewster, and Alfred Guzzetti. Bloomington: Indiana University Press, 1977.

Modleski, Tania. "Time and Desire in the Woman's Film." Reprinted in *Home Is Where the Heart Is: Studies in Melodrama and the Woman's Film,* edited by Christine Gledhill, 326–38. London: BFI Publishing, 1987.

Mulvey, Laura. "Afterthoughts on 'Visual Pleasure and Narrative Cinema' inspired by *Duel in the Sun.*" Reprinted in *Feminism and Film Theory,* edited by Constance Penley, 69–79. New York: Routledge, 1988.

———. "Hollywood Cinema and Feminist Theory: A Strange but Persistent Relationship." *Iris* 26 (Autumn, 1998): 23–32.

———. "Visual Pleasure and Narrative Cinema." *Screen* 16, no. 3 (Autumn 1975): 6–18.

Nichols, Bill. "The Voice of the Documentary." *Movies and Methods,* vol. 2, edited by Bill Nichols, 258–73. Berkeley: University of California Press, 1985.

Odin, Roger. "A Propos d'un couple de concepts 'son in' vs. 'son off.'" *Linguistique et Sémiologie* 6 (1979).

Oudart, Jean-Pierre. "Cinema and Suture." *Screen* 18, no. 4 (Winter 1977/78): 35–47.

"Poetry and the Film: A Symposium with Maya Deren, Arthur Miller, Dylan Thomas, Chairman Willard Maas. Organized by Amos Vogel." In *Film Culture Reader,* edited by P. Adams Sitney, 171–86. New York: Praeger Publishers, 1970.

Pope, Rebecca A. "The Diva Doesn't Die: George Eliot's *Armgart.*" In *Embodied Voices: Representing Female Vocality in Western Culture,* edited by Leslie C. Dunn and Nancy A. Jones, 139–51. Cambridge: University of Cambridge Press, 1994.

Poizat, Michel. *L'Opéra ou le cri de l'ange: Essai sur la jouissance de l'amateur d'Opéra.* Paris: A.M. Métailié, 1986.

Renov, Michael. *Hollywood's Wartime Woman: Representation and Ideology.* Ann Arbor and London: UMI Research Press, 1988.

———. "*Raw Deal:* The Woman in the Text." *Wide Angle* 6, no. 2 (1984): 18–22.

Restivo, Angelo. "Lacan According to Žižek." *Quarterly Review of Film and Video* 16, no. 2 (1997): 193–206.

———. "Recent Approaches to Psychoanalytic Sound Theory." *Iris* no. 27 (Spring 1999): 135–41.

Robertson, Pamela. "Structural Irony in *Mildred Pierce,* or How Mildred Lost Her Tongue." *Cinema Journal* 30, no. 1 (Fall 1990): 42–54.

Rolfe, Hilda. "The Perfectionist." *Film Comment* 28, no. 11–12 (1992): 3–4.

Rose, Jacqueline. "Introduction II." In *Feminine Sexuality: Jacques Lacan and the école freudienne,* edited by Juliet Mitchell and Jacqueline Rose, 27–57. Translated by Jacqueline Rose. New York: W. W. Norton, 1982.

Rosolato, Guy. *Eléments de L'Interpretation.* Paris: Gallimard, 1985.

———. *Essais sur le symbolique.* Paris: Gallimard, 1969.

———. *Le Relation d'Inconnu.* Paris: Gallimard, 1978.

Rowe, Kathleen. *The Unruly Woman: Gender and the Genres of Laughter.* Austin: University of Texas Press, 1995.

Salaci, Renata, and Slavoj Žižek, eds. *Gaze and Voice as Love Objects.* Durham, N.C.: Duke University Press, 1996.

Silverman, Kaja. *The Acoustic Mirror: The Female Voice in Psychoanalysis and Cinema.* Bloomington: Indiana University Press, 1988.

———. "Dis-Embodying the Female Voice." In *Re-Vision: Essays in Feminist Film Criticism,* edited by Mary Anne Doane, Patricia Mellencamp, and Linda Williams, 131–49. Frederick, Md.: University Publications of America, in association with the American Film Institute, 1984.

———. "A Voice to Match: The Female Voice in Classical Cinema." *Iris* 3, no. 1 (1985): 57–69.

Smoodin, Eric. "The Image and the Voice in the Film with Spoken Narration." *Quarterly Review of Film Studies,* no. 8 (Fall 1983): 19–32.

———. *Voice-over: A Study of the Narration within the Narrative.* PhD diss., University of California—Los Angeles, 1984.

Stewart, James G. "The Evolution of Cinematic Sound: A Personal Report." In *Sound and the Cinema: The Coming of Sound to American Film,* edited by Evan William Cameron, 38–67. Pleasantville, N.Y.: Redgrave Publishing Company, 1980.

Studlar, Gaylyn. *In the Realm of Pleasure: Von Sternberg, Dietrich, and the Masochistic Aesthetic.* Urbana: University of Illinois Press, 1988.

———. "Masochistic Performance and Female Subjectivity in *Letter from an Unknown Woman.*" *Cinema Journal* 33, no. 3 (Spring 1994): 35–57.

Suter, Jacquelyn. "Feminine Discourse in *Christopher Strong.*" Reprinted in *Feminism and Film Theory,* edited by Constance Penley, 89–103. New York: Routledge, 1988.

Telotte, J. P. "Narration and Incarnation: *I Walked With a Zombie.*" In *Film Criticism* 6, no. 3 (Spring 1982): 18–31.

———. "The Sounds of *Blackmail:* Hitchcock and Sound Aesthetic." *Journal of Popular Film and Television* 28, no. 4 (Winter 2001): 184–91.

———. *Voices in the Dark: The Narrative Patterns of Film Noir.* Urbana: University of Illinois Press, 1989.

Turk, Edward Baron. "Deriding the Voice of Jeanette MacDonald: Notes on Psychoanalysis and the American Film Musical." In *Embodied Voices: Representing Female Vocality in Western Culture,* edited by Leslie C. Dunn and Nancy A. Jones, 103–119. Cambridge, Eng.: University of Cambridge Press, 1994.

Vasse, Denis. *Le poids du réel, la souffrance.* Paris: Editions du Seuil, 1983.

———. *L'ombilic et la voix: Deux enfants en analyse.* Paris: Éditions du Seuil, 1974.

Vernet, Marc. Seminar on psychoanalysis and cinema, University of Paris IV, Fall 1986.

Waldman, Diane. "Architectural Metaphor in the Gothic Romance Film." *Iris,* no. 12 (Spring 1991): 55–69.

Walsh, Andrea. *Women's Film and Female Experience 1940–1950.* New York: Praeger, 1984.

Weis, Elisabeth, and John Belton, eds. *Film Sound,* New York: Columbia University Press, 1985.

Wexman, Virginia Wright. "The Transfiguration of History: Ophuls, Vienna and *Letter from an Unknown Woman.*" In *Letter from an Unknown Woman: Max Ophüls, Director,* edited by Virginia Wright Wexman, 3–14. New Brunswick, N.J.: Rutgers University Press, 1986.

White, Hayden. "Writing in the Middle Voice." *Stanford Literature Review* 9, no. 2 (1992): 179–87.

White, Susan. *The Cinema of Max Ophüls: Magisterial Vision and the Figure of Woman.* New York: Columbia University Press, 1995.

Williams, Alan. "Historical and Theoretical Issues in the Coming of Recorded Sound to the Cinema." In *Sound Theory Sound Practice,* edited by Rick Altman, 126–37. New York: Routledge, 1992.

———. "Is Sound Recording Like a Language?" *Yale French Studies,* no. 60 (1980): 51–66.

Žižek, Slavoj. *Looking Awry: An Introduction to Jacques Lacan through Popular Culture.* Cambridge, Mass.: MIT Press, 1991.

Index

musical scenes in, 191–95; paradox in, 192, 193, 196; Selma's character in, 190, 191, 192; "star"-voice in, 192–95; synch relations in, 194–95; visual style of, 190; vortexical narrative in, 192, 193, 196

Dark Passage, 108, 112, 140, 225n75

Dee, Frances, 158, 208n104

De Lauretis, Teresa, 28

Deleuze, Gilles, 8, 215n39

Deren, Maya, 68

Derrida, Jacques, 159

Detour, 65

Diana Productions, 115

discourse: definitions of, 131–32, 220n1; feminine, 154–55, 157, 158; in Hollywood films, 133–35

disembodied voice, 37–38; characteristics of, 35, 50–52; types of, 6–7

dissolves, 58–59, 209n120

diva, the, 26, 228n107

D.O.A., 139

Doane, Mary Ann, 18, 27, 28, 137, 155, 199n4, 220n1; on cyclical film structure, 97; on degrees of directness in voice-off address, 141, 222n29, 224n73; on discursive form, 205n61; on disembodied voice, 207n99; on enunciation, 152–53; on female voice as feminist tool, 40, 63; on heterogeneity exposed by voice/sound, 11, 34–35, 36, 41, 61; on hybrid cinema, 204n50; on interior monologue, 140; on *Secret beyond the Door,* 111, 112, 213n4, 217nn54–57, 218n61, 218n69; on sound/image hierarchy, 134; on synch vs. non-synch, 34–35, 40; taxonomies of voice, 6–8, 38–39, 83, 137, 221n23; on voice and space, 38–40, 41, 62, 137–38; on voice and the body, 34, 36–40, 47, 137–38

documentary, 221n21, 222n29; and voice-of-God, 6, 51, 141, 208n99

Double Indemnity, 108

Dubois, Jean, 220n2

Duras, Marguerite, 206n80, 213n1, 214n14

Echo, 26

Eddy, Nelson, 211n141

Eisler, Hanns, 205n57

Eliot, George, 128

embodiment: and taxonomies of voice, 7, 37, 138–39, 221n23

Enchanted Cottage, The, 81, 143; internal vision in, 22–23, *24,* 192

female voice-off: and address of female spectator, 9–10, 155–59, 225n75; fluidity of, 83, 107, 157–58, 163, 186, 222n40; and genre, 2; and hallucination, 226n90; vs. male voice-off, 65, 108, 121, 123, 126, 140, 157, 160, 225n75; and music, 65, 66, 104, 105, 216n50, 225n77; and omniscient camera, 156–57; prevalence of, 2

feminine subjectivity, 13, 200n13

feminist films, 9, 47, 48, 49, 51, 196, 206n80, 226n84

feminist film theory: and the body, 37, 52; on classical Hollywood cinema, 2–3, 136–37, 150–51, 196, 198; and difference, 198; on discursive interiority, 147–48; and female subjectivity, 151, 197; and studies of voice, 197

Fischer, Lucy, 56, 211n146, 212n173

Flaubert, Gustave, 74

Flitterman-Lewis, Sandy, 221n16

floating voice, 7, 9

Fontaine, Joan: in *Letter from an Unknown Woman,* 66, 211n143, 225n77; in *Rebecca,* 16, 146, 147, 155, 225n77, 226n90

Foucault, Michel, 14, 17, 26; on contradiction and coherence, 148–49, 153; on paradox, 149; on speech, 128, 135, 155

free indirect style, 74, 212n158. *See also style indirect libre*

Freud, Sigmund, 68, 74, 210n128; on fantasy, 96; on middle voice, 26; on the primal scene, 133; on sado-masochism, 72; on the uncanny, 201n8, 207n91

Gardner, Ava, 143

Garfield, John, 128, 131

gaze, the, 10: and blindness, 21; dialectic to eye, 21–22; dialectic to voice, 10; panoptical, 14; relationship to sound, 22; Sartre's description of, 22; and spectator, 27–28. *See also individual film titles*

textual analysis: need for, 18, 49, 145, 150, 198; in sound theory, 18
Thin Red Line, 82
thought-voice, 31, 82, 226n87
Tierney, Gene, 225n76
Touch of Evil, 120, 223n52
Trevor, Claire, 225n78
Trinh, T. Minh-Ha, 189, 198
Turk, Edward Baron, 11, 65, 211n141, 217n60
Two Mrs. Carrolls, The, 82, 226n90

uncanny, the, 61, 201n8, 207n91

Vasse, Denis, 13, 14, 59–60, 74, 210n128; on the "between," 62–64, 67; on grain of the voice, 61; on the mother's voice, 61, 62, 63; on the umbilical, 62; on the unconscious and the conscious, 210n135; on voice as petit object (a), 61–62, 73; on writing, 210, 126
vocal writing, 126
voice: contradictory representations of, 25; grain in, 17, 23, 25, 61, 66; relations to the body, 7, 24–26, 36–38, 40, 137–38; relation to the gaze, 10; sexual difference in, 64–65; taxonomies of, 6–7, 137–38; as "traverse," 13
voice-off: as act of enunciation, 152–53; as authorial position within text, 27, 59, 155; definition as term, 6, 8–9; and direct address, 140–41, 155–59, 225n75; and embodiment, 7, 11; fluidity of, 9, 83, 107, 145, 157–58, 163, 186, 222n40; and genre, 2; and madness, 114, 115; male vs. female, 50–51, 65, 108, 121, 123, 126, 140, 157, 160, 225n75; preva-

lence in Hollywood, 2; and representations of consciousness, 31, 90–91; and subjectivity, 81; and textual interiority, 11, 27, 137; typologies of, 6–7, 137–38
voice-of-God, 51, 208n99, 219n75. *See also* documentary
voix-off, 6
von Trier, Lars, 189, 196
vortexical narrative: in *All about Eve,* 122–25; and contradiction, 186, 197; and discursive empowerment, 147; and dissolves, 209n120; and feminine subjectivity, 13, 58, 196, 197; in *Humoresque,* 128; in *Secret beyond the Door,* 73, 96–100, 120; structural complexity of, 18–19, 215n39; and temporality, 67–68, 73, 209n121

Waldman, Diane, 217n53
Wanger, Walter, 214n29, 218nn65–66
White, Hayden, 26, 72–73, 201n11
White, Susan, 57, 211n144
Williams, Alan, 28–29, 202n20, 202n23, 203n29
Wollen, Peter, 9
women directors, 9, 146, 150, 151, 221n16
women's films: address to audience, 2, 4, 10, 17, 49, 132, 166; ambivalence to men/patriarchy in, 116, 143, 164; discursive conflict in, 87; discursive production in, 92, 201n23; financial success of, 4; home front themes/connections, 2, 4, 199n4, 217n53, 225n76

Young, Robert, 23, 143

Žižek, Slavoj, 210n128

Britta Sjogren is a filmmaker and an associate professor of cinema at San Francisco State University, where she teaches film production, theory, and screenwriting. Her work has been published in *Iris,* and she has an article on French films of the 1930s slated for publication in the forthcoming anthology *Reclaiming the Archive: Feminism and Film History* (eds. Vicki Callahan and Alison McKee). Sjogren has received a number of major grants, including the American Film Institute Independent Filmmaker Grant and the Western States Regional Media Arts Grant. Her films include *Jo-Jo at the Gate of Lions* (1992), *A Small Domain* (1996—Grand Jury Prize for Best Short Film–Sundance Film Festival), and *In This Short Life* (2005).

The University of Illinois Press
is a founding member of the
Association of American University Presses.

Composed in 9.5/13 ITC Cheltenham
with ITC Franklin Gothic display
by Jim Proefrock
at the University of Illinois Press
Designed by Dennis Roberts
Manufactured by Thomson-Shore, Inc.

University of Illinois Press
1325 South Oak Street
Champaign, IL 61820-6903
www.press.uillinois.edu